CONCORDIA UNIVERSITY

BF181.G31930
GREAT EXPERIMENTS IN PSYCHOLOGY NE

W9-ACO-227

3 4211 000004937

WIT   WN

GREAT EXPERIMENTS
IN
PSYCHOLOGY

The Century Psychology Series
Richard M. Elliott, Editor

GREAT EXPERIMENTS IN PSYCHOLOGY

BY HENRY E. GARRETT

ASSISTANT PROFESSOR OF PSYCHOLOGY
COLUMBIA UNIVERSITY

150.72
G 239 G

12752

STUDENTS LIBRARY
CONCORDIA TEACHERS COLLEGE
RIVER FOREST, ILLINOIS

THE CENTURY CO.

NEW YORK : LONDON

COPYRIGHT, 1930, BY THE CENTURY CO.
COPYRIGHT ASSIGNED TO HENRY E. GAR-
RETT, 1932. ALL RIGHTS RESERVED, IN-
CLUDING THE RIGHT TO REPRODUCE THIS
BOOK, OR PORTIONS THEREOF, IN ANY
FORM.   3122

150.72
G239G

37

PRINTED IN U. S. A.

12752

BF181/.
G3

PREFACE

It is the common experience of many who have attempted
to teach general psychology to undergraduates, that frequently students are inclined to compare the experimental
foundations of psychology with those of physics and chemistry—usually to the detriment of psychology. The opinion
is pretty well established, I think—certainly among the more
capable students—that traditionally, at least, the first course
in psychology has contained too much dialectic, too many
fine verbal distinctions, and too many technical definitions;
and that it has made too little appeal to concrete, objective,
experimental evidence. In part this objection has been met
by the more recent text-books, but the text-book, by its
very nature, must confine itself largely to the exposition
of general principles. This leaves to the Instructor the task
of elaborating and emphasizing the more specific experimental findings; or in lieu of this, the student is given reading lists and supplementary references from which he is
supposed to fill in the details. The percentage of undergraduates who "go to the literature," however, is lament-
ably small; while the percentage of those who are capable
of evaluating what they read is still smaller. This, plus the
fact that the time of the Instructor is usually limited, often
restricts considerably the time which may be devoted to
presenting the experimental evidences of psychology.

The present book has been written with the specific idea
of meeting the situation outlined above. Its avowed object is
to present concretely the experimental foundations of psy-

chology and to outline in some detail those great or classical
experiments upon which modern psychology takes its stand,
and stakes its claim to be called an experimental science.
Every effort has been made to enliven and clarify the material so that it will have a real appeal to undergraduates,
without at the same time compromising its exactness. The
book is intended to be used primarily as a supplementary
or second book in connection with one of the standard texts;
but it could be used also in a first course in experimental
psychology. Not the least of its virtues, I hope, is that it will
not deter the beginning student because of its length, nor
discourage him because of its aridity.

A word of explanation is in order regarding the use of
the adjective "great" in the title. What I have tried to do is
to select those experiments which owing to their intrinsic
value or historical significance or both are generally ac-
knowledged by competent psychologists to deserve such a
description. I am laboring under no delusion that I have
included *all* of the great experiments in psychology in this
little book. Probably few psychologists if asked to enumerate
those experiments which they consider fundamental or great
would make exactly the same choices. Many experiments,
however, would certainly be found in nearly all lists, and
it is such experiments as these, upon which there is fairly
general agreement, that I have tried to select for presentation. I shall be entirely satisfied if my colleagues agree that
the experiments herein described are "great," even though
they may consider that I have been guilty of omitting many
equally important contributions. In this event, at least, my
sins will be those of omission rather than of commission.

It is a pleasant duty to acknowledge one's gratitude for
aid generously given by colleagues and friends. I am much
indebted to Professors R. S. Woodworth, H. L. Holling-
worth, Hulsey Cason, and to Dr. Heinrich Klüver for sup-

plying lists of great experiments. Professors R. S. Woodworth, A. T. Poffenberger, C. J. Warden, Dr. R. A. McFarland, Mr. Prescott Lecky, and Miss Anne Anastasi of Columbia, as well as Dr. M. R. Schneck of the City College of New York and Professor Miles A. Tinker of the University of Minnesota read one or more chapters and offered many helpful criticisms and suggestions. To all of these I am exceedingly grateful. My thanks are due also to those psychologists from whose printed works I have quoted or have taken diagrams or figures, and specific acknowledgment is made elsewhere in appropriate places in the text. Finally, I wish to express my particular indebtedness to Professor R. M. Elliott, the editor of the Century Psychology Series, for countless aids, suggestions, ideas, criticisms. It is a pleasure to acknowledge this obligation even though there is little possibility of my fully discharging it.

HENRY E. GARRETT

Columbia University
March, 1930

EDITOR'S INTRODUCTION

Is there in the college curriculum any subject in which it is more easy to interest the student, and more difficult to instruct him, than psychology? At present the student is usually taught first what is known in psychological science (factual content, as in the typical beginning course), second how it has been found out (experimental methods and laboratory), and third how to discover something himself (research). The student's contacts with these three kinds of opportunity are step-wise, one after the other.

This procedure is unjustified traditionalism. The honors student should be treated as a graduate student, less competent perhaps, but recognized as employing the same mental operations of criticism and research. The sophomore or even freshman student should be shown the living methods of psychology, if possible in practice. With or without laboratory facilities to draw upon, the use of a single standard text in the first course is not to be recommended. Habits of skimming acquired in rapid reading courses in history, literature, and the like, may not affect the study habits of the student when he is up against a mathematics or physics assignment. They do undoubtedly tend to keep him from taking a ten page psychology assignment seriously.

There has long been need for a *supplementary* text like the present one, stressing experimental methods, giving the student some idea how psychological facts have been discovered, who the men are who have contributed to the upbuilding of psychology, and what problems await immediate solution. Dr. Garrett's book, used parallel with a text of standard content, will punctuate with question marks the stores of knowledge so authoritatively displayed and will soften the rigidity of the system—behavioristic, experiential, organismic, or what not—which we force upon the unsuspecting and all too gullible beginner. In its pages psychology appears to the student as a live growing enterprise with a personal history and with a future to which it is not at all impossible to contribute.

R. M. E.

CONTENTS

Contents

ILLUSTRATIONS

FIGURES

Figures

GREAT EXPERIMENTS
IN PSYCHOLOGY

Chapter 1

BINET'S SCALE FOR MEASURING GENERAL INTELLIGENCE

(1)

IN 1904 the French Minister of Public Instruction appointed a commission of physicians, educators, and scientists which was assigned the task of formulating methods and making recommendations for the instruction of feeble-minded children in the public schools. One member of this commission was the eminent psychologist, Alfred Binet, at that time Director of the Laboratory of Physiological Psychology at the Sorbonne. Binet was born in Nice, France, in 1857, and was educated to be a physician. His interests, however, early directed him into abnormal and child psychology, and it is in the latter field that he is best known. In 1895 Binet founded the journal *L'année Psychologique*, in which a number of his own studies and those of his students are published. As a direct outgrowth of his work as a member of the commission mentioned above, Binet in 1905, with the collaboration of Thomas Simon, published his first rough scale for measuring general intelligence. This set of tests was followed by an enlarged and revised edition in 1908, and by a third and last revision in 1911, published shortly before Binet's untimely death.

It has often been said—and truly—that the development of the Binet-Simon Scale marks the real beginning of intelligence testing as we know it to-day. However, it must not be thought that Binet's scale is merely of historical interest.

After twenty years of revision, criticism, discussion, and experimentation, it is to-day still the prototype of the best modern scales for measuring general intelligence, while Binet's conception of intelligence is in remarkably close agreement with the views of present-day psychologists. Less than ten years after the publication of its final revision, the Binet-Simon Scale was being extensively used in America, Canada, England, Australia, New Zealand, South Africa, Germany, Switzerland, Italy, Russia, and China, and had been translated into Japanese and Turkish. Such widespread and immediate popularity indicates clearly the great need that was felt for just such an intellectual measuring device as was supplied by Binet's tests.

(2)

How can we explain the remarkable response to Binet's simple set of tests? Perhaps the best way of answering this question is to consider just how Binet made his scale, how it differed from previous tests, and what it was designed to do. First, let us look at Binet's conception of intelligence, upon which the method and scale were built. Before Binet, mental tests had been devised chiefly with the notion of measuring rather narrow aspects or phases of mental ability, such as rote memory, attention-span, speed and accuracy of perception and discrimination in checking numbers or recognizing forms, speed and accuracy of voluntary movements, sensory acuity, etc. Binet criticized tests of this sort as being too restricted in scope to be good measures of general ability. For this purpose, he said, we must tap the "higher mental faculties," such as reasoning, imagination, judgment, as it is here that differences in intellectual ability are most likely to be manifested. Attention and adaptability, along with good judgment, were for Binet the most important contributors to general intelligence. Intellect, he says, is com-

Courtesy of C. H. Stoelting Co., Chicago

ALFRED BINET

(1857–1911)

pounded of "judgment, common sense, initiative, and the ability to adapt oneself." Again he stresses "insight" into one's own capabilities (notoriously absent in the feeble-minded), the ability readily to adapt one's behavior to a definite end or goal, and persistence in sticking to a task once undertaken. Binet distinctly marked off intelligence from mere information which may be acquired in school or in a cultural environment, although he insisted that the intelligent person, unless deprived by untoward circumstances of a normal environment, will always acquire more information than the unintelligent one.

Binet did not attempt to analyze intellect into its parts and then to devise simple tests to measure the elements. On the contrary, he considered it more promising to estimate intelligence by measuring the *combined* effects of attention, imagination, judgment, and reasoning, as shown in the performance of fairly complex tasks. His first scale consisted of thirty carefully selected questions, or problems. These were arranged in a rough order of difficulty, determined by trying them out experimentally on about 200 normal children. The tests were not grouped according to ages; Binet simply indicated how many tests a normal child of say five or seven years should be expected to perform. In his second scale, that of 1908, the tests were for the first time arranged into age-groups, constituting the first age-scale. This scale contained from four to eight tests for each age from three to thirteen, each test allotted to an age-group in the following manner. Whenever a test was passed by from two thirds to three fourths of a given age-group, Binet considered it to be a fair test for children of that age. If all or practically all of his five-year-olds failed in a given test, he regarded it as obviously too hard for children of that age; while if it were passed successfully by practically all of his ten-year-olds, it was clearly too easy for that age-group.

This method of discovering at what age a given test should be put was somewhat rough and ready, to be sure, but it possessed the virtue of being based upon experimental data.

The 1908 scale is of more than ordinary interest because here for the first time Binet employed the concept of "mental age." A child's mental age (M A) depends upon the number of tests in the scale which he can pass successfully. If he performs all of the tests assigned to the eight-year-old group, for instance, he has a mental age of 8 years, no matter what his chronological age (C A) may be. If he happens to be five years old chronologically, he is, of course, advanced three years; if eight years old, just normal; and if ten years old, retarded two years. Description of performance in terms of mental age has proved to be extremely useful in mental measurement. For one thing, it is more easily understood than other kinds of scores by the non-psychologically trained person; and furthermore, it permits a quick and meaningful comparison of a child's years of mental growth with his years of physical growth.

The 1911 scale represents three years of work with the 1908 scale and is the final form in which his tests were left by Binet. There are fifty-four tests in the 1911 scale, arranged in age-groups as follows:

Binet's 1911 Scale

Age III.
1. Points to nose, eyes, and mouth.
2. Repeats two digits.
3. Enumerates objects in a picture.
4. Gives family name.
5. Repeats a sentence of six syllables.

Age IV.
1. Gives his sex.
2. Names key, knife, and penny.

3. Repeats 4 digits.
4. Compares two lines.

Age V.
1. Compares two weights.
2. Copies a square.
3. Repeats a sentence of ten syllables.
4. Counts four pennies.
5. Unites the halves of a divided rectangle.

Age VI.
1. Distinguishes between morning and afternoon.
2. Defines familiar words in terms of use.
3. Copies a diamond.
4. Counts thirteen pennies.
5. Distinguishes pictures of ugly and pretty faces.

Age VII.
1. Shows right hand and left ear.
2. Describes a picture.
3. Executes three commands given simultaneously.
4. Counts the value of six sous, three of which are double.
5. Names four cardinal colors.

Age VIII.
1. Compares two objects from memory.
2. Counts from 20 to 0.
3. Notes omissions from pictures.
4. Gives day and date.
5. Repeats five digits.

Age IX.
1. Gives change from twenty sous.
2. Defines familiar words in terms superior to use.
3. Recognizes all of the pieces of money.
4. Names the months of the year in order.
5. Answers easy "comprehension questions."

Age X.
1. Arranges five blocks in order of weight.
2. Copies drawings from memory.
3. Criticizes absurd statements.
4. Answers difficult "comprehension questions."
5. Uses three given words in not more than two sentences.

Age XII.
1. Resists suggestion.
2. Composes one sentence containing three given words.
3. Names sixty words in three minutes.
4. Defines certain abstract words.
5. Discovers the sense of a disarranged sentence.

Age XV.
1. Repeats seven digits.
2. Finds three rimes for a given word.
3. Repeats a sentence of twenty-six syllables.
4. Interprets pictures.
5. Interprets given facts.

Adult.
1. Solves the paper-cutting test.
2. Rearranges a triangle in imagination.
3. Gives differences between pairs of abstract terms.
4. Gives three differences between a president and a king.
5. Gives the main thought of a selection which he has heard read.

Of the tests which had appeared in the edition of 1908, several were omitted from Binet's final revision of 1911 as a result of various criticisms. For instance, Binet left out certain tests which had been found to depend chiefly upon specific information obtained in school, as well as such routine tests of common knowledge as knowing one's age and the days of the week. Several tests which were found to have been misplaced (being either too simple or too difficult) were either eliminated or else shifted up or down in the scale, and several new tests were introduced. In making this last revision, as in preparing his two earlier scales, Binet attempted to include only tests which were not difficult to administer, were relatively short, covered an extensive range of mental processes, and did not depend directly upon specific information obtained in school. Such, in his opinion, were the requirements of a good intelligence test.

(3)

Among the criticisms which from time to time have been leveled against the Binet scale, probably the most common is that a child's performance depends more upon his training and social surroundings than upon his native ability.[1] For this reason, it is said, the child from an educated and cultured home has a distinct advantage over one not so favored. This is quite generally true, provided the cultural gap is wide, and has never been disputed by psychologists. Native capacity is of little value *per se* unless an environment suitable for development is supplied. For example, an American white child, brought up from birth among Eskimos would undoubtedly test as feeble-minded on the Binet scale, no matter how great his potential ability. Or to take a less striking illustration, it is clearly unfair to compare children from the slums of New York City with children from cultured and well-to-do homes. Many recent experimental studies have brought out clearly this fact of the differential effect of environment. S. S. Colvin (1922), for example, found that children from a wealthy suburb of Boston ranked, on the average, nearly two years in mental age above children from the poor sections of another large city. Cyril Burt (1921) an English psychologist, found decided differences in Binet test performance in favor of children of superior social status in London. The same investigator found also that children from superior schools were on the average one to two years in mental age ahead of those from inferior schools. These results emphasize concretely the importance of considering a child's environment in interpreting his mental test rating.

Binet was fully aware that his tests did not measure innate ability completely divorced from the influence of en-

[1] In the present connection, read the discussion in Chap. 2, pp. 44-47.

vironment. He consistently held that a comparison of the mental ages of two children was valid only when both had had approximately the same schooling and the same common background of experience. But when these conditions are satisfied, he considered test ratings fair measures of comparative ability on the reasonable assumption that normal children will be exposed to much the same facts, and hence will acquire much the same information. Binet's tests, it must be remembered, were constructed with the express purpose of reducing to a minimum the influences of special training. Unless, therefore, the cultural gap is wide or the deprivation from normal contact with the environment is serious, mental ages are usually close estimates of "real" ability. To be sure, responses in the test make use of verbal expressions which are clearly learned. But the abilities required to see relations, interpret meanings (in a picture, for instance), give sensible definitions, detect absurdities or incongruities, and comprehend social and other situations demand thought, reasoning, and judgment—and these are the important indices of ability. In short, although the Binet-Simon Scale draws heavily upon language, it exacts a high degree of sagacity, cleverness, and mental alertness, rather than the ability simply to reproduce parrot-like facts learned by rote.

Another criticism sometimes brought against the Binet tests is that they fail to detect character defects, such as bad temper, laziness, and abnormal sex habits, which are as important as intellect in daily living. Also, it is sometimes charged that they fail to discover exceptional gifts in music, art, or mechanics. The reply to this is that Binet set out to locate the general intellectual level at which the child habitually functions, not to analyze character traits or to discover exceptional aptitudes. Still, in spite of this recognized limitation of the scale, a knowledge of the mental age is a decidedly valuable asset even though one is interested primarily in problems of delinquency and emotional maladjustment. Time and again juvenile courts and children's clinics have demonstrated the intimate connection between crime and immorality on the one hand, and low-grade intellect on the other. The method to be followed in treating character defects and delinquencies will depend to a large degree upon the intellectual level of the person to be treated. Also, knowing the mental age rating simplifies to a considerable degree the search for causes, even though the problem be largely an emotional one.

What may in practice be a decided limitation in the value of the Binet score should be mentioned at this point. This is that, in striking an average or mean of an individual's capacities, one is apt to forget that abilities are rarely if ever evenly developed, and that in consequence a gross total score fails to tell us in what respects our subject is especially good or especially poor. The same situation is met with in every test which gives a single score intended to be taken as indicative of general intellectual level. Practically, it is often far more valuable to know that a child is advanced or above age in ability to handle numbers, say, or in knowledge of words and word relations, or in retentivity, than to know that his I Q is 90 or 100 or 120; for vocational or educational guidance may then direct the child into those courses of study or that kind of work for which his abilities peculiarly fit him. A trained psychologist always studies his test results for evidence of special development or special deficiencies. Sometimes, too, he supplements the mental age rating with special tests of learning or memory or reasoning, or even tests of manual dexterity, such as speed and coördination of movement. These special test scores may be put in the form of a "psychograph"—a chart wherein the testee's various records are represented by a series of points plotted above or below the mean line or "norm" for his age-group. Relative superiorities as well as inferiorities are clearly presented by this graphical method.

An illustration of a psychograph representing the standing of a ten-year-old boy, A. F., in several selected measures of ability will be found in Figure 1.

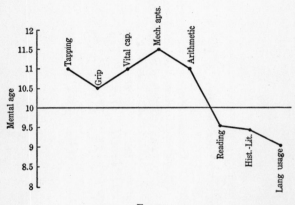

FIG. 1

A PSYCHOGRAPH SHOWING PERFORMANCE ON A VARIETY OF TESTS
This is the record made by a ten-year-old boy, A. F., whose I Q is 104

The data from which this psychograph has been constructed are given in Table I opposite.

The norms for these physical and motor tests were taken from Pyle's *The Examination of School Children* (1913), and the other records from the instruction booklets accompanying the Stanford Achievement Test, Advanced Examination, and the Stenquist Mechanical Aptitudes Tests, Test II. It is at once apparent from the chart that A. F. is physically above par for his age. He is also advanced in arithmetic and in mechanical ability, but lags behind somewhat in language-usage, history-literature, and reading. Offhand it

TABLE I

SOME TEST RECORDS OF A 10-YEAR-OLD BOY, A. F., I Q 104

	Tapping rate, right hand, 30"	Strength of grip, right hand, in kgs.	Vital capacity in ccs.	Mechanical aptitudes (Stenquist Test II)	Arithmetic, Stanford Achievement Test	Reading, Stanford Achievement Test	History-literature, Stanford Achievement Test	Language-usage, Stanford Achievement Test
A. F.'s record	165	17.5	1,750	28	124	64	8	5
Equivalent age record	11	10-6	11	11-6	11	9-5	9-6	9-1

might seem that this boy would do best, vocationally, in work requiring good physique, manual dexterity, and mathematical and mechanical knowledge. A further check-up on his interests, ambitions, financial situation, and personality would, of course, be necessary before venturing a more definite opinion. Several interesting examples of psychographs of special aptitudes will be found in C. L. Hull's *Aptitude Testing* (1928), pages 173-177.

A minor limitation of such language tests as the Binet lies in the fact that they cannot be used with foreign-born children nor with adults who do not speak English, with the deaf, nor very reliably with those who stutter, stammer, or have some similar language handicap. This general inadequacy is inherent in all tests employing verbal expression and has been remedied to a large extent by the construction of performance tests. Such tests require that the testee fit blocks into a board (form-board tests), reconstruct puzzle pictures, learn mazes, and, in general, perform mental activities which demand ingenuity and insight with a minimum of language.[2]

To summarize briefly what has been said in this section, the Binet-Simon Scale and its derivatives are valid measures of general intelligence when—and only when—given and scored in a standard manner; when the subjects come from a normal environment; and when they labor under no marked language handicaps. For the best results, individual intelligence tests should be supplemented by careful observation, in order to detect peculiarities and abnormalities which might affect the testee's record. Whenever possible and practicable, too, the personal history, medical record, and habits of industry of the subject should be investigated as well as his social and moral habits. In the case of children, play

[2] See Pintner, R., and Paterson, D., *A Scale of Performance Tests* (1921).

habits and the traits exhibited in school should be carefully noted. The Binet tests and their later revisions have been especially valuable in schools in detecting the low-grade as well as in selecting children of superior ability. In many progressive schools to-day special work is provided for the dull group fitted to their limited abilities; while for the second group there are provided enriched courses of study and accelerated classes.

(4)

Binet's tests were quickly taken up in America, where they were adapted and revised to fit American children and the conditions of American life. Goddard (1911) was the first to introduce Binet's tests into America. He translated the scale into English, made some changes in the position and wording of certain tests, and used the scale extensively in his work with the feeble-minded at the Vineland Training School. Several later revisions of the Binet scale have appeared; one by Terman in 1916, and two by Kuhlman in 1912 and 1922. In addition Yerkes, Bridges, and Hardwick (1915) and Herring (1922) have published revisions in which the classification of the tests into age-groups has been abandoned in favor of a "point scale" method. In point scales the tests are first arranged in an order of difficulty; and credits or points are then allowed in accordance with the number of tests passed successfully. This point score may be translated into a Coefficient of Mental Ability, the child's score divided by the norm for his age (Yerkes), or into the more familiar M A or I Q (Herring).

By far the best known, and the most widely used, of the revisions of the Binet-Simon Scale of tests is that of Professor L. M. Terman of Stanford University. This revision is known generally as the "Stanford Revision," or often simply as "Stanford-Binet," and is a careful and thorough working-over of the old Binet scale. Terman found that Binet's tests were too few and too difficult at the upper age-levels; that many were misplaced in the scale; and that the instructions for giving the tests were often indefinite. To insure uniformity of procedure in making his revision, one half-year was spent in training examiners to give the tests, and another half-year in supervision of the testing. In all, forty new tests were tried out, 1,000 school-children of average social status furnishing the chief experimental group. As finally drawn up, the Stanford Revision contained ninety tests, thirty-six more than Binet's 1911 scale. Six tests and one alternate test were placed in each age group from the age of three to the age of ten; eight tests were placed at age twelve, six at age fourteen, six at "average adult" level (taken at sixteen), and six at the "superior adult" level (taken at eighteen). In addition to the mental age score, Terman used the expression *intelligence quotient,* or I Q, to express mental development or brightness.[3] This term is simply the ratio of the mental age to the chronological age. For example, a child of eight with an M A of 8 years has an I Q of 8/8 or 1.00; if the child's M A is 6 years, his I Q is 6/8 or .75; if his M A is 10, his I Q is 10/8, or 1.25. The mental age expresses the intellectual *status* of the child—his position on the mental growth curve —while the I Q tells us how bright or how slow he is relative to the average child, whose I Q is always 1.00, or 100, as it is more commonly written. In the Stanford Revision, each of the six tests within a given age-group counts for two months of mental age (except at ages twelve, fourteen, sixteen, and eighteen, where each test has greater value), so that mental ages of so many years plus so many months may be calculated from the scale.

The child of six years and six months, say, who is strictly

[3] The term *intelligence quotient* was first used by the German psychologist William Stern (1913).

Courtesy of Science Service

LEWIS M. TERMAN

(1877–   )

average should pass *all* of the tests for six years and *below,* and three tests at age seven. As it happens, however, a strictly average child probably exists only in textbooks, and so in almost every case there is some scatter in a child's record of passes: that is to say, he fails on some of the tests below his true mental age and passes some of those above it. In the end, however, these failures and successes balance each other, so that the normal child of seven years and four months finally comes out with a mental age of 7 years and 4 months, and an I Q of 100. A superior child, of course, will go higher than his actual age, while a retarded child will find tests which he cannot do below his chronological age-group.

Before this section closes, a word of warning is in order regarding the administration of the Stanford-Binet, or for that matter, any individual mental scale. Because the tests seem so easy to give, many people mistakenly imagine that they can administer them without previous supervision in test-giving or training in psychology. The unfortunate part of it is that they can give these tests after a fashion, but the results will almost certainly be worthless and will usually be downright misleading. Such "testers" forget that the object of the examination is to see whether a child can do certain things *under carefully prescribed conditions,* not whether he can do them when given plenty of time, and often plenty of suggestion and prodding, too, by the examiner. A trained examiner, first of all, knows the tests by heart; he is careful to see that he has the child's confidence, and has stimulated his interest, so that he will do his best; and he gives and scores the tests strictly according to the directions laid down in the manual. A year's graduate study in psychology plus at least six months' practical experience in giving mental tests under supervision is a minimum requirement for a trained examiner.

(5)

As indicated in the last section, the average adult level of general intelligence was placed by Terman at sixteen years. The view that intelligence matures or reaches the adult level at this relatively early age is generally regarded with surprise not unmixed with doubt by non-psychologists. Many people are inclined to contend that intelligence surely continues to grow well into middle life; and they resent—when they do not scoff at—the idea that they are no smarter at forty than at sixteen. The confusion here is due entirely to a misunderstanding of what the psychologist means by *intelligence* and by *matures*. By intelligence, it must be remembered, psychologists mean ready adaptability to new situations, mental alertness, keenness, and ingenuity, and *not* knowledge or experience, which are products of these, and which usually do increase with age—at least beyond sixteen years. Generally speaking, it is obvious, of course, that the average father has more general—and more special—knowledge than his sixteen-year-old son, that he can do many more things and has wider experience, though he may be no more alert nor readily adaptable (potentially intelligent) in the psychologist's sense. Carefully repeated measurements of the same and of different individuals over a period of years have shown that native ability (in so far as it is measured by mental tests) increases rapidly during the early years; then advances more and more slowly as the teens are reached, until somewhere between fourteen and sixteen years the average individual does as well as he will do at twenty or thirty years, or ever. At this comparatively early age, most people possess as much natural keenness and sheer native ability, apart from experience, as they will ever have.[4]

Curves showing the growth of intelligence in bright, aver-

[4] See further Chap. 2, pp. 37-39.

age, and dull children are represented in Figure 2. The middle curve shows the course of average, the upper curve of superior, and the lower curve of inferior intellect. Note that average intelligence rises rapidly during the first four or five years; that from five to ten or eleven, growth, while evident, is considerably slower; and that from this point on the curve gradually ceases to rise, becoming level somewhere between fourteen and sixteen years. The curve for superior

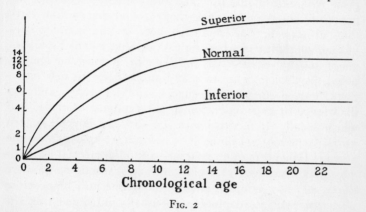

FIG. 2

MENTAL GROWTH CURVES FOR SUPERIOR, NORMAL, AND DULL CHILDREN
FROM BIRTH TO MATURITY

intelligence rises more rapidly and goes higher than the average curve, probably not reaching its level until two or three years later. As shown by the lower curve, mental growth in the retarded (those of inferior intelligence) is distinctly slower than in the normal and superior. Also, mental growth reaches its maximum from two to three years earlier than in the normal, or average, growth curve. Except in the matter of speed and quickness of response, the loss in general ability from twenty to forty or forty-five years appears to be relatively slight. In old age general intelligence wanes slowly.

(6)

The widespread application of intelligence tests to large numbers of children and adults has established quite clearly the various degrees of intelligence to be expected in the population at large. In statistical language, intelligence is said to be "distributed normally," that is, in accordance with

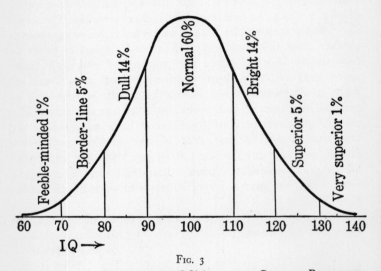

Fig. 3

<small>DISTRIBUTION OF INTELLIGENCE (IQ's) IN THE GENERAL POPULATION</small>

the law of normal probability. Figure 3 shows the normal probability distribution or normal curve, with the percentages of the different grades or degrees of intelligence which might be expected to occur in a very large sample of people.

A normal distribution of people with respect to any trait, such as height, speed of movement, or general ability, simply means that the majority possess a medium amount of the trait in question; that lesser and lesser amounts are possessed by fewer and fewer individuals; and that greater and greater amounts are possessed by steadily decreasing numbers. To put it in a different way, if we begin at the average, the proportion of individuals becomes smaller and smaller as the amount of the trait grows either larger or smaller. The normal distribution of a human trait or characteristic is well illustrated in the case of height. By far the greater number of men are close to five feet eight inches in height (the average); fewer men will be found two inches taller or two inches shorter than this average; still fewer four inches taller or four inches shorter; while the number of very tall (over seven feet) and very short, (under five feet) men is exceedingly small indeed. What is true of height is true also of general intelligence, and probably of all mental traits. Repeated measurements of intelligence have established the fact that about 60 per cent of the general population are of average intelligence; 18-19 per cent are somewhat higher or somewhat lower than this average; while roughly 1-2 per cent are very superior or very inferior. (See Figure 3.)

A description of intellectual level in terms of I Q may be expressed as follows:

I Q	Classification	Approximate % in the population
130 and above	Very superior	1
120-129	Superior or very bright.... }	
110-119	Bright .... }	19
90-109	Average or normal	60
80-89	Dull normal—backward ... }	
70-79	Border-line, very dull...... }	19
0-69	Feeble-minded	1

Of course, the number of feeble-minded in the general population (here put at 1 per cent) will depend upon where the line of demarcation between the normal and the feeble-minded is drawn. At present the best opinion seems to be that all individuals below 70 I Q should probably be classified as feeble-minded. Three classes of the feeble-minded are generally recognized by psychologists, viz., idiots, imbeciles, and morons. Idiots, who are the lowest in intellect, range in I Q from about 0-25; their mental ages rarely go above 2 years. Imbeciles range in I Q from 25 to about 50, with mental ages of from 3 to 7 years. Morons have I Q's from 50 to about 70, their mental ages ranging from about 8 to about 10 years. Scales like the Stanford-Binet have proved to be extremely useful in differentiating quickly and accurately among these different grades of feeble-mindedness. In many institutions for the feeble-minded, the kind and the extent of the training attempted depends in large part upon the preliminary mental test rating.

Worth mentioning in the present connection is a contribution made to theoretical psychology by the Binet and other mental tests. This is the experimental finding that the feeble-minded are not a distinct species separated off from the normal human, as, for instance, animals are separated from man.[5] There is no sharp division between normal and feeble-minded so far as performance on intelligence tests is concerned, but a gradual progression from one group to the other. The difference between the two groups is *quantitative* rather than *qualitative;* a matter of more available and more complex behavior units rather than a matter of a different *kind* of intellectual activity.

As Binet's original tests were constructed with the express purpose of locating the feeble-minded, for a long time this was regarded as the chief function of general intelligence

[5] Norsworthy, N. *The Psychology of Mentally Deficient Children* (1906), Columbia University Contributions to Philosophy and Psychology XV, 2.

tests. Probably a good deal of the suspicion with which tests were (and still are, to some degree) regarded is a reflection of this view. The expression to "submit" to an intelligence test describes it exactly. Recently, however, the importance of mental tests in locating superior children has been recognized. Intelligence tests are now being widely employed as a means of finding bright children who should be rapidly advanced or given special attention. Terman's recent studies (1926) of 1,000 children with I Q's of 130 and above has shown that these very superior children tend to be above the average in height, weight, and general health, as well as in looks and social and emotional maturity (see further page 179). This flatly contradicts the old idea—still widely prevalent, unfortunately—that precocious children are usually poorly adjusted socially, that they tend to be puny and undersized, and that they usually die at an early age! The parents of Terman's very bright children were for the most part from the professional and the semiprofessional classes (80 per cent), only a small fraction (6 per cent) coming from the semi-skilled and laboring classes. One fourth of the children had at least one parent who was a college graduate, while the average schooling of both parents was about twelve grades—twice that of the general adult population. These results indicate that both the heredity and the environment of these bright children were distinctly above average.

(7)

The question of the constancy or stability of an individual's general level of intelligence throughout life is bound up with the prior consideration of whether intelligence is inborn and native, and hence largely if not entirely determined at birth; or whether it is only loosely native in the sense that all behavior is fundamentally and potentially native, and hence is generally and highly susceptible to training. There is considerable evidence in favor of the view that intelligence is inborn, inherited after much the same manner as physical characteristics.

In the first place, we have the facts of common everyday observation. Bright boys and bright girls tend to grow into bright men and women, while the history of stupid people reveals more often than otherwise a record of stupidity in childhood. Nearly every one can cite instances from his own experience of dull children, who, in spite of every advantage socially and educationally, have grown into dull and mediocre men and women; while we all know of bright children, who, despite marked disadvantages, have insisted upon remaining bright and becoming successful. Among children who grow up in the same community, attend the same school, play together, see the same movies, and, all in all, possess about the same opportunities, some will learn more rapidly and progress faster than others. Such an outcome must be largely the resultant of native differences in endowment.

There are exceptions, of course. Disease, deafness, poor eyesight, unkind treatment, a restricted or vicious environment—all of these serve to complicate the nature-nurture problem. But when all of these are allowed for, the fact still remains that some people are natively better equipped mentally than others.

The biographies of men of genius reveal the fact that exceptional gifts usually appear early in childhood. A famous illustration is the case of Sir Francis Galton, who could read when he was two and one-half years old. The day before his fifth birthday he wrote the following note to his sister: "My dear Adele, I am 4 years old and can read any English book. I can say all of the Latin substantives and adjectives and active verbs besides 52 lines of Latin poetry. I can cast up any sum in addition and multiply by 2, 3, 4, 5, 6, 8, 10. I can also say the pence table. Francis Galton. Febuary [sic] 15, 1827." Terman (1917), after studying Galton's biography and later career, estimates that his I Q must have been close to 200. Voltaire began to read at three and at twelve wrote a tragedy. Sir Isaac Newton, as a child, was "constantly occupied during his play hours" in devising all sorts of contrivances and machines, especially water-clocks and kites. At seventeen, Goethe was familiar with the poetry of the leading nations; he had done extensive reading in German, French, Latin, and Hebrew; he knew the history of the European countries in detail; he played the piano and the flute, and was considered a promising art student.[6] Other illustrations abound. Macaulay could read at four, and at eight wrote a "treatise to convert the natives of Malabar to Christianity"; Jonathan Edwards wrote a paper on spiders at twelve which actually increased the scientific knowledge on the subject; Walter Scott and John Stuart Mill were considered to be infant prodigies. Childhood histories of Francis Bacon, Descartes, Spinoza, and many others all give early promise of later greatness.

Not all geniuses, however, have been recognized as precocious in youth. Darwin, for instance, was considered rather dull by his teacher, partly, no doubt, because he carried insects and small animals around in his pockets, oftentimes disturbing the serenity of the class-room. Napoleon's record in military school was just average. Of David Hume it was said by his mother that he was good-natured but "uncommon wakeminded." Thomas A. Edison was usually at the foot of his class in school, and considered "addled" by his teacher, despite the fact that he read Gibbon's *Decline and Fall of the Roman Empire,* Hume's *History of England,* and Burton's *Anatomy of Melancholy* before he was twelve.

[6] For numerous illustrations see *Genetic Studies of Genius* (1926), Vol. II.

It is hardly probable that these illustrations are exceptions to the rule, "bright child, bright adult." Many brilliant children are hopelessly misunderstood by their parents as well as by their teachers. Uninterested in the (to them) simple facts taught in school, they often neglect their lessons, meanwhile concerning themselves with matters far beyond the capacity or interests of the ordinary child. Bright children, too, are frequently mischievous and problem cases, because, quickly grasping what is taught, they idle or play instead of dutifully paying attention and doing assigned tasks. Intelligence tests are doing much to discover and provide for the exceptional child. Special classes, extra studies, and other expedients of a like nature offer opportunity for initiative and creative endeavor, so that the energy of the bright child is usefully conserved and applied.

To take the other extreme of the intelligence scale, we have much evidence, too, that intelligence is native and inherited from the way in which feeble-mindedness tends to run in families. Authorities estimate that fully 90 per cent of all feeble-mindedness is native and inherited, the remaining 10 per cent being due to disease or injury at birth or in early childhood (Tredgold, 1922). Normal parents who come from families in which there is no mental defect rarely have a feeble-minded child. If, however, one parent is normal and the other feeble-minded, some of the children are likely to be feeble-minded or very dull; while if both parents are feeble-minded, *all* of the children will be feeble-minded or low-grade. Many studies have been made which show that feeble-minded tend to mate with feeble-minded, thus passing on the defect from one generation to the next. Goddard (1914) in his study of the Kallikak family (a fictitious name) went back five generations to Martin Kallikak, a man of good ability (presumably), who, during the American Revolution, had an illegitimate son by a girl known to be feeble-minded. From this son have come 480 descendants. Of these, 143 were feeble-minded, forty-six probably normal, and the rest doubtful. Among the total lot, thirty-six were illegitimate, thirty-three were sexually immoral, mostly prostitutes, twenty-four were drunkards, three were epileptics, eighty-two died in infancy, three were criminals, and eight were keepers of houses of ill-fame. Of this family tree Thorndike remarks (1914), that it constitutes "a horrid array of human incompetence." After the Revolution, Martin Kallikak married a normally intelligent woman of Quaker stock. Fortunately Goddard was able to trace 496 descendants from this union, and the records of these offspring furnish an effective "control" experiment, as it were, to the other line. All of these legitimate progeny, except possibly two, were normal mentally and morally, and several were evidently of superior intellect. In this group we find lawyers, physicians, governors, professors, and college presidents. After surveying all of his evidence, Goddard writes, "The fact that the descendants of both the normal and the feeble-minded mother have been studied and traced in every conceivable environment, and that the respective strains have been true to type, tends to confirm the belief that heredity has been the determining factor in the formation of their respective characters."

Experimental evidence of the influence of inheritance in determining the degree of intelligence has come from the study of mental resemblances among members of the same family. Galton, and later Thorndike and Merriman, among others, have shown that twins are much more alike than siblings (ordinary brothers and sisters) in traits little affected by training as well as in those upon which the school concentrates its influences (see also pages 182-3). The relationship between the mental traits exhibited by members of a family is as high as or higher than the relationship exhibited by physical traits, such as height, weight, hair, and eye-color.

Since the physical resemblances of twins and brothers and sisters are accepted as due to native factors, it would seem that mental traits must also have a native basis.

If, as seems highly probable, intelligence is largely determined by native factors, it follows that the I Q (assuming it to be a fair measure of mental ability) should remain constant throughout life. Many recent studies have demonstrated that this is substantially true.[7] Repetitions of the Stanford-Binet test on the same child after one, two, or more years have shown that an I Q rarely varies more than four or five points up or down from the initial value. This result holds, of course, only for normal children who have had pretty much the same social and educational advantages and opportunities. Children brought to institutions from bad homes will often show a decided increase in I Q after a few months of kind treatment, good food, and medical attention, such as removal of diseased tonsils and adenoids. Also, children raised in isolated environments or under peculiar or restraining conditions will many times exhibit the same phenomenon of I Q increase when given normal surroundings and fair opportunity. Cases such as these are to be attributed not to any real increase in intellectual ability, but rather to the fact that the potential capacities have not hitherto been given a chance to function normally. Such I Q increases are really measures of the effect of a normal social environment, education, and fair treatment.

By way of summary, it may be said fairly that on the whole the Binet-Simon tests and their revisions have amply justified their existence and their widespread use. Their promise for the future is all in the direction of fairer treatment for the incorrigible and inferior child as well as for

[7] See, as an example, Rugg, H. O., and Colloton, C., *Constancy of the Stanford-Binet I.Q. as Shown by Re-Tests,* Journal of Educational Psychology (1921), 12, pp. 315-322.

the normal and superior by providing an opportunity commensurate with individual ability and fitted to individual needs. It would seem that inevitably such a program must lead to better adjustments and increased human happiness.

Suggested Readings

There are many books on mental testing to which the interested student may refer. The following are suggested.

1. A brief history of the testing movement is given in R. Pintner's *Intelligence Testing* (1923), Chapter I.
2. L. M. Terman's *The Measurement of Intelligence* (1916) gives a complete account of the Stanford Revision of the Binet-Simon Scale.
3. For the rôle of low-grade intellect in delinquency, see W. Healy and A. F. Bronner, *Delinquents and Criminals* (1926).
4. There is a clear account (with illustrations) of many of the measures of intelligence developed since Binet in R. Pintner's *Educational Psychology* (1929), Chapter V.

12752

Chapter 2

ARMY ALPHA AND THE RISE OF GROUP TESTS FOR MEASURING GENERAL INTELLIGENCE

(1)

THE extensive use of intelligence tests [1] in the American army during the World War, for the purpose of measuring the ability of large groups of men at the same time, constitutes psychology's greatest experiment in human engineering. During the years 1917-1918, intelligence examinations were given to slightly less than 1,750,000 men. As an immediate result of these tests, about 8,000 men were recommended for discharge because of defective intelligence; something like 10,000 were assigned to labor battalions or to other service requiring low-grade ability; and about 10,000 more were recommended to be sent to special development battalions for observation and further training. Nearly one third of the men examined were unable to read or write, or else did so too poorly to be classed as literate, and to these was given a special examination prepared for illiterates.

The army mental tests were not, as is sometimes supposed, simply a series of questions, puzzles, and other "stunts," thrown together without purpose or design. On the contrary, they were carefully selected and methodically put together in accordance with the best scientific principles of test-making then available. A brief outline of the steps leading up to

[1] For a discussion of what psychologists mean by the term *general intelligence*, see Chap. 1, p. 18.

the construction of a group test for measuring general intelligence, designed especially for soldiers, will show the care which was exercised. In April, 1917, a committee was appointed by the American Psychological Association, and to this committee was entrusted the task of preparing an adequate test for measuring the general intellectual level of large groups of men at the same time. This committee consisted of five psychologists who were specialists in the field of mental testing, and was under the direction of Robert M. Yerkes as chairman. All of the material previously used in measuring intelligence was culled over, especially a group test devised by A. S. Otis, which had not at that time been published. The committee decided that a general intelligence examination intended for use with soldiers should, as far as possible, meet certain definite requirements. These, in brief, were as follows: (1) It should as nearly as possible be independent of specific school information, since its aim was to discover a man's *native* ability rather than his degree of formal school training. (2) It should be steeply graded in difficulty, i.e., hard enough to tax the high-grade men, and at the same time easy enough to measure those of lesser ability. (3) Scoring must be simple, rapid, and objective, so that little might be left to the personal judgment of the scorer. (4) It should require a minimum of writing on the part of the testee, in order to eliminate speed of writing as a large factor in determining the score. (5) A number of different forms approximately equal in difficulty must be drawn up to prevent coaching. In addition to these more formal requirements, an effort was made to utilize material which would be interesting in itself and varied enough to keep the man "on the job." How well these principles were adhered to we shall see in later sections.

After much experimentation and trial, two tests, one for men who could read and write, and one for those who could

STUDENTS LIBRARY
CONCORDIA TEACHERS COLLEGE
RIVER FOREST, ILLINOIS

do neither (or else do so very poorly) were devised. The test for literates was called the Alpha, that for illiterates the Beta, examination. In preliminary trials, Alpha was tried out on elementary and high school children; large groups of students in schools, colleges, and officers' training camps; more than 5,000 enlisted men; and inmates of various institutions for the feeble-minded. The *validity* of the examination, that is, its value as a measure of general intellect, was checked against all available criteria: among the students and the feeble-minded, by such measures of aptitude as school grades, teachers' estimates of ability, and other intelligence tests, such as the Stanford-Binet; among the soldiers, by officers' ratings for ability, rank attained, ability shown in training, previous civilian accomplishments, and the like. The correlations [2] between the Alpha test and these various criteria ranged from .50 to .95, which means that statistically the test is a reasonably valid measure of general ability as here defined. The Beta test gave returns nearly as good as those obtained with Alpha. The consistency or *reliability* with which Alpha and Beta measure ability proved also to be satisfactory. For example, on taking a second form of Alpha, a man's score will rarely deviate more than four or five points from his first rating, so that an obtained Alpha score may be taken as an adequate measure of performance.

(2)

The Army Alpha Intelligence Examination [3] consisted of eight tests which may be described briefly by the following

[2] Correlation is a mathematical method of measuring relationship between two sets of test scores or other measures. Correlation coefficients range from + 1.00, or perfect relationship, through .00, just no relationship, down to − 1.00, perfect inverse relationship. A correlation of .50 denotes a fair, one of .95 a very high, relationship.

[3] As the Alpha test was given to literates, results from it are generally more enlightening and valuable than those from Beta. For this reason

titles: (1) Following Directions; (2) Arithmetic Problems; (3) Practical Judgment; (4) Synonym-Antonym; (5) Disarranged Sentences; (6) Number Series Completion; (7) Analogies; (8) General Information. The items in each of these tests were arranged so as to be progressively more difficult from the beginning to the end of the test. Time-limits were set for each test short enough to prevent any but the very fastest worker from finishing. This precaution is readily appreciated when one considers that the man who finishes a test before time is called is actually unmeasured, for we cannot say how much more he might have done had more material been available. It is just as true, of course, that the man who scores zero on a test is also unmeasured, as he might have done a very few items, at least, had still easier ones been provided. Five forms of Alpha were constructed, all approximately equal in difficulty.

Just exactly what the Alpha Examination was designed to do will be clearer if we consider the separate tests in somewhat greater detail. In Test (1),[4] Following Directions, each item was to be marked by the soldier in accordance with certain definite directions given by the examiner. For example, in the second item there are nine circles each containing in order a number from 1 to 9. The directions are as follows:

"Attention! Look at 2, where the circles have numbers in them. When I say 'Go,' draw a line from Circle 1 to Circle 4 that will pass *above* Circle 2 and *below* Circle 3. Go!" (Allow not over 5 seconds.)

There are twelve items in this test, the later ones being more difficult than those which come earlier.

we shall deal chiefly with Alpha in the following pages, but important results from Beta will also be presented.

[4] The following illustrations of the different tests are taken from Form 5.

Test (2), Arithmetic Problems, consisted of twenty ordinary problems of the "reasoning" or "mental arithmetic" variety. The tenth problem reads as follows:

10. If it takes six men three days to dig a 180-foot drain, how many will dig it in half a day?...Answer (   )

Five minutes are allowed for the entire test.

In Test (3), Practical Judgment, the directions were to indicate the best of three possible answers to a given question by placing an (X) in the "box" before it. Item 7, for example, proposes the following question:

7. Why is wheat better for food than corn? Because
   ☐ it is more nutritious
   ☐ it is more expensive
   ☐ it can be ground finer

Only one and one-half minutes are allowed for this test, which contains sixteen items. It is meant to be a test of practical "common sense."

Test (4), Synonym-Antonym, was designed to gauge ability to apprehend relations of likeness and difference. The ability to see relations is believed by many psychologists to play a highly important rôle in intelligence. Items 26 and 36 may be taken as examples:

26. Fallacy-verity .... same-opposite   26
36. Innuendo-insinuation .... same-opposite   36

Instructions are to underline "same" if the two words mean the same or nearly the same, and if they do not, to underline "opposite." There are forty items in this test, and one and one-half minutes are allowed.

The Disarranged Sentences Test, No. (5), was planned to measure the testee's ingenuity and cleverness as shown in his ability to rearrange jumbled words into a sentence. To illustrate with items 16 and 21:

16. ninety canal ago built Panama years
    was the ....true-false   16
21. employ debaters irony never........true-false   21

The twenty-four items in this test are answered by drawing a line under "true" or "false." Two minutes are allowed.

Test (6), Number Series Completion, was designed to measure "reasoning" ability. The task set was the completion of given series of numerical arrangements in a logical fashion. The thirteenth and sixteenth items read:

11	13	12	14	13	15	.14.	.12.
81	27	9	3	1	1/3	.1/9.	.1/27.

The directions are to write on the dotted lines the two numbers which should come next in the series. There are twenty items in the test, and three minutes are allowed.

Test (7), Analogies, was selected as another test of ability to "reason out" or "see" relations, of a verbal sort. To illustrate with items 17 and 36:

17. lion-animal :: rose—**smell leaf plant thorn**   17
36. tolerate-pain :: welcome—**pleasure unwelcome
    friends give**   36

The problem is to find the relation between the second and first words, and then underline that one of the four alternatives that is related in the same way to the third word. There are forty items, and a time allowance of three minutes is given.

General Information, Test (8), was included in order to give an estimate of the extent to which the individual has picked up common information from his surroundings. This test has been much criticized on the ground that it draws upon experience and knowledge rather than upon intellectual ability. It proved, nevertheless, to be a fairly adequate intelligence test. If we are justified in assuming roughly the same environment, it seems reasonable to suppose that those who are mentally alert will garner more information from their surroundings than those who are stupid and dull. Items 21 and 37 will serve as illustrations:

> 21. The **dictaphone** is a kind of **typewriter   multigraph   phonograph   adding machine**...... 21
> 37. **Mauve** is the name of a **drink   color   fabric   food** 37

Instructions are to underline that one of the four possible answers which makes the best or "truest" sentence. There are forty items in all, and four minutes are allowed.

(3)

The total score on the Army Alpha Examination is obtained by adding together the separate scores on the eight sub-tests. The maximum score possible is 212 points. When a soldier's total score had been found, the next step was to translate this numerical rating into a letter grade by means of Table II.

TABLE II

LETTER GRADES ON THE ARMY ALPHA EXAMINATION

Letter rating	A	B	C+	C	C—	D	D— and E
Range of Alpha scores corresponding.	212-135	134-105	104-75	74-45	44-25	24-15	14-0
Per cent of white soldiers receiving each letter grade.	4	8	15	25	24	17	7

The letter grades corresponding to the different score-ranges given in the table were found by drawing up a "distribution" or tabulation of Alpha scores made by a large and representative group. This distribution was then sub-divided into seven sections: high scores (A), fairly high

(B), average (C + and C), low (C —), and very low (D, D — and E). Letter designations, therefore, are to be taken as measures of *relative* performance and are not to be confused with *absolute* measures (those taken from a true zero), such as height and weight. Any score from 212-135 is given an A rating; any score from 134-105 a B rating, and so on. About 4 per cent of the white soldiers were assigned A ratings, and about 12 per cent A and B ratings, while nearly two thirds (64 per cent) fell into the C +, C, and C — groups. The average score made by the white enlisted men was 59 Alpha points, which corresponds to a letter rating of C. The white officers made on the average a score of 139 points, nearly all of them scoring A or B.

Shortly after the war, certain popular writers aroused indignation and much confusion by the unqualified statement that the mental age of the average American soldier was about 14 years. The first reaction of the individual unacquainted with tests and test technology, upon learning that the mental age of the average soldier was about equal to that of a first-year high school boy, was usually one of doubt, derision, or amusement, his specific attitude depending largely, perhaps, upon his age, education, experience, and sophistication. Among many uncritical people, however, the prevailing attitude was—and still is to some degree—one of uneasiness and even dismay at what might well be regarded as the precarious outlook of the nation in view of the mental immaturity of a large share of its citizenry.

This conclusion, fortunately, is entirely unwarranted; it grew out of an almost complete misunderstanding by the writers mentioned of what the army tests are and what they really do. This may be readily seen if we look carefully into the method whereby the average mental age of 14 years was obtained. First, the correlation or correspondence between the Alpha scores and the mental ages—as determined by the Stanford-Binet examination [5] —of a large group of men was calculated. It was then discovered that the Alpha score made by the average white soldier (C in letter grades) corresponded to a mental age of about 14 years on the Stanford-Binet scale. The statement of Alpha performance in terms of mental age, then, simply means that the average soldier did about as well on the test as the average fourteen-year-old school-child. Certainly there need be nothing alarming, nor even especially disconcerting, about this finding. Reference to Figure 2, page 19, will show that the rise in the growth curve for normal intelligence from 14 to 16 years is extremely slight. This means that the average white soldier was but little below the level (16 years) set by Terman in the Stanford Revision as the point at which intelligence reaches its maturity. There are several facts which will account even for this deficiency. In the first place, many psychologists are now convinced that Terman's 16-year level is too high, and that normal intelligence matures somewhat earlier, very probably at 14 years. Also it must be remembered that the schooling of many of the drafted men was years removed, which put them at a disadvantage when compared with school-children on a paper and pencil test. Again, it is well known that specialized training and the routine of adult occupation often play havoc with whatever skill a man may have had at one time in reading and figuring rapidly.

It should be added further, by way of defense of the soldier, that the Alpha test gave no measure of manual ability nor of skill in performing mechanical tasks; of ability to exercise good judgment and restraint in business relations; of ability to control one's temper, or to get along on amicable terms with one's neighbors. Ingenuity, mental alertness, and the ability to solve problems involving language and numbers

[5] See Chap. 1, pp. 15-17.

with ease and despatch, i.e., to deal with "ideas," are admittedly important; and these capacities are clearly measured by the Alpha test. But skill in abstract thinking and in dealing with ideas does not exhaust the gamut of human achievement by any means; and so, all in all, we need not be greatly perturbed that the average soldier had a mental age of only 14 years on the Stanford-Binet scale.

(4)

Since all of the men inducted into the army were required to give their former civil occupations, important data regarding the comparative intelligence of different occupational groups may be gleaned from the army records. In the groups scoring A and B on the tests, we find the professions, for the most part, the civil engineers, mechanical engineers, physicians, lawyers, teachers, and business executives. In the C + group were men who described themselves in civil life as stenographers, bookkeepers, clerks, photographers, and workers at skilled trades. In the C group were carpenters, policemen, tailors, butchers, printers, farmers, and small storekeepers. Store clerks, cooks, fishermen, firemen, barbers, and day laborers made up the lowest groups (C — and D). Common observation and experience, as well as such other studies as have been made of the subject, all emphasize the wide differences in mental level among occupational groups. The army tests confirmed these findings. We must not forget, however, that early environment, lack of formal education, opportunity, and temperament, as well as many other less tangible influences play highly important rôles in determining one's vocation. Such factors should always be considered before judging a man's probable intelligence from his occupation. But this does not discount, of course, the importance of the relation disclosed by the army tests between occupation and intelligence.

We have previously commented upon the fact that officers for the most part made much higher Alpha scores than enlisted men. This result was to be expected, as was also the further finding that officers in those branches of the service which require technical training or special preparation rank highest in general intelligence. Officers in the Engineering and Artillery Corps, for example, ranked higher than officers in the Machine-Gun and Field Signal Battalions; while these, in turn, made better scores than the officers in the Quartermaster Corps and the Infantry. One rather surprising result was the relatively low average rating of the officers of the Medical Corps. Wide differences in age and training, as well as the methods of military selection, are no doubt responsible to a large extent for this poor showing. It is a well-known fact that the Medical Corps contained some of the ablest and at the same time some of the weakest men in the profession. For this reason an "average intelligence score" is hardly representative of either group.

(5)

Owing to the size of the groups and the lack of special selection, the army test data yield probably the fairest and most unbiased comparison of negro and white intelligence which we possess. Negro soldiers scored lower than white on the Alpha test, the average score of the white soldier being 59, that of the Northern negro 39, and that of the Southern negro 12. Since Alpha was a test designed for literates, it may be argued—and with much reason—that the better educational equipment of the whites, and not their superior native ability, led to their better showing on Alpha. To a considerable extent, this is undeniably true, but it is hardly the whole story. The educational opportunities of the negro have been—and still are—poorer than those of the white, especially in the South, and these inequalities must surely be reflected in any test involving language and a knowledge of numbers. Yet when illiterate whites and negroes are compared for intelligence, the whites are still ahead. On the Beta test, for example, which it will be recalled is a non-language examination, the average score of the uneducated white soldier was 43 points, that of the uneducated northern negro 33 points, and that of the uneducated Southern negro 20 points. The gap here is not as great as on the Alpha test, to be sure, but it is still fairly large; so that, whether literate or illiterate, the negro is still *on the average* somewhat below the comparable white in general intelligence as measured by our tests. Of course the overlapping of scores in the two groups is large, and many negroes surpass the average white score. This is especially true where the selection of negroes is stringent, as in the case of officer material. For instance, about 40 per cent of the negro officers made A or B ratings on Alpha as against 80 per cent of white officers, but only 12 per cent of the white draft made A or B scores.

The Northern negro was superior to the Southern both on Alpha and Beta. Again it is impossible to tell just how much of this superiority comes from better educational equipment and how much from better native ability. Probably it is usually the more intelligent and more ambitious negro who moves to a Northern State where better educational and better working conditions may presumably be secured. If the Northern negro is first selected for intelligence, his better schooling would serve simply to increase still further the intellectual and cultural gap between him and his Southern kinsman.

(6)

An interesting comparison of the intelligence ratings of various nationalities may be secured from the scores made by foreign-born men who were drafted into the American army. The intelligence scores of these national groups were put in terms of a "combined scale"—a scale made up of the eight Alpha tests, the Stanford-Binet tests, and four tests from Beta. The maximum score on the "combined scale" was 25 points. The average scores of the men who were born in various foreign countries, together with the number of men in each group, is given in Table III.

TABLE III

Country of birth	Number of men	Mean Intelligence Score
England	411	14.87
Scotland	146	14.34
Holland	140	14.32
Germany	308	13.88
Denmark	325	13.69
Canada	972	13.66
Sweden	691	13.30
Norway	611	12.98
Belgium	129	12.79
Ireland	658	12.32
Austria	301	12.27
Turkey	423	12.02
Greece	572	11.90
Russia	2,340	11.34
Italy	4,009	11.01
Poland	382	10.74

It is apparent from the table that men born in northern European countries rank consistently higher, though the differences are slight, than men born in southern European countries. These variations in the average scores of the different national groups have led to acrimonious discussions and to some ill feeling. On the one hand are the supporters of the theory of "Nordic superiority" who hold that the Nordics (mostly northern Europeans) constitute a group quite distinct racially from the Alpines (mostly middle Europeans) and the Mediterraneans (mostly southern Europeans).[6] The Nordics, their champions insist, are more intelligent than their neighbors, and they point to the results of the intelligence tests as experimental evidence of this fact.

Arguing on the other side, the opponents of the Nordic claim explain the variations in intelligence test score as due entirely to differences in language, customs, training, and educational background. The high standing of the English and Scotch they take as concrete evidence of the influence of the language factor. Moreover, while disputing the actuality of the threefold racial division into Nordics, Alpines, and Mediterraneans, they hold that even if such classification were possible, we still have no idea how representative of each country (or each race) our small samples are. This last is undeniably true, as is also the further fact that our immigrants are rarely samplings from the same social and intellectual strata of the various countries from which they come. It would seem then that, all in all, the army tests hardly prove the Nordic claim to superiority.

Interesting evidence of the apparent decline in intelligence of American immigration over the last quarter-century may be gleaned from the army test results. For instance, those immigrants who had lived more than twenty years in this country scored higher on the "combined scale" than those who had lived here from ten to twenty years. These latter individuals, furthermore, scored higher than the very recent arrivals—those with less than five years' residence. Either we must conclude, apparently, that our immigration has become steadily less and less intelligent, or else take

[6] For a fuller discussion, see Brigham, C. C., *A Study of American Intelligence* (1922), pp. 119-210. Compare this reference with Brigham's recent statement in which he recedes from his earlier position; see *Eugenics News*, 1928, 13, 67-69.

the view that foreign-born men long exposed to American customs, language, and ways of life are enabled thereby to make higher scores on a general intelligence test than men equally intelligent by and large, but with shorter residence. The issue is far from settled. As is well known, our earlier immigrants were drawn mainly from northern European countries, Germany, the British Isles, and Scandinavia, and are generally and popularly believed to have been an exceptionally sturdy stock. Of late, American immigration has come largely from southern Europe, and there is much evidence that the influx from these countries has not been from the most desirable elements of the native populations. Southern Europeans scored lower in general on the "combined scale" than northern Europeans, and their scores were lower on the non-language as well as on the language parts of the test. We have pointed out above that these differences are scarcely significant, but at least they are hardly in favor of the lower groups. It seems probable, then, that our immigration has actually declined somewhat in intelligence; but the many unknown factors at work, such as differences in ability to understand and use the English language, more or less unfamiliarity with American social customs with resulting hesitation and timidity, and inadequate or different educational preparation, prevent any definite conclusion being drawn from the army test results as they stand.

(7)

In Section (3) it was pointed out that a soldier's intelligence score is evidently related to his amount of schooling. The degree of this relationship is still a moot question even among psychologists. Some hold that intelligence tests are little more than measures of scholastic achievement; others, that they measure, to a high degree, native ability. The following table in which are given the median Alpha scores made by officers and enlisted men who had completed, respectively, none to four school grades, five to eight school grades, high school, and college may serve to throw some light on this question.

Table IV

Group	*Median Alpha scores for given amounts of education*			
	0 to 4 grades	5 to 8 grades	High school	College
White soldiers (native-born)	22.0	51.1	92.1	117.8
White soldiers (foreign-born)	21.4	47.2	72.4	91.9
Negro soldiers (Northern)	17.0	37.2	71.2	90.5
Negro soldiers (Southern)	7.2	16.3	45.7	63.8
White officers	112.5	107.0	131.0	143.2

Striking evidence of the importance of education to success in the Alpha test is seen in the fact that the median scores of all groups (with a single exception) increase regularly with increases in schooling. In fact, the general rule would seem to be the more the schooling, the better the intelligence score. This might seem to dispose of Alpha as a measure of anything but school training did we not have equally striking evidence of the influence of mental alertness on Alpha score. The officers, for instance, score consistently higher than the native-born white soldiers for each grade of education, while the latter group, in turn, regularly exceeds the other three groups. At each educational level the order of Alpha score is: officers, native-born whites, foreign-born white, Northern negroes, and Southern negroes. These regular and consistent gaps in Alpha performance, for a *con-*

stant amount of schooling, bear significant testimony to the part played by native ability.

A comparison designed to test specifically this matter of the influence of schooling on Alpha may be cited in this connection. The median Alpha score made by the group of 600-odd officers (see Table IV) all of whom had completed eight grades or less of school was compared with the median Alpha score of the 14,000 white soldiers, all of whom had gone *beyond* the eighth grade. The officers' score was 107, that of the enlisted men 97—a difference of ten points in favor of the *less* educated officer group. This result has often been taken as a conclusive demonstration that native ability and not education is the "crucial" factor in determining an Alpha score. While this is probably true, note, nevertheless, that when the officers who had completed five to eight grades are compared with white soldiers of the *same* educational status (see Table IV), the difference is fifty-six points in favor of the officer group! Presumably, then, lack of education *reduced* the superiority of the first officer group from 56 points to 10 points.

Such comparisons as these lead inevitably to but one conclusion, namely, that the more able men made the highest Alpha scores and also, generally, had the most schooling. This is doubtless the result to be expected when we remember that education is in itself a highly selective process; that the stupid and unintelligent child simply does not get through school except rarely, and then, perhaps, not by reason of his own ability. Of every 1,000 children [7] who start out in the fifth grade, only 600, on the average, will complete the eighth grade; only about 140 will complete high school; and not more than twenty will go through college. No doubt there are many reasons, economic and otherwise, for this

[7] See pamphlet by Phillips, Frank M., *A Graphic View of Our Schools* (1927), p. 45.

enormous elimination; but certainly the most powerful is the inability to do the work of the school satisfactorily, with resulting discouragement and loss of interest.

The discovery that the more extensive the education the higher the Alpha score is not, therefore, proof positive that Alpha is a measure of school information and not a test of intelligence. Individuals who have completed high school and college are by virtue of that accomplishment alone highly selected as to intellect, and hence should be expected to score high on any valid measure of intelligence. Again, we must remember that the educational demands made by the Alpha test are not excessive. Granted a common-school education and ordinary acquaintance with current American life—which was true of the majority of the men who took the Alpha test in the army—a man's score must inevitably be principally a measure of his general intelligence, of his ability to learn and to profit by experience. No intelligence test can ever hope to measure "raw brain-power," and it would be of little value if it could; for intellect, by any reasonable definition, can be measured only as it expresses itself in the activities and tasks of everyday life. For men of meager education—owing to no fault of their own—as well as for those who through misfortune or untoward circumstances have been deprived of a normal environment, the Alpha test is admittedly an unfair measure of ability. This simply means that an Alpha score must always be interpreted with due regard for obvious handicaps and limitations.

(8)

Immediately after (and during) the war, the army Alpha test was given to hundreds of students in our colleges and universities. A comparison of the scores made by college students with those made by soldiers will prove interesting in view of the discussion in Section (7). The median Alpha scores made by college freshmen from many institutions fall between 130 and 140, which compares favorably with the median Alpha score of 139 made by the white officers, but is enormously higher than the 59 made by the average white soldier. Within the departments of a university, rather distinctive variations in Alpha score appear. In one large university, for instance, the post-graduate students scored highest (median 154), followed closely by the undergraduate students in arts (145), engineering (144), and business (143). Somewhat lower in the scale were the students in education, agriculture, pharmacy, and dentistry. The differences in score here must be almost entirely the result of differences in native ability, as the minimum schooling necessary for Alpha is substantially constant throughout.

If a candidate for college has an Alpha score below 100 points (120 for the better colleges), he will have an extremely hard time of it in college. Sometimes, of course, a student who scores not much over 100 points may "get by" in college, while another who scores high may be dropped because of poor scholarship. But these upsets do not occur often, and, when they do, can generally be explained as the result of great persistence, determination, and hard work on the part of those students who are average or below average in intellect, and by distractions, outside interests, laziness, or character defects in those able students who are eliminated. It is true, of course, that success in college does not depend wholly upon general intelligence; but we may be sure that intellectual ability is by far the most influential factor. The marked correlation (.50 — .65) between scholarship and the more discriminative and better-constructed group intelligence examinations, such as the Thorndike Intelligence Examination for High School Graduates and the Thurstone Psychological Examination, serve to demonstrate experimentally the close relation between general intelligence and school achievement.

The army tests were the starting-point for a host of group tests designed to measure general intellectual level. Many of these are now being widely used in our schools and colleges, chiefly as a means of selecting the more promising material, or for the purpose of classifying students into medium, slow, and accelerated groups in accordance with their ability. More and more, too, intelligence tests are being introduced into business for the purpose of diagnosis and selection. Many workers throughout the country are devoting their energies to the problem of increasing the validity and the accuracy of existing examinations and to the construction of new instruments. Every indication is that intelligence testing has come to stay. If due care is exercised in the interpretation of results and due regard is taken of emotional and temperamental (non-intellectual) factors, we may be certain that the future of the movement is a bright one.

Suggested Readings

1. An interesting and fairly comprehensive account of the army tests may be found in R. M. Yerkes and C. S. Yoakum's *Army Mental Tests* (1920).
2. For a further discussion of the relation between intelligence test scores and school achievement, and for the educational uses of intelligence tests, see F. N. Freeman's *Mental Tests* (1926), Chapter XIV.
3. The value and uses of mental tests in business are described in A. W. Kornhauser and F. A. Kingsbury's *Psychological Tests in Business* (1924).

Chapter 3

EBBINGHAUS'S STUDIES IN MEMORY AND FORGETTING

THE importance to experimental psychology of the experiments of Hermann Ebbinghaus on memory lies in the intrinsic value of the work itself as well as in the impetus and inspiration which it gave to literally scores of later investigations. Ebbinghaus was born in 1850 near Bonn, Germany. He attended several German universities, but returned to take his doctor's degree in philosophy at the University of Bonn at the age of twenty-three. For eight years (1886-1894), Ebbinghaus was a professor at the University of Berlin, from which post he went to the University of Breslau. He died in 1909 while in the midst of preparing a third edition of his book *Principles of Psychology*.

In his experimental work on memory, Ebbinghaus was much influenced by Fechner,[1] from whom, apparently he got the idea of mental measurement. The results of his memory experiments were published in 1885 after several years of interrupted work. They mark the first real attempt to apply precise scientific method to the study of the "higher mental processes." Such phenomena had been regarded as too "subjective," too fleeting, even too personal, perhaps, for exact and quantitative treatment. It is Ebbinghaus's contribution to have shown conclusively that memory products are as amenable to experiment and to measurement as any other natural facts with which science deals.

[1] For Fechner's work on the measurement of sensation, see Chap. 12.

HERMANN EBBINGHAUS
(1850–1909)

Ebbinghaus devised several valuable methods for measuring memory which can be employed with different kinds of material. In addition, he introduced a new kind of memory material—the so-called *nonsense syllables*—which possess among other advantages the very real one of being relatively free from "ready-made" associations. Nonsense syllables as used by Ebbinghaus were meaningless combinations of three letters, each combination consisting of two consonants separated by a vowel or diphthong. Examples are *bap, tox, muk,* and *rif.* Nonsense syllables of four letters, e.g., *nult, rulb, selx,* are often constructed also, and are perhaps more widely used in memory experiments at the present time than those of three letters.

To illustrate the very real advantage of using nonsense syllables in memory experiments, let us suppose that one sets out to measure the memory ability of a small group of educated adults, using as material Lincoln's "Gettysburg Address," or Poe's "Raven." Differences in memory ability will quickly appear, a considerable part of which may be attributed forthwith to the varying degrees of acquaintance with the material possessed by the subjects. In fact, probably as much individual variation will result from differences in familiarity as from differences in native ability to learn. One man may be favored because he is already slightly familiar with the selection, or because he is of literary bent and hence accustomed to such memory tasks. Another man may be at a decided disadvantage because he is a mechanical engineer in whose everyday activities literary selections and poems are seldom encountered. This unequal initial state of acquaintanceship and familiarity will always be present for such material when subjects differ greatly in age, education, cultural background, or training; and it exists, but to a somewhat lesser extent, even among children.

It was to overcome these handicaps, and as far as possible

to equalize the backgrounds of different subjects so that each will start with a clean "memory slate," that Ebbinghaus invented his nonsense syllables. An equally important advantage of nonsense syllables is that the same individual can be tested under different conditions and at different times with material sufficiently equal in memory value and homogeneous in content to yield closely comparable results. All told, Ebbinghaus constructed about 2,500 nonsense syllables which he employed in the experiments to be described.

(2)

All of Ebbinghaus's experiments were carried out upon himself as subject and were performed in an extremely careful and highly controlled manner. In each group of experiments, Ebbinghaus proposed a general problem which he attempted to answer by means of specific experiments. These problems may be conveniently grouped under the following five heads:

1. What is the relation between the amount of material to be memorized and the time and effort required to learn it? Specifically, what effect does the *length* of a series of nonsense syllables have upon the *rapidity* with which it can be memorized?

2. What is the relation between amount or degree of learning and retention? What effect does the *number of repetitions* of a given series have upon its *retention*?

3. How is *forgetting* related to the time-interval between learning and recall? What effect does the passing of time have upon one's memory for comparable series of nonsense syllables?

4. What effect do *repeated learning* and frequent review have upon one's ability to retain what he studies?

5. What sort of connections are formed in learning: do

they run forward serially from one term to the next following only, or do they skip terms in the forward direction, and even sometimes in the backward direction? What is the relative strength of these different associations, assuming them to be so formed?

These questions may appear at first glance to be pretty closely restricted to nonsense-syllable learning, and hence to be of minor value in clearing up the vexed questions of learning and forgetting so common in everyday life. Closer inspection of Ebbinghaus's work, however, will show that its bearing upon the more complex problems of memory is considerable; and that Ebbinghaus approached such problems in the only really scientific way possible, namely, through the use of a rigorously controlled method and of standard material which avoided to a high degree the complications of unequal initial memory value.

(3)

Let us consider the five problems listed above in order.
1. What is the relation between the amount of material to be memorized and the time and effort required to learn it?
Common experience tells us that the longer a poem or a prose memory lesson, the harder it is to learn up to the point where it can be repeated "by heart." Will the learning of ten verses of a poem require twice as long, three times as long, or six times as long as the learning of five verses? Probably no one would care to commit himself to a definite arithmetical answer to such a question as this, though doubtless every one would be perfectly certain that it would take considerably longer. Ebbinghaus attacked this problem in the following way. First, he recorded the time and the number of repetitions necessary for him to learn different lists of seven, ten, twelve, sixteen, twenty-four, and thirty-six

nonsense syllables each, up to the point of *one* errorless reproduction.[2] He then calculated the average time put on each syllable in the different lists to give a comparative measure of effort. Ebbinghaus's results may be stated in tabular form as follows:

TABLE V

Length of lists	Number of readings	Time for lists	Average time per syllable
7	1	3 secs.	.4 secs.
10	13	52	5.2
12	17	82	6.8
16	30	196	12.0
24	44	422	17.6
36	55	792	22.0

From this table it is clear that the *time* as well as the *number* of repetitions necessary for learning increases much faster than the length of the list to be learned, and that neither of these measures of memory ability increases in simple arithmetic or geometric progression. There, is relatively speaking, an enormous jump in the number of readings needed as we go from seven to ten syllables; but after this the increase is roughly constant and at the rate of about 150 per cent from each syllable list to the next following. If we disregard the again comparatively large increase in time of learning from the seven-word to the ten-word list, the time increment also is roughly constant and at the rate of about 200 per cent. It is interesting to compare the effort involved in learning twelve, twenty-four, and thirty-six syllables, as these lists are in the ratio 1:2:3. Taking the "average time per syllable" for a list of twelve, i.e., 6.8 seconds per syllable, as our datum or reference point, the list of twenty-four syllables requires two and one-half times,

[2] This method is called the "learning method."

and that of thirty-six, three and two-tenths times as much time expenditure per syllable as the list of twelve. The absolute increase is about 11 seconds per syllable, on the average, from twelve to twenty-four syllables and about 5 seconds per syllable from twenty-four to thirty-six; hence it is clearly harder to go from twelve to twenty-four syllables than from twenty-four to thirty-six.

As the memory task increases in length, not only do we get an increase in the number of readings and the time required—which is to be expected—but a marked increase in the *time per syllable* as well. This suggests that the greater the number of associations required, the greater is the effort which must be expended on each association; and that learning a long list is not, therefore, simply a matter of adding on *more* syllables to a short list. A partial explanation of this finding would seem to lie in the need of linking together parts or sections of the longer lists into a coherent whole as well as of tying together the separate syllables or elements. It is highly probable, too, that in the longer lists the later-formed associations serve to confuse and to be confused by those which come earlier, and as a result all require better fixation, i.e., more learning. This interference of one set of associations with another set is called *retroactive inhibition* when it extends in the backward direction, and *proactive inhibition* when it extends in the forward direction. Both kinds of confusion have been much studied by psychologists.[3] The moral for the practical learner lies in recognizing the fact that in learning a long lesson not only must he expend more time and effort than in learning a short lesson, but more time and effort per element or detail as well.

[3] See, in this connection, Robinson, E. S., *Some Factors Determining the Degree of Retroactive Inhibition*, Psychological Monographs (1920), 28, 128.

By way of contrast with these results from nonsense material, it is interesting to compare some results got by Ebbinghaus with meaningful subject-matter. In seven tests, each test comprising six stanzas from Byron's "Don Juan," Ebbinghaus found that he required on the average about eight repetitions to reach his standard of one errorless recitation. Each stanza contained about eighty syllables. On the basis of the results given in Table V above, Ebbinghaus estimated that he would probably have required about seventy to eighty repetitions to learn eighty nonsense syllables up to his standard of one errorless recitation. A comparison of these figures for meaningful and meaningless material gives us, then, a ratio of 10:1 in favor of the meaningful, and furnishes, in Ebbinghaus's words, "an approximate numerical expression for the extraordinary advantage which the combined ties of meaning, rhythm, rime, and a common language give to the material to be memorized."

An objection may be raised to Ebbinghaus's standard of learning, namely, the time and the number of repetitions necessary to reach the *first* errorless reproduction. Impetuous subjects, it may be said, will attempt to reproduce a list before it has been well learned, and hence run the risk of becoming confused and discouraged; while cautious individuals will study longer than is necessary, and hence tend to "overlearn." This "error of variable standard" can be controlled in a practical way by requiring the subject to attempt reproduction fairly early—but not too early—in his learning, thus making sure that the first errorless reproduction is really the first reproduction of which he is capable. With trained subjects little difficulty arises on this account. Probably no one since Ebbinghaus has been better trained or more careful than he; hence his results are highly reliable, although based upon data from only one person.

(4)

2. *What is the relation between the amount or degree of learning, and retention?*

The reader will readily understand that the results quoted in the last section are limited in scope, since in every case Ebbinghaus learned his lists up to the point of one correct reproduction only. Ordinarily, of course, we memorize to a considerably greater degree than this, and in general the slower the learner, the more often and the more painstakingly does he go over his task. What is the influence of this overlearning [4] upon retention? Ebbinghaus undertook to answer this question in the following experiment: He read over the lists of sixteen syllables in exactly the same way and at the same rate, except that the number of readings varied from eight to sixty-four. This means, of course, that some of the lists were overlearned to a very high degree. Twenty-four hours later he studied these same lists until he could just recite them once. He then figured the percentage saved in relearning each list—i.e., he found how many repetitions *less* were required to relearn than to learn twenty-four hours before, and what per cent this saving was of the original learning time. This method of studying memory was devised by Ebbinghaus and is known as the "saving method." Following are some of his results based on several lists:

TABLE VI

Number of readings on the first day....	8	16	24	32	42	53	64
Per cent saved in relearning the lists 24 hours later	8	15	23	32	45	54	64

[4] According to Ebbinghaus's standards, any learning over and above that necessary to secure one correct reproduction would be considered overlearning.

Evidently each original repetition brought about a saving of almost exactly 1 per cent in the relearning necessary on the following day. The remarkable uniformity of these results suggests that 100 readings on the first day should logically make it possible to reproduce a list on the next day without any additional learning—the saving would be 100 per cent! But Ebbinghaus found that it was impossible for him to read through a list 100 times without serious lapses of attention, fatigue, and drowsiness. This indicates that the regular saving of 1 per cent for each previous day's reading will eventually break down as the learner's "physiological limit" is reached; and that beyond this point further repetitions will be of little or no value.

The clear implication of this experiment is that degree of retention depends directly upon the amount of work done (overlearning), as well as upon the amount to be learned. In memorizing nonsense syllables, at least, the strength of the connections formed, the saving in relearning, is, up to a certain point, roughly proportional to the amount of study put on them. This fact throws light upon the widely held view that the slow learner retains better than the fast learner. Perhaps the truth of the matter is that the slow learner does more overlearning than the quick learner, and hence saves more in relearning. In this connection the following data from Radosavljevich [5] are of interest. This experimenter compared children with adults in the learning of twelve syllable nonsense lists and the relearning of the same lists after twenty-four hours. His results were as follows:

[5] A later investigator (1907), who repeated much of Ebbinghaus's work using more subjects. See Ladd and Woodworth, *Elements of Physiological Psychology* (1911), p. 576 ff., for a more extensive account of his experiments.

TABLE VII

	No. readings in first learning	No. readings needed to relearn 24 hours later	Per cent of saving
Adults	20	6	70
Children	42	7	83

The children took twice as many readings to learn the lists originally, but they saved a considerably larger per cent in relearning than the adults. Very probably this is what happens in the case of the slow but sure learner, and accounts for his apparent superiority in retention over the rapid learner. For when the amount or degree of learning is kept constant, the quick learner retains better than the slow learner (Luh, pages 68-72).

Of the many studies of degree of learning and retention which have followed those of Ebbinghaus, probably the most thorough is that of Luh (1922). This experimenter had ten subjects memorize lists of twelve nonsense syllables to four degrees or stages of completeness: 100 per cent, 150 per cent, 67 per cent, and 33 per cent. In 100 per cent learning each subject memorized his lists up to the point of *one* errorless recitation; in 150 per cent learning he was allowed as many repetitions as in 100 per cent learning plus a bonus of half as many again; in 67 per cent learning he was given two-thirds as many repetitions as in 100 per cent learning; and in 33 per cent learning, one-third as many. Retention was tested by three methods: written reproduction, recognition, and reconstruction (for description, see later page 66). Luh's results showing the amounts retained after three time-intervals are given in Table VIII.

TABLE VIII

Memory method	Amount retained after three time-intervals		
Written reproduction	4 hours	1 day	2 days
150% learning	82%	39%	31%
100%	65	46	40
67%	66	42	25
33%	43	26	14
Recognition			
150% learning	93%	83%	73%
100%	92	78	79
67%	85	74	62
33%	55	45	26
Reconstruction			
150% learning	91%	43%	44%
100%	75	49	44
67%	65	57	32
33%	48	26	20

On the whole these results support Ebbinghaus in so far as they indicate that increasing the repetitions (up to a certain point) leads to better retention. The "diminishing returns" from overlearning, commented upon by Ebbinghaus, are quite clearly shown in Luh's records, since after intervals of one day and two days better results are obtained from 100 per cent than from 150 per cent learning. However, the loss from overlearning appears much sooner in Luh's than in Ebbinghaus's results. From Table V we find that it took Ebbinghaus thirty repetitions to learn sixteen nonsense syllables up to the standard of one correct recitation. If we take thirty-two repetitions by Ebbinghaus (see Table VI) as roughly equivalent to Luh's 100 per cent learning, it would seem that Ebbinghaus overlearned his material up to 200 per cent (sixty-four repetitions) without any diminishing return appearing. Unfortunately, Tables VI and VIII are not strictly comparable, as Luh used different methods of presenting his material (see page 66) and of measuring memory retention; also his lists were shorter than those of Ebbinghaus, viz., twelve vs. sixteen syllables. Again, Table VIII is based upon the average returns of ten persons, while Table VI gives Ebbinghaus's results alone. Doubtless much of the apparent discrepancy between the two tables may be fairly attributed to differences in method; but, on the whole, Luh's results appear to be the more reliable. Summarizing our results from these experiments, it appears certain that overlearning up to a certain point (which must be determined experimentally) definitely increases retention.

(5)

3. How is forgetting related to the time-interval between learning and recall? What effect does the passing of time have upon one's memory for comparable series of nonsense syllables?

No doubt most of us have had the experience of finding that a poem memorized long ago, although it cannot be recited now, can be relearned in a much shorter time than it takes to memorize a new poem of the same length and the same approximate difficulty. Fortunately, too, this quicker relearning holds for most of the facts learned in school for which retention appears to be almost zero. Indeed, the ability to "get back" material once learned but now forgotten seems oftentimes to be the only real justification for having learned it at all. It is common experience, too, that the more recently we have studied a topic the fresher it tends to be. Just how is this forgetting related to the passing of time? Do memories dim gradually and progressively, or is comparatively a large amount lost quickly, some facts with possibly a vague outline remaining for a longer time? Ebbinghaus attacked this particular problem in what is probably his most important, and is certainly his best-known, experiment. Eight lists of thirteen nonsense syllables each were learned up to the point of *two* errorless recitations. Then, after a lapse of twenty minutes, the lists were again taken up and studied as before until each list could be recited twice without error. The actual time saved in relearning was then expressed as a *per cent* of the original learning time. (This is called the saving method.) To illustrate how this was done, it took Ebbinghaus on the average about eighteen minutes (1,080 seconds) to learn twelve lists of thirteen nonsense syllables each up to his new standard of two correct reproductions. After a lapse of twenty minutes it required only about eight minutes (498 seconds) for him to relearn the same lists. This means that there was a saving of about 10/18, or 56 per cent,[6] of the time which Ebbinghaus required to learn the lists originally. This figure (56 per cent) measures the retention, or the amount which "stuck" over a period of twenty minutes, and shows that the forgetting during this time was 100—56, or 44 per cent. Other lists of thirteen syllables each were learned by Ebbinghaus in the same manner and relearned again after periods of one hour, nine hours, one day, two days, six days, and thirty-one days in duration. The per cent of saving in each case was calculated as above illustrated. Many lists were learned and then relearned after the intervals stated, Ebbinghaus being careful so to distribute his experiments as to prevent any one period from being unduly favored by practice. Table IX summarizes his principal results:

[6] This percentage was determined more accurately to be 58 per cent by Ebbinghaus when all of his data were considered.

Table IX

Interval between learning and relearning	Percentage of work saved (retention)	Loss due to forgetting
20 minutes	58	42
1 hour	44	56
9 hours	36	64
24 hours	34	66
2 days	28	72
6 days	25	75
31 days	21	79

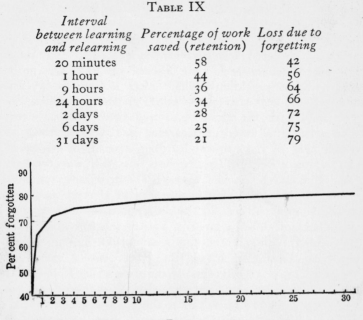

Fig. 4

Curve of Forgetting (Ebbinghaus) for Nonsense Syllables

The percentages forgotten are laid off on the vertical line, the time elapsed since learning along the horizontal base-line.

If we draw a graph of these results, laying off the time-intervals between learning and relearning along the base-line and the per cents forgotten on the vertical axis, we get Ebbinghaus's Curve of Forgetting, shown in Figure 4. The obverse of this curve, Figure 5, in which the per cents retained are plotted against the time-intervals between learning and relearning, is the Curve of Retention. This retention curve, which has been a classic in psychology for all of forty years, has the general character of an inverse logarithmic relationship.[7] It indicates that, after the large initial drop from twenty minutes to two days, forgetting proceeds more and more slowly until there is very little difference between the loss after ten days and after thirty days. A certain minimum, presumably, sticks almost indefinitely; and it is just this minimum which tips the balance against the uneducated man and in favor of the educated man even when the latter has been long out of school.

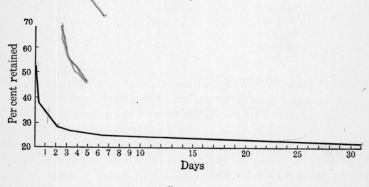

Fig. 5

Curve of Retention (Ebbinghaus) for Nonsense Syllables after Various Time Intervals

Later investigators working with many subjects and with meaningful material as well as with nonsense syllables have obtained results different in some respects from those of Ebbinghaus, but not markedly so. The following table from Radosavljevich gives the records from several subjects both for nonsense syllables and poetry.

[7] Its equation is $b = \dfrac{100k}{(\log t)^c + k}$, in which $b =$ per cent retained, $t =$ time-interval elapsing, and k and c are constants.

TABLE X

Interval between learning and relearning	Percentage of retention for nonsense syllables	Percentage of retention for poetry
5 minutes	98	100
20 minutes	89	96
1 hour	71	78
8 hours	47	50
24 hours	68	70
2 days	61	67
6 days	49	42
14 days	41	30
30 days	20	24
120 days	3	7

In Table X, forgetting proceeds at a slower rate than in the experimental results of Ebbinghaus, but the general shape of the two curves of forgetting is much the same. Radosavljevich's curve is less regular than that of Ebbinghaus, the extremely poor record after eight hours being explained as owing to the unfavorable time of day at which the relearning fell (Ebbinghaus had taken account of this factor in his work). The immediate retention for poetry is, as might have been expected, somewhat better than that for nonsense syllables, though, surprisingly enough, after twenty-four hours the difference between the two is negligible.

The differences between the records of Ebbinghaus and Radosavljevich are attributable, in part at least, to the fact that the latter's subjects probably overlearned their material, since they were in general neither so well trained nor so uniform in their learning methods as Ebbinghaus. Radosavljevich considered his results to be far superior to those of Ebbinghaus, but it is doubtful whether they actually discredit the earlier work.

Beside the matter of individual differences and overlearning, the retention of nonsense syllables depends to a large degree upon the method employed in measuring retention. This has been clearly shown by Luh in an experiment in which five relearning methods were compared: anticipation, relearning (or saving), written reproduction, reconstruction, and recognition. The presentation of the nonsense syllables throughout Luh's work was effected by a rotating drum apparatus which exposed the twelve syllables one at a time through an aperture in a screen. In the anticipation method, the subject attempted in his reproduction to anticipate each syllable before it was shown; the relearning method is the saving method of Ebbinghaus previously described; in written reproduction the subject simply wrote down all of the nonsense syllables which he could remember in a stated time; in reconstruction he was given the twelve syllables, each on a separate slip of paper, and was instructed to rearrange them in the original order of presentation; and in recognition he attempted to select from twenty-four syllables the twelve which he had seen. Luh's results are shown in Table XI and his retention curves in Figure 6.

TABLE XI

Method	Per cents retained after				
	20 mins.	1 hour	4 hours	1 day	2 days
Anticipation	68	50	39	18	10
Relearning (saving).	75	66	55	52	48
Written reproduction	88	82	61	39	27
Reconstruction	92	88	75	51	39
Recognition	98	95	93	75	72

The outstanding fact in Table XI is the discrepancy in percentages retained after the five given intervals. Clearly the method employed in recording amounts retained is sufficient in itself to make the losses after various time-intervals appear decidedly different in size. The hardest method is anticipation, which is almost pure recall, with a minimum of "cues"; the easiest method is recognition, where the loss after two days is slightly less than the loss after twenty minutes by the anticipation method. This result, i.e., that recognition is decidedly easier than recall, has been frequently shown by other investigators.[8]

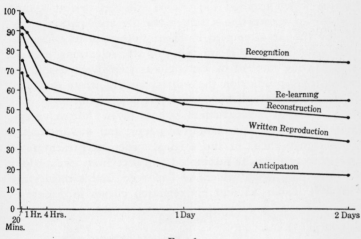

Fig. 6

Curves of Retention for Twelve Nonsense Syllables Learned by Five Different Methods

Percentages retained are laid off on the vertical axis; times between learning and relearning on the horizontal axis. (From Luh, 1922.)

The percentages retained by the relearning method are the only results directly comparable to those of Ebbinghaus (see Table IX), since Ebbinghaus employed only the relearning (i.e., saving) method. A comparison of the percentages saved for four time-intervals as found by Ebbinghaus and Luh is as follows:

[8] See for example Strong, E. K., *Effect of the Time Interval upon Recognitive Memory, Psychological Review* (1913), 20, 339 ff.

	20 mins.	1 hour	1 day	2 days
Ebbinghaus	58%	44%	34%	28%
Luh	75%	66%	52%	48%
Difference	17%	22%	18%	20%

Ebbinghaus's results run regularly from 18 to 20 per cent below those of Luh for comparable time-intervals. Perhaps part of this difference is due to the fact that Ebbinghaus learned thirteen nonsense syllables, while Luh's subjects learned only twelve. From Table V we know that the addition of two extra syllables (the jump from ten to twelve) increases the number of readings necessary for learning from thirteen to seventeen; hence an increase of one syllable might be expected to have some effect, at least, on the saving from relearning. But the greater part of the difference is undoubtedly due to the method of presentation. Luh's presentation was rigidly controlled, each syllable being shown as an isolated unit so that connections must have been almost 100 per cent in the forward direction. On the other hand, Ebbinghaus's lists, which were spread out before him, offered ample opportunity for backward as well as forward associations and for associations with the list as a whole (see page 75 later). If learning was easier in Ebbinghaus's procedure than in Luh's, the enforced over-learning of the latter's subjects as compared with Ebbinghaus would inevitably have made forgetting less rapid.

One further recent experiment on memory retention may be cited, an experiment this time in which highly complex and meaningful material was used. H. E. Jones (1923) has studied the retention of lectures by college students, after the passage of various time-intervals. Using a large group of subjects, this investigator found that, at the close of a forty-minute lecture, students can reproduce on the average about 62 per cent of the material just presented; after three or four days, about 45 per cent is remembered; after one week, 35 per cent; after two weeks 31 per cent; and after eight weeks, 24 per cent. The retention curve plotted from these data falls off in much the same fashion as that of Ebbinghaus for nonsense syllables: i.e., the loss is rapid at first and progressively slower as time goes on.

These results on forgetting are of considerable practical import to the student interested in retaining as long as possible the material which he has learned. Since forgetting is relatively very much faster during the time immediately following learning, obviously the thing to do is to review early and often. In this way what one has learned will be held, so to speak, above the "memory threshold." It must be kept in mind, however, that Ebbinghaus barely learned his material in the first place. We have found already how enormously retention is affected by overlearning. Therefore, when a memory lesson is exceedingly well learned to begin with, forgetting must proceed at a very much slower rate than that exhibited by Ebbinghaus's curve (see Figure 4). The effect of repeated learning will be considered in the next section.

(6)

4. What effect do repeated learning and frequent review have upon one's ability to retain what he studies?

We have seen in the last section that material just barely learned tends to be forgotten very rapidly at first and then more slowly as time goes on. Also, that the amount forgotten depends upon the method of recording retention, as well as upon the labor expended in the original learning, appears clearly in Ebbinghaus's and Luh's results (Tables VI and VIII). What effect, we may now ask, does repeated learning (review) have upon retention? Ebbinghaus attempted to answer this question in the following experiment. First, series of twelve, twenty-four, and thirty-six nonsense syllables as well as stanzas from Byron's "Don Juan" were learned. They were then relearned at the same hour on six successive days, each time up to the standard of one correct recitation. Table XII shows the number of repetitions required at each period and the per cent saved over the first day's record.

TABLE XII

No. of syllables in series		No. of repetitions which (on the average) were necessary for relearning the series on successive days; also per cent saved on successive days over the first day's record

			Days					
			I	II	III	IV	V	VI
12	Number of repetitions..		16.5	11	7.5	5	3	2.5
	% saved over first day.	...		34	55	70	82	85
24	Number of repetitions..		44	22.5	12.5	7.5	4.5	3.5
	% saved over first day.	...		49	72	83	90	92
36	Number of repetitions..		55	23	11	7.5	4.5	3.5
	% saved over first day.	...		58	80	86	92	94
1 stanza "Don Juan"								
	Number of repetitions..		7.75	3.75	1.75	.5	0	0
	% saved over first day.	...		52	77	94	100	100

The important fact in Table XII is that the necessary amount of relearning becomes progressively less and less on each succeeding day. In other words, the much exercised or older associations are forgotten more slowly than the less exercised or newer associations. On each succeeding day, Ebbinghaus brought his learning up to the standard of the previous day—one correct recitation. If this means that the associations formed were left in the *same* condition at the end of each day's learning, then logically we should expect the loss to be about the same from one day to the next, no matter how often the learning was repeated. To use an analogy, forgetting according to this view might be conceived of as the running down of a clock which must be rewound to the same point each day in order to bring it back to its original efficiency. So if it took eleven repetitions on the second day to bring the twelve nonsense syllables up to their original strength on the first day, it should take eleven repetitions to bring them up to the same standard on the third day, the fourth day, the fifth, and the sixth. On the contrary, however, we find that the loss due to forgetting became less and less after each learning period. This can mean but one thing, namely, that connections are more strongly established the more often they are exercised. So the multiplication table, the months of the year, and the names and relations of common coins are rarely forgotten except by very old persons or by those suffering from mental disease.

It is interesting to note in Table XII that the required repetitions, when the learning was repeated at stated intervals, were relatively fewer for the longer lists. This is owing to the fact that many more repetitions were needed originally to fixate the longer series; hence from the beginning the associations in these lists were more firmly established. The saving, for example, in relearning thirty-six nonsense syllables after twenty-four hours (Table XII) was 58 per cent as against a saving of 34 per cent for twelve nonsense syllables after the same interval. But nearly three and one-half times as many repetitions were needed to learn the longer list in the first place.

An important discovery made by Ebbinghaus in the present connection has to do with the relative value of *distributed* versus *concentrated* learning. Ebbinghaus found that sixty-eight successive readings of a twelve-syllable list made it possible for him to relearn the same list on the following day after only seven repetitions. When his readings were spaced over three days, the same result was not attained until the fourth day—but only thirty-eight preceding readings were necessary! In other words, by a judicious distribution of effort over three days, a result was secured which when packed into a single day required *twice* as much labor. The superiority of distributed over concentrated learning has been since verified by other experimenters. Jost (1897), for example, using lists of nonsense syllables, compared ten repetitions a day for three days with thirty repetitions in a single day, and found an added saving of about 15 per cent in favor of distributed learning. Lyon (1914) found distributed learning to give better retention than learning confined to a single sitting. In a recent well-controlled experiment Robinson (1921) found distributed learning of three-place numbers to be superior to concentrated learning both with respect to amount retained and accuracy of recall. Robinson gives a bibliography of thirty titles on the topic of the relative efficiency of distributed versus concentrated learning.

Closely related to the question of the best distribution of learning and review is that of the value of recitation during the learning itself. Some experiments of Gates (1917) bearing on this point are instructive. Gates gave his subjects nine minutes in which to study lists of sixteen nonsense syllables. Some were told to devote their entire time to reading the lists over and over. Others gave one fifth of their time to "self-recitation"; that is, each subject spent this time in attempting to recite the list to himself, prompting himself when necessary with frequent reference back to the list. Still other subjects gave two fifths, three fifths, and even four fifths to self-recitation. The results of the tests given at the end of the learning period showed that recitation is a decided aid in memorizing. Those who gave four fifths of their time to recitation, for instance, remembered twice as much as those who simply read the lists over silently. In every case, in fact, it was found that recitation gave better retention than simple reading; and this was true for meaningful material the same as for nonsense syllables.

The results quoted in the last few paragraphs are of considerable importance in school work, for they show clearly that repetition and frequent review are more effective and more saving of time and labor than learning concentrated into one great effort. It is sometimes true, of course, that the clever student will be able to "cram" enough information to pass the next day's examination. However, he will almost certainly retain less of the content than his more sagacious brother who has distributed his learning throughout the course in the manner recommended by the professor. So in the matter of retention, at least, it would seem that virtue is rewarded!

By the way of summary, let us list the main factors which we have found influential in determining the rate of forgetting. *First* of all, the length of the lesson to be learned is clearly an important fact. *Second,* there is the amount of labor expended on learning: the more repetitions and the longer the time spent in learning, the greater (within limits) the retention. *Third,* there is the distribution of effort to be considered. Judiciously spaced review is nearly always superior to massed or concentrated learning, while self-recitation is better than merely reading the material. *Fourth* and last is the character of the material to be learned. Meaningful material is more easily "fixated" and better retained than nonsense material.

(6)

5. What sort of connections are formed in learning: do they run forward serially from one term to the next following only, or do they skip terms in the forward direction, and even sometimes in the backward direction? What is the relative strength of these different associations, assuming them to be so formed?

In any kind of learning, it often seems that in addition to simple *1, 2, 3,* or *a, b, c* forward associations formed serially, other connections are set up in various ways within the material to be learned, as well as with what we already know. In the experiments of Ebbinghaus hitherto described, repetition always proceeded regularly from one syllable to the next following. Hence, it would appear that only serial connections could be made, and that these connections must be formed in the forward direction only. Are there any other associations formed in nonsense syllable learning?

Ebbinghaus set out to answer this question by learning lists of sixteen syllables up to the point of one correct recitation, and then twenty-four hours later learning "derived" lists made up in a variety of ways from the original lists. If we designate the syllables of an original list by numbers, as 1, 2, 3 . . . 16, a sample derived list might be:

1, 3, 5, 7, 9, 11, 13, 15, 2, 4, 6, 8, 10, 12, 14, 16.

Such a derived list would clearly benefit from forward associations between one term and the second following if such associations had been formed in learning the original list. It should be easier, then, to relearn such a derived list than an entirely new one. Another derived list might skip two syllables in the forward direction:

1, 4, 7, 10, 13, 16, 2, 5, 8, 11, 14, 3, 6, 9, 12, 15,

thus giving more remote forward associations a chance to

operate if present. Still other derived lists drawn up by Ebbinghaus skipped three, four, and up to seven intervening syllables. In addition to these, other lists were constructed in which the syllables were reversed in regular order from 16 to 1, or were simply jumbled up or arranged in chance order. Thus forward associations, both near and remote, backward associations, and any other incidental connections were given a chance to operate in the relearning if present in fact.

The average saving in terms of repetitions in learning these derived lists twenty-four hours after the original lists had been learned is shown in Table XIII.

TABLE XIII

Saving in relearning original lists unchanged........	33%
Saving in learning lists derived by skipping 1 syllable	11%
2 syllables	7%
3	6%
7	3%
Saving in learning reversed lists...................	12%
reversed lists, 1 syllable skipped..	5%
lists, syllables arranged by chance	0.5%

The percentages of saving shown in the table are rather small in several cases, but they are based upon six or more lists and are statistically reliable. It seems clear that connections were actually formed in learning these lists not simply from one syllable to the next following, but to the second, the third, and even more remote terms. To quote Ebbinghaus. "As a result of the repetition of the syllable series, certain connections are established between each member and all of those that follow it. These connections are revealed by the fact that the syllable pairs so bound together are recalled to mind more easily and with the overcoming of less friction than similar pairs which have not been previously united." The more remote the terms, the weaker the connection tends to be. Only in the case of derived lists in which the syllables are simply thrown together by chance or reversed with one syllable skipped is there no real saving.

The explanation of "backward," "remote forward," and "incidental" associations is *probably* to be found in the learning method employed by Ebbinghaus rather than in any reversible neural mechanism. With his lists of nonsense syllables spread out before him, it was almost impossible for Ebbinghaus to refrain from glancing backward and forward as he read slowly through a list. Hence his method might account for the adventitious connections which showed up later on in learning the derived lists. It seems likely that much of the benefit obtained from overlearning is brought about by a strengthening of the essential forward associations together with a gradual weakening of indirect and useless connections. With continued repetitions, bonds which might easily cause confusion and interference when learning is imperfect are minimized in favor of the more necessary direct ones.

In attempting to summarize in brief space Ebbinghaus's chief contributions to experimental psychology, we must certainly list (1) his introduction and use of quantitative methods in the study of learning and forgetting; (2) his measurement of the factors governing fixation, retention, and recall in verbal learning; and (3) his invention of nonsense syllables. Ebbinghaus's memory methods are to-day standard procedures in the psychological laboratory. His main results may be accepted substantially as he left them. Of his invention of nonsense syllables Titchener remarks,[9] "It is not too much to say that the recourse to nonsense syllables, as a means to the study of association, marks the

[9] *Textbook of Psychology* (1913), p. 380.

most considerable advance, in this chapter of psychology, since the time of Aristotle." In brief, Hermann Ebbinghaus was the founder of the quantitative study of association.

Suggested Readings

1. Ebbinghaus's own account of his experiments will be found in *Memory, A Contribution to Experimental Psychology* (1885), translated in 1913 by H. A. Ruger and Clara E. Bussenius.
2. A comprehensive survey of the experimental work on memory and learning may be found in Walter S. Hunter's Chapter 15 in *The Foundations of Experimental Psychology* (1929).
3. Luh's study, *The Conditions of Retention,* is published in the Psychological Monographs (1922), vol. 31, 3.
4. Chapter XIII, *Memory,* in E. S. and F. R. Robinson's *Readings in General Psychology* (1923) contains much suggestive material on this topic.

Chapter 4

PAVLOV AND THE CONDITIONED REFLEX

(1)

THE researches of the great Russian scientist, Ivan Pavlov, on the conditioned reflex date roughly from the year 1904, in which Pavlov was awarded the Nobel prize in medicine. Pavlov's early results were published only in Russian, and hence for some time they were little known to scientists of other countries. When finally they began to be available, however, they were seized upon with avidity in America, especially by those younger psychologists who were dissatisfied with the introspective psychology then widely current. Here at last, it seemed to them, was the foundation upon which could be constructed a straightforward and naturalistic description of human behavior. So it happened that Pavlov's method and his findings became the mainstay of behaviorism, the modern revolt against introspective psychology, and are to-day still the chief scientific weapon of the strictly objective psychologist. In addition, however, and happily, Pavlov's researches have broad and important implications for general psychology as well. They have, for instance, thrown much light upon the mechanics of learning and habit-formation, and have led to an ingenious explanation of the age-old problem of sleep. Besides, Pavlov and his students have succeeded in producing abnormal mental states in animals akin to those widespread modern nervous ailments called neuroses, which are thought by many physicians and sociologists to be largely a by-

Courtesy of Science Service

IVAN P. PAVLOV

(1849–   )

product of present-day intense and complex civilization. To-day, at the age of eighty, this remarkable man, the son of an obscure peasant priest, still enthusiastically carries on his work, aided by a devoted group of students and followers. Experimental reports from his laboratory are eagerly awaited and read by scientific men the world over.

Pavlov's researches began with a well-known and frequently observed fact. Every one of us has seen the saliva drip from a dog's mouth as he waits in eager anticipation for his food. Probably most of us, too, have felt our mouths

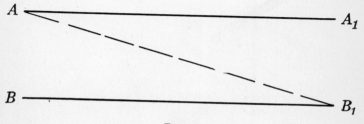

Fig. 7

<small>Simple Scheme to Show the Mechanism of a Conditioned Reflex</small>

"water" at the sight or odor of appetizing food. Originally, i.e., in young animals or very young children, saliva does not flow until food is actually taken into the mouth: in other words, it is an automatic and purely reflexive glandular reflex, the adequate stimulus being food-in-the-mouth. In time, however, as we all know, the sight or the odor of food alone is able to initiate the saliva flow. Such a reflexive act which is brought about by a situation other than its original, and biologically adequate, stimulus is a "conditioned reflex." The associated stimulus—the sight or odor of food—is called the conditioned stimulus, oftentimes the substitute stimulus, and the response to the conditioned or substitute stimulus is the conditioned reflex. The scheme is better shown, perhaps, in Figure 7.

Call A the adequate or unconditioned stimulus for the reflex A'; likewise let B represent the biologically adequate stimulus for B'. If A becomes an effective stimulus for the reflex B', A is the substitute stimulus and B' is the conditioned reflex. Theoretically, all of our native or reflexive activities are capable of being conditioned. The salivary reflex is particularly well adapted for experiment, however, because responses to other than the original stimulus can be accurately ascertained and their strength measured by noting the amount of saliva secreted.

The conditioned reflex has been widely employed in modern textbooks on psychology to explain how we learn or how we acquire new responses and new forms of behavior. But it would be a mistake for us to conclude that, because the conditioned response or C R [1] is a new term, it represents a new explanatory principle in psychology. In reality the idea is distinctly old, and is clearly implicit in the time-honored laws of association by similarity, contrast, and contiguity in space and time. Essentially what the laws of association attempted to explain was how one idea or thought grows out of, or is connected with, or substitutes for, another. As early as 1690, John Locke in his *Essay Concerning Human Understanding* gave illustrations to show how individual peculiarities, likes, and dislikes can be explained on the principle of association or conditioning. Locke also applied his explanatory principle of the association of ideas to the learning of language by children. He writes: "If we will observe how children learn languages, we shall find that

[1] C R stands for *conditioned response*. This is a better general term than *conditioned reflex* because the meaning of the term *reflex* is restricted to simple innate forms of behavior; and because the principle of conditioning has become so widely current in psychology as an explanation of complex forms of behavior which are clearly not reflexive.

to make them understand what the names of simple ideas, or substances, stand for, people ordinarily show them the things whereof they would have them have the idea; and then repeat to them the name that stands for it, as white, sweet, milk, sugar, cat, dog." Much later William James (1890) stated the law of contiguity, to which the other laws of association may be reduced, in the following passage: "When two elementary brain processes have been active together or in immediate succession, one of them on recurring, tends to propagate its excitement into the other." This is substantially the same principle as that of "conditioning."

If the idea of the conditioned response is by no means modern, how, we may ask, does the work of Pavlov differ from that of the older association psychologists? The difference lies essentially in the fact that Pavlov dealt not with "ideas," but with objective facts of behavior, i.e., with sensory stimuli and glandular responses which can be measured and compared. The great merit of Pavlov's method is that results are always measured. Without measurement there can be, ordinarily, no definiteness, no accuracy, and no objective facts. Without definiteness, accuracy, and objective facts there can be no science.

(2)

In his studies of the conditioned reflex, Pavlov has worked almost entirely with dogs and with the salivary reflex. Implicit in all of his work is the theory that everything the dog learns from puppyhood on is the result of the association of certain events which happen to occur at the same time with the biologically adequate stimulus to some native response, such as withdrawing, struggling, eating, sex behavior, or the like. What the dog can learn, i.e., what stimuli can be conditioned, how fast he learns, and how rapidly he forgets, is studied by measuring the saliva flow under rigidly controlled conditions. Pavlov chose to work with the salivary reflex mainly because the strength—or the degree—of a response, and not simply its occurrence or non-occurrence, is readily determined by the *amount* of saliva secreted. Besides, the salivary glands form a simple organ and not a composite one consisting of several muscles; there are no tonic reflexes present to interfere with or complicate the experimental control; and the response (secretion) can be measured with great precision in units as small as one tenth of a drop.

Pavlov's method of measuring the saliva flow is relatively simple. By means of a small incision, a fistula or opening is made in the dog's cheek through which a glass tube is inserted into the opening of the parotid, or submaxillary (two of the salivary) glands. The saliva which drips from the tube is collected and measured in finely graduated containers. As the salivary reflex is delicate and readily interfered with, the greatest precautions are taken in Pavlov's laboratory against any disturbances. All experiments are conducted in especially built windowless sound-proof rooms (there are eight in all), the walls of which are of turf, two feet thick. Both the food and the substitute stimuli are presented automatically, the food by an ingenious pneumatic device. Meanwhile the experimenter watches the dog from another compartment through a periscope in the wall, so that by no chance can the dog respond to him rather than to the stimuli. Each dog is put through a long training period which sometimes lasts many weeks, until he is thoroughly accustomed to the man who is to work with him. He is taught to stand still upon a small table in the experimental room on which he is secured by a collar and other restraining but not uncomfortable bonds. It is reported that the dogs look forward with every appearance of eagerness to the experiment, jump upon the table without command and place themselves in the correct position for the experiment. A diagram of the laboratory set-up is shown in Figure 8.

FIG. 8

DIAGRAM TO ILLUSTRATE PAVLOV'S METHOD OF ESTABLISHING A CONDITIONED SALIVARY REFLEX

The unconditioned stimulus (food) is presented automatically in the small dish through the window. At the same time, or prior to this, the conditioned stimulus, e.g., the ringing of a bell, is given. The saliva which flows from the dog's mouth is collected in the graduated glass receptacle. As the saliva flows into the receptacle, it strikes a small disc which depresses the lever just in front of the animal. This downward movement is transmitted to the lever behind the screen, and an automatic tracing is thus secured upon a smoked drum or kymograph. The kymographic record tells the experimenter how many drops of saliva have been secreted and how regular the flow has been. (From Yerkes and Morgulis, 1909.)

(3)

The simplest technique in conditioned reflex experiments is to apply over and over again the conditioned or substitute stimulus together with the unconditioned or natural stimulus. In Pavlov's experiments, olfactory, auditory, visual,

and tactual stimuli are all used as substitute stimuli, food
in every case being the unconditioned or adequate stimulus.
With the dog standing quietly on the table, a small dish
of food is presented, and at the same time a note, say, is
sounded or a bell is rung. This is repeated time after time
on successive days, the number of joint stimulations averaging from eight to ten per experiment. At first the saliva
flows only to the food plus the sound, but finally, after
repeated joint stimulations, usually from twenty to forty,
the saliva will begin to flow at the sound alone. The sound
is now a conditioned stimulus for food, and the dog's salivary
response is said to be conditioned. Figure 9 will show this
more clearly.

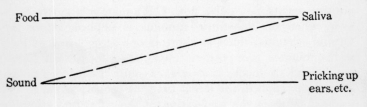

FIG. 9

How the Salivary Secretion May Be Conditioned to a Sound
Stimulus

Food and sound coming together often enough, the sound
gradually becomes an effective stimulus for the salivary flow.
Not only auditory stimuli, but olfactory stimuli, such as
the odor of camphor; visual stimuli, such as letters and
geometrical forms; tactual stimuli, touches or light scratches
on the skin—all have been substituted for food and made
to produce the saliva flow. In all such experiments as these,
the dog's brain and nervous system may be considered to
have formed a connection between the two stimuli, or
learned that the substitute stimulus stands for the food.

Through such associations, the range of stimuli which lead to a given simple reflexive act may become enormously increased. Part of the widespread activity of both dog and human is doubtless acquired through just such simple conditioned reflexes.

The factor of time is important in conditioned reflex experiments. When the conditioned, or substitute, stimulus is given simultaneously with the natural stimulus, the C R can usually be secured. But if the substitute stimulus comes for even as short a period as one second *after* the natural stimulus, there is no C R. Krestovnikoff, one of Pavlov's workers, made 1,000 trials in which the substitute stimulus, a scratch on the skin, was applied from one to three seconds after the unconditioned stimulus (food) without securing positive results, i.e., saliva flow. C R's may be secured, however, when the substitute stimulus is applied *before* the natural stimulus; times as short as one second, and as long as five minutes, give positive results. If a substitute stimulus, e.g., sound or touch, is *continued* until the unconditioned stimulus is applied, the latent time [2] is roughly equal to the interval between the application of the substitute stimulus and the natural one. Thus, if a note is sounded on a horn, and two minutes later food is given, the saliva will not begin to flow, once the C R has been established, until the horn has been sounding for two minutes. This is called a "delayed reflex." The longer the interval between the substitute and the natural stimulus, the more numerous the applications needed to build up the C R.

When the substitute stimulus is applied *before* the natural stimulus (food), it is not always necessary that it be continued until the food is presented. For instance, the substitute stimulus may first be applied, a pause allowed, and

[2] The time between the application of the stimulus and the appearance of the C R.

then the food presented. This pause between substitute and natural stimulus may be of considerable length; even three minutes is not unusual. The latent period in these experiments almost exactly equals the period between the application of the substitute stimulus and the food. For example, a note may be sounded once, and two minutes later food given, and this process be repeated many times. Eventually, when the animal is conditioned, saliva will begin to flow just two minutes after the sound, at the time when the food ordinarily appeared. This type of delayed response is called a "trace reflex." That the intervening period is not simply one of inactivity is shown by the fact that any extra stimulus (if it be a strong one) which by chance or otherwise is applied during the waiting period will cause a secretion of saliva immediately (see later page 90). The restraining mechanism at work during this wait is apparently like a delicate balance which is upset by any strong supervening stimulus.

Another phenomenon closely akin to the trace reflex is called simply the "time reflex." If a dog is fed at stated intervals, say every ten minutes, he soon becomes conditioned to this time-interval so that saliva will flow every ten minutes in anticipation, as it were, of the food. It would seem in such cases that some rhythm or periodicity had been established in the nervous system which "sets off" the response at the proper time, much as a "repeater" alarm-clock rings every two minutes or so. Examples of such rhythms or time reflexes in everyday life will at once come to mind. Some people awaken at the same time every morning, oftentimes just before the alarm-clock rings, while many, through vague but unmistakable inner cues, know when their regular lunch-time has arrived without consulting their watches. Periodicity in efficiency during the day—physiological C R's possibly—seem to be well established.

(4)

Closely bound up with the question of the time relations between substitute and natural stimulus is that of the degree of differentiation or selection possible among various coacting stimuli. This is clearly an important problem, for obviously there must be a high degree of selection and choice among stimuli. Otherwise, the dog's salivary secretion would be general and uncontrolled, since dogs are continuously being bombarded by a multiplicity of sounds, smells, sights, and touches when eating. How is this selection made, and how fine is a dog's differentiating ability? Pavlov and his workers have attacked the problem in many experiments, one of which is here described. First, two spots A and B on the dog's flank were selected. The A spot was lightly scratched, and at the same time food was given. In like manner B was touched, but no food was given. After many repetitions and many weeks of work, A with food, B without food, the point was finally reached whereupon touching A always gave the salivary reflex, and touching B never gave it. The negative spot B was then moved closer and closer to A, in order to study the fineness of differentiation, until the two spots were separated by only a few millimeters. Still A gave the reflex, while B invariably failed to give it. Inevitably, however, this very fine differentiation broke down when a certain point was reached. If the negative stimulus, for instance, is almost identical with, or very similar to the positive stimulus, both will produce the C R, the degree of response, i.e., amount of saliva, in the case of the negative stimulus depending upon its nearness or similarity to the conditioned stimulus. This phenomenon of spread of stimulation has been called by Pavlov "irradiation." The degree of irradiation can be somewhat reduced by frequently reinforcing the conditioned stimulus: i.e., by applying the conditioned stimulus together with the unconditioned stimulus (food).

Clean-cut differentiation of stimuli to a quite high degree has been secured by Pavlov's workers with other than tactual stimuli. Bieliakoff trained his dogs to differentiate between tones of 800, and of 812 and 825 vibrations per second. This investigator found that he must begin with the least similar (825 vibs.) and proceed to the more similar (812 vibs.) tones in order to secure differentiation, as the reverse procedure failed to give positive results. In other experiments, it was found that the dog could distinguish between metronome beats at the rate of 96 and 100 per second; and in the case of visual stimuli between a circle and an ellipse seven-eighths as large.

All of the results just cited were secured with *simultaneous stimulation*. When there is a time-interval between the conditioned and the natural stimulus, the fineness of differentiation is considerably reduced, being inversely proportional (roughly) to the length of the pause. No high degree of differentiation is possible if the pause between the conditioned and the natural stimulus is long; apparently, irradiation, or spread of stimulation, prevents a clear-cut differentiation from occurring in these delayed responses.

(5)

The ability of the brain and nervous system of the dog to differentiate between two closely similar stimuli, sounds, touches, or visual objects, is attributed by Pavlov to an actively restraining neural mechanism called "inhibition." Inhibition is roughly analogous to the braking of an automobile which is gathering too much speed on a hill. This concept is well illustrated by an experiment in which were selected four spots, *A1, A2, A3,* and *A4,* on a dog's flank

(Figure 10). When each of these spots was touched, food was given, and this process was continued until all of the spots called out the salivary reflex. These may be called positive spots. Another spot, *B*, in the same region was next selected and touched over a long period, no food being given on the successive stimulations. At first, touches on the *B*

FIG. 10

HOW INHIBITION MAY BE STUDIED

Spots *A¹*, *A²*, *A³*, and *A⁴* are positive spots; *B* is a negative spot. For full description see text.

spot led to a saliva flow due to irradiation; but finally, as no food was ever given, the C R ceased, and the spot became negative. Now, when the negative *B* was touched and afterwards any one of the positive *A* spots, no saliva flowed in spite of the fact that all of the *A's* were positive! This highly interesting result is explained by Pavlov as due to the spread of the inhibiting, or restraining action set up in that part of the dog's nervous system controlling the B spot to the part controlling the A spots. Such "inhibition of an excitation" is a general fact encountered in all C R's— it occurs with auditory, visual, and olfactory, as well as tactual stimuli.

Ordinarily, as we have seen, the negative B spot does not give a saliva flow. But if when B is touched, a bell or note is sounded at the same time, the C R will at once appear— saliva will begin to drop as though B were a positive A spot. This "inhibition of an inhibition" is fairly common in C R experiments, and has been mentioned before in describing the trace reflex (page 86). It will be remembered that the C R does not appear until a given time *after* the substitute stimulus, the exact time depending upon the period originally intervening between the substitute stimulus and the food. During the waiting period the reflex is held in check or inhibited by the dog's nervous system until the proper time arrives for releasing the brake. But, as noted above, any strong extraneous stimulus will lift the brake, causing the salivary reflex to appear. For example, in an experiment conducted by Anrep, one of Pavlov's students, an irritating odor caused twenty-eight drops of saliva to flow during a trace reflex; while on another occasion the buzzing of a fly had the same disorganizing effect. Perhaps the reader will the more readily understand now the need for sound-proof, windowless rooms, and for the other extreme precautions taken in C R work.

If any one of the positive A spots is touched and at the same time an indifferent spot—one not producing the reflex— is stimulated, the reflexive response to A will gradually diminish and finally drop to o. This blocking of a positive stimulus by an indifferent one is called a "conditioned inhibition." It may be irradiated to other stimuli. Thus if A is the positive substitute stimulus, and X the indifferent stimulus, the response may be inhibited not only to A plus X, but also to A plus X plus Y plus Z. The degree of inhibition—diminution of saliva flow—depends largely upon the similarity of the added stimuli to the indifferent stimulus X. When a C R is not occasionally reinforced by its natural stimulus, it soon dies out or becomes extinguished—fails to produce the salivary flow. This is known as the "extinction" of the C R. Sometimes it happens that the C R will again function after a period of extinction, due probably to the fact that some inhibiting or suppressing stimulus has gradually lost its force. But usually reinforcement is necessary.

Without doubt, the outstanding finding in Pavlov's experiments on differentiation is the tremendous value of this inhibitory power in the life of the dog. Without his "braking power," the dog would be unable to choose or select. He would respond hit or miss to every stimulation, unimportant as well as important; in short, his existence would be a riotous confusion of events.

What happens when the dog loses his ability to discriminate is clearly shown in a case of "experimental neurosis" produced by Pavlov and his group in a dog. Krestovnikova, one of Pavlov's students, conditioned a dog so that saliva was secreted whenever a circle of light was thrown upon a dark screen. As in previous experiments, the C R was built up by giving the dog food whenever the circle appeared and continuing this combination, food plus circle, until at last saliva flowed to the circle alone. Next the dog was shown again and again a small ellipse, no food ever being given along with it. Eventually, the point was reached where the saliva flowed at the sight of the circle, but never at the sight of the ellipse. To test the dog's differentiating ability, he was shown larger and more circular ellipses, always without food, until finally he could distinguish—as shown by the appearance of the reflex—between the circle and an ellipse whose axes were in the relation 7:8. This would seem to have been a sufficient feat in itself, but the experimenter was not yet satisfied, and attempted to have her dog distinguish between the circle and an ellipse whose axes were as 8:9—a figure scarcely different from a perfect circle. This task proved to be too much for the dog's inhibitory ability. Saliva flowed first at sight of the ellipse, then at the circle, then at sight of either or both without any distinction. The dog began to whine, barked fiercely at the screen, tore at his restraining apparatus with his teeth, and attempted to jump down from the table. After this experiment the dog was useless as an experimental animal. Saliva would flow at sight of the experimenter, or at sight of the experiment room, or at almost any stimulus. Apparently what had happened was an almost complete collapse of the dog's differentiating ability, due to too great strain being placed upon the brake. When finally the brake gave way, response became general and riotous.

This loss of discriminative ability in humans, which fortunately is rarely if ever as complete as that in the dog which we have described, is often associated with nervous diseases or neuroses. The neurotic individual cannot discriminate between really dangerous and really harmless objects. Hence he may be afraid of cats, dark rooms, crossing bridges, or a thousand other things intrinsically harmless. Nor can he choose between really important and really unimportant tasks, and so is impelled to perform useless acts such as washing his hands ten times a day, touching every other lamp-post, going up the steps two at a time, or the like. Possibly a large share of the fatigue characteristic of neurasthenia comes from the large amount of lost motion indulged in.

To be sure, even in normal people, confusion often arises

when undue strain is placed upon the discriminatory function. Teach a child two foreign languages at the same time,
for instance, or two methods of subtracting or dividing, and
for a time at least efficiency will be markedly impaired as
the result. Intelligent behavior in dog or man depends to no
small degree upon a judicious choice and selection from
among the many competing stimuli seeking entrance. In
Pavlov's method the continuous struggle between entering
stimuli and the checking and selective activity of the nervous
system may be studied and accurately measured.

(6)

One of the most interesting of Pavlov's findings is the
discovery that sleep is closely linked up with the inhibitory
phenomena encountered in the experiments on differentiation and the trace reflex. It will be remembered that in the
trace reflex the conditioned salivary flow does not appear
until some time after the substitute stimulus has been given.
This period depends upon the original time-interval between
the substitute stimulus and the natural stimulus. Whenever
this delay was one-half minute or more, a peculiar thing
happened; the dog usually became drowsy and often went
sound asleep. This even happened in delayed reflexes when
the conditioned stimulus was continued throughout the period
intervening between the substitute stimulus and natural
stimulus; for example, the dog would fall asleep with the
bell or buzzer going loud enough, apparently, to keep a dozen
dogs awake. Annoyed by this unforeseen happening, at
first Pavlov and his workers tried to get exceptionally lively
and active dogs, thinking that the sleep which came so
readily might be an individual peculiarity of the dog used.
Even the most active dogs, however, regularly went to
sleep, indicating that some general, and not individual, con-

dition was at work. What is the nature of the sleep which occurs in these experiments? It must, said Pavlov, be a condition of general cortical inhibition analogous to, but greater than, the local inhibition or brake effect which we have already met with in previous experiments. During the waiting period between substitute stimulus and conditioned reflex, the brain and nervous system are actively inhibiting or holding in check the salivary reflex; that this must be true is shown by the sudden appearance of the reflex when any strong stimulus comes in to lift the brake. In like manner, when the dog's salivary flow has been positively conditioned to a note of 800 vibrations and negatively conditioned to a note of 812 vibrations, there must again be a delicate balance between the excitation and inhibition of the glandular (motor) response. (We have already described in Section (5) what happens when too much strain is placed on the brake.) This inhibition is evidently at first a matter of the local negative stimulation of a small sector in the dog's brain. But if this focus of negative stimulation is continued for a fairly long period of time, which happens in the trace reflex, apparently the inhibition gradually spreads over the entire cortex, the dog meanwhile becoming more and more drowsy until finally he goes to sleep. Normal sleep in man is readily explained after the same fashion as this experimentally induced sleep in the dog. The natural stimulus for sleep is fatigue, which induces first drowsiness (local inhibition) and then sleep (general inhibition). When the brake is lifted— the inhibition removed from the cortex—the sleeper awakens. It is interesting to note how readily sleep as a response is itself conditioned. Ordinarily sleep follows the natural stimulus, fatigue, with which is associated (usually) a comfortable bed, darkness, a certain hour, and quiet. These latter elements in the total situation often become such effective substitute stimuli for sleep that many individuals will fall asleep when in their customary situation, even though not especially fatigued. Again, for many people these associated stimuli become so important that they cannot sleep without them, no matter how tired they may be. Insomnia, according to this view, might be thought of as occasioned oftentimes by a negative stimulus which represses or inhibits the positive stimuli to sleep. Worry, excitement, fear, and other emotional conditions may readily act as negative stimuli to sleep.

(7)

Pavlov's success in conditioning the salivary reflex of the dog has stimulated many investigators, particularly in America, to undertake experiments with the C R. Much work has been done with animals other than the dog, and with various reflexes; in fact, conditioning experiments have been attempted all the way from protozoa to man. Some of this work is extremely interesting as showing the possibilities of measuring and comparing the learning processes in the lower animals. Although many of these lower orders are thought of as possessing few activities which can be called mental, we find, nevertheless, that they can often form definite associations. To illustrate, in studying the behavior of the snail, E. L. Thompson (1916) found that the pressure of a piece of lettuce on the mouth of the snail provoked a chewing movement which did not appear when the pressure was applied to the foot. Here, he thought, is the opportunity of discovering whether the snail is capable of making a connection between pressure on the foot and chewing. To test out this hypothesis, the mouth was repeatedly stimulated with lettuce, causing a chewing movement, and simultaneously with this, pressure was applied to the foot. Continued repetition of these stimuli led to the formation of an association, or a C R: whenever the foot was pressed, the snail began to chew. This learned response was actually retained for four days—not a bad memory feat for a snail! An extremely interesting and carefully devised series of experiments on the formation of C R's in fish have been reported by H. O. Bull (1928) in England. Using food as the natural or unconditioned stimulus to approach, this investigator conditioned fish to a number of substitute stimuli such as a slight rise in temperature of the water, as small as 4° C.; changes in the salinity of the surrounding water; and to auditory (probably vibratory) and visual intensities. Even discrimination between one and two sources of light was obtained after differential training, the C R's being fairly stable.

If a dog's foot is pricked with a pin or given an electric shock, it will be pulled away quickly and involuntarily, in the same way that a man's hand is suddenly withdrawn when it accidentally touches a hot stove. This avoiding response is called a withdrawal reflex. J. B. Watson (1916) by applying an electric shock to a dog's foot and at the same time sounding a note, so conditioned the dog's withdrawal reflex that the animal's foot jumped back at the sound alone. Watson also reports having secured a differential response by applying the shock with one of two tones. After training, the dog's foot was pulled back at the positive sound only, remaining quiet at the negative one. These C R's were, apparently, not long retained.

There are numerous instances of animal learning, apart from these more exact studies, which are more or less explicable in terms of the C R mechanism. Performing animals, dogs, horses, elephants and others, are usually responding to many substitute stimuli, such as the trainer's voice, a movement of his head, or a movement of his hand, all of which have been previously associated over and over again with the desired response. Several illustrations showing how the C R is employed in the training of animals are given in Chapter 5, pages 117-19.

As children are able to introspect little if at all better than animals, the C R method would seem to be especially well adapted to the study of their behavior.[3] Krasnogorski (1909), one of Pavlov's students, seems to have been the first investigator to study learning in young children by the C R method. He conditioned the salivary reflex in several young children with a fair degree of success to a variety of stimuli, the sight of food, a bell, sound of a reed pipe, a slight scratch on the skin. As an indication of the amount of saliva secreted, Krasnogorski noted the number of mouth-openings and swallowing movements made by the child. He states that C R's can be built up as early as the first year of life; and that almost any stimulus can serve as a substitute stimulus for a reflex motor or secretory activity. An important discovery was that C R's break down more readily in normal than in abnormal and feeble-minded children. Apparently the feeble-minded child is less mobile and more mechanical in his associations than is the normal.

In 1918 Florence Mateer in America extended and substantially verified Krasnogorski's work. This investigator worked with more than fifty normal children from about twelve to eighty-nine months of age, and with a half dozen or so feeble-minded children. She studied the formation of the C R, its retention over a period, its dying-out or extinction (unlearning), and the ease with which conditioned stimuli could be reassociated. Mateer worked with the salivary reflex, noting the number of swallowings as did Krasnogorski, but her experiments were much better controlled than his. C R's in normal children were learned and un-

[3] In Chap. 7 will be found illustrations of the C R method used by Watson in studying emotional responses of young children.

learned [4] in about one-half the number of trials necessary (on the average) for the feeble-minded. Mateer also established a substantial relationship between the ease of C R-formation and mental ability as measured by mental tests. This author regards the C R method as especially valuable in work with young children, as it gives a direct measure of native learning ability; and in any case she considers it to be a valuable supplement to other clinical methods.

(8)

The problem of just how fundamental the C R is in human learning, that is, in the acquisition of new behavior patterns, has been approached experimentally by psychologists. Some of the most interesting and valuable work in this field has been done by investigators who worked with involuntary muscle reflexes, which are not ordinarily under conscious control. The possibility of the acquisition of behavior patterns even below the level of conscious awareness has been clearly demonstrated in these experiments. A few of the more striking results may be cited. R. Dodge (1924) succeeeded in obtaining a conditioned lid reflex (wink) to a knee-jerk stimulus after many simultaneous stimulations. The normal stimulus to the knee-jerk is a smart tap on the patellar tendon just below the knee-cap. This stimulus was substituted for the normal stimuli which lead to the entirely different protective wink reflex. H. Cason (1922) conditioned the pupillary response, i.e., the change in the size of the pupillary aperture, by ringing a bell each time a beam of light was thrown in the subject's eye. After 400-odd joint stimulations of bell plus light, the pupil dilated to the sound of the bell alone. In one subject,

[4] The measure of unlearning is the time it takes the C R to die out when not reinforced with the natural stimulus.

also, the pupil was conditioned to contract to the bell. These
C R's persisted for only a short time. J. B. Watson (1916),
who has worked with the C R both in adults and in children,
has conditioned the withdrawal movement of the foot as well
as the withdrawal of the finger. In these experiments an
electric shock was the unconditioned or natural stimulus,
while a bell, a buzzer, and a bright light were among the
substitute stimuli. This last experiment did not, of course,
deal with smooth muscle reflexes.

(9)

In the last two sections we have given a brief sketch of
some of the later developments in C R experimentation since
Pavlov's pioneer work. Just what the final judgment of
psychologists as to the value of the C R in human psychology
will be is at present hard to estimate. To the behaviorist
the C R seems to be well-nigh an all-inclusive explanatory
concept for human as well as for animal learning, while
many other psychologists have used the concept widely.
Smith and Guthrie (1921), for example, regard perception,
as well as learning and habit-formation, as C R systems
gradually built in during the course of the individual's lifetime; while apparently Watson (1925) would now explain
all behavior in terms of C R's. Burnham (1924) makes wide
and extended use of the concept as a basic phenomenon in
explaining how we acquire bad habits, personality defects,
and the like. Allport (1924) regards social responses, language, gesture, and emotional and personality adjustments as
constructs which have grown up as a result of the conditioning of reflexes. Other psychologists, more conservative
perhaps, consider the C R to be descriptive mainly of animal and the simpler forms of human learning; that is, to
be one method of learning, but no by means the only method.

Among writers who have given recent systematic accounts from this standpoint are Woodworth, Dashiell, Dunlap, Gates, Hunter, and McDougall.

Leaving out the question of ultimate value, let us attempt to summarize briefly the facts at hand in trying to get an idea of the present worth of the C R. First of all, the C R technique is clearly an important instrument for research in animal psychology. Animals give neither verbal reports nor introspections. But by means of carefully controlled set-ups we can, nevertheless, obtain exact and quantitative data on learning, forgetting, and fineness of discrimination to tones, lights, tactual stimuli, and so on. There is apparently, no way whereby we can tell whether a dog distinguishes a note of 800 vibrations from one of 810 vibrations, except by the general method of the C R.

In experiments with humans as well as in experiments with animals, the C R method substitutes objective records for verbal report. This has obvious advantages. It is possible, for instance, to determine whether an individual senses stimuli below his threshold by conditioning him to subliminal sounds or lights. No report is asked for, nor could one be given if required. Again we have already seen in Mateer's results that normal children differ from abnormal in the ease with which C R's are formed and lost. Here would seem to be, then, a method of measuring native endowment uncomplicated by differences in training or nurture.

The C R as a method appeals to objectivists because it conceives complex behavior as composed of simpler links forged into a behavior series. Furthermore it substitutes for explanations in terms of trial-and-error, satisfyingness, and the like a more exact cause-effect relationship. This is all good as far as it goes. It must always be remembered, however, that the explanation of *all* habits as groups of C R's has not yet been demonstrated, and that formulations to this effect go beyond the experimental evidence. To indicate some of the difficulties which must be met by those inclined to explain all learned behavior as basically C R , we need only point to the extreme sensitiveness of most laboratory-determined C R's; to the difficulty of securing many of them; to the ease with which extraneous stimuli may inhibit them; and to their extinction without frequent reinforcement with the natural stimulus. When we contrast some of these fragile constructs with our highly integrated and deeply ingrained habits, our attitude may well be skeptical. We are in no sense detracting from the machine-like accuracy of Pavlov's technique, nor his striking results with animals, in concluding that it is not yet possible to explain adequately all human acquisitions as conditioned responses.

Suggested Readings

1. Pavlov's own account of his work will be found in his *Lectures on Conditioned Reflexes* (1928). This reference will probably prove to be "hard going" for most beginning students.
2. A simpler and more readable account of conditioned responses is given in the first six chapters of W. H. Burnham's *Normal Mind* (1924).
3. For a comprehensive review of the experimental work on conditioned responses, see H. Cason's article *The Conditioned Reflex or Conditioned Response as a Common Activity of Living Organisms,* Psychological Bulletin (1925), Vol. 22, 8.
4. For illustrations of the use made of the conditioned response concept by the extreme behaviorist, see J. B. Watson's *Behaviorism* (1925).

Chapter 5

THORNDIKE'S ANIMAL EXPERIMENTS AND LAWS OF LEARNING

(1)

EDWARD L. THORNDIKE'S studies in animal psychology (1898) mark the real beginning of the modern laboratory approach to problems of learning and habit formation in the comparative field. Thorndike began his experimental work at Harvard (1897), where as an undergraduate he did several experiments with chicks in the cellar of William James's house. Later, he came to Columbia to work in Cattell's laboratory; and from Columbia in 1898 he received the doctor's degree in psychology, his dissertation embodying a series of studies under the title *Animal Intelligence: An Experimental Study of the Associative Processes in Animals.* While he has retained his interest in animal psychology, Thorndike's work for the past twenty-five years has been largely in the field of educational psychology, where he has conducted a large number of important studies.

It must be admitted at once that much of the work with animals of investigators before Thorndike, of Lloyd Morgan, Lubbock, and Romanes, for instance, can be called experimental although performed without adequate laboratory control or special apparatus. For the most part, however, writers on animal psychology were content to occupy themselves with anecdotes and with uncontrolled though highly interesting observations of the doings of some pet dog or horse. Many of these accounts are impressionistic and highly col-

EDWARD L. THORNDIKE

(1874–   )

ored, with little or no emphasis upon the real stupidity shown by most animals. To be sure, animals were scarcely credited with the ability to "reason" or "think"—these being considered as strictly human accomplishments—but they were regarded as the equal of many men, and the superior of some, in their ability to form associations and build up habits. That they learned many things through imitation and the use of "ideas" seems not to have been questioned. As we shall see later, Thorndike's studies furnished experimental evidence which was flatly contradictory to these somewhat naïve views.

Although they were performed upon animals, Thorndike's experiments have broad and important implications for human as well as for animal learning. Certain definite principles, for instance, have emerged from these studies which characterize quite accurately the way in which children and adults form new associations and learn new things. Thorndike's two fundamental laws of learning, the *law of exercise* and the *law of effect*, are still to-day, in spite of criticism and later work, the basis of modern pedagogical theory. And it is highly probable that they will long be regarded as among the most valuable empirical generalization with which educational psychology must deal.

(2)

Thorndike's experiments were carried out upon fish, chickens, cats, dogs, and monkeys. The fish, a common variety resembling the minnow, were kept in an aquarium measuring four feet by two feet, with a water depth of about nine inches. These fish shun sunlight, and one end of the aquarium was covered over to protect them from light; here all food was given, and here the fish remained most of the time. An experiment consisted in gently forcing a fish from the shady to the sunny end of the tank, by gradually moving across the tank a glass slide placed behind the fish to cut off its retreat. A second glass slide containing a small opening was then placed between the fish and the shady end of the tank. The object was to see whether the fish could find the opening and escape. At the beginning, the fish's behavior, motivated by its desire to escape from the sunlight, consisted in swimming up and down the length of the slide, bumping against it here and there and looking for a place to get through. Eventually it would strike the opening and swim through to the shady section. Upon being replaced in the same situation again and again, the fish soon indicated clearly that it had profited by previous experiences, that is to say, it swam with less and less loss of time and fewer and fewer random movements directly to the opening. This experiment was repeated with a number of fish, and with slides containing openings at different points. Always the result was the same, viz., in every instance the fish ultimately learned the trick of finding and getting through the opening in the slide. It is clear from this experiment that learning, in the sense of simple connection-forming, can be demonstrated in vertebrates rather low in the evolutionary scale.

In his experiments with chicks, Thorndike used a number of pens or mazes, one of which is illustrated in Figure 11. When a chick is placed in section *A* of the maze, there are four possible exits as shown in the drawing. If the opening on the extreme right is followed by the chick to the second turn, it will lead out of the maze and into an enclosure in which are to be found other chicks and food. The other three exits are blind alleys. The problem is to see how long it will take a chick to select the pathway which will carry him out of the maze. The behavior of a chick when first placed in the pen resembles closely that of a fish which is trying to avoid the sunlight. Taken away from the other

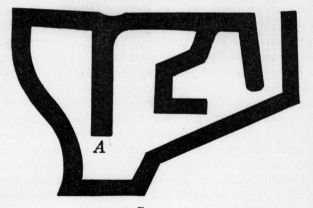

FIG. 11

PEN USED BY THORNDIKE IN STUDYING THE PROCESS OF LEARNING
IN CHICKS

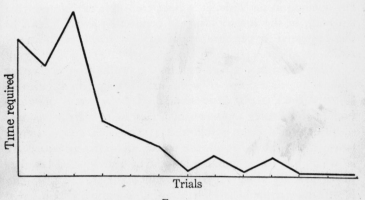

FIG. 12

LEARNING CURVE OF A CHICK

This curve shows the time required in successive trials to escape from
the pen shown in Figure 11. (From Thorndike.)

chicks and from food, for example, and dropped into the pen at *A*, the chick runs back and forth, in and out of the blind alleys, peeps loudly, and tries to jump out of the pen and to squeeze through any available opening. At length it will pick the right exit "by accident" and get out. Put back again and again, for the first few trials the chick's behavior is much as before; soon, however, it begins to eliminate useless movements, such as repeatedly entering the blind alleys, until finally it can run directly to the right exit. A good picture of how a chick learns the trick of escaping from such a pen as the one described is shown in Figure 12.

In this figure the separate trials are laid off along the horizontal or *X*-axis, and the time in seconds required to escape on the vertical or *Y*-axis. Note that after a fairly long practice period the chick will run directly to the proper exit.

(3)

The task set by Thorndike for his cats was to escape from various "puzzle boxes," the general construction of which may be seen from Figure 13. These boxes were so designed that escape from them could be effected in a variety of ways: e.g., by turning a button, pulling a string, depressing a lever, or pulling a wire loop. Each of these escape mechanisms, when operated by the animal, released a door which was at once pulled open automatically by a weight attached to it. Only one escape device was employed with the simpler boxes; but with the harder ones, two or more separate acts, such as pulling a string and depressing a bar, were required to open the door. An experiment consists in placing a hungry cat in the box with a small piece of fish or meat lying just outside. This situation usually results in immediate activity on the part of the cat. It tries to creep through the slats of the box; claws at the bars of wire; thrusts its paws through any opening large enough; works vigorously at anything loose or movable: and in general gives a perfect picture of impulsive hit-or-miss effort to escape. In time the animal nearly always succeeds in operating the escape device (hitting the wire noose or turning the button) by accident, and getting out. It is then allowed to eat a bit of the fish or meat,

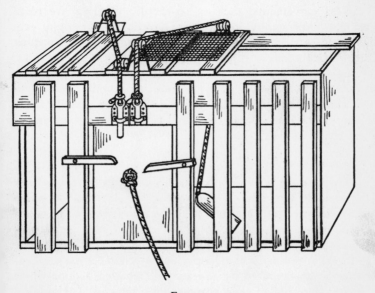

FIG. 13

PUZZLE-BOX USED BY THORNDIKE IN LEARNING EXPERIMENTS WITH CATS

and immediately returned to the box for a second trial. During this next trial, and for several trials thereafter, the cat's plan of attack remains much the same as before; but in succeeding trials its activity becomes more and more restricted to the button or other escape device, as useless clawings and scratchings are gradually eliminated. Finally the animal, on being placed in the box, goes almost at once to the door, works the mechanism, and escapes.

A cat may take twenty or more trials and an hour or so to reach the point where its escape-responses are prompt, sure, and accurate. During this process, improvement is nearly always quite irregular, the escape time seesawing up

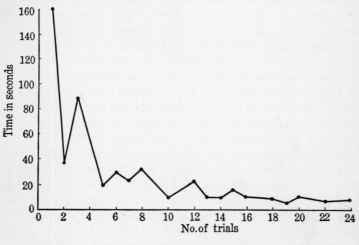

Fig. 14

LEARNING CURVE OF A CAT

The time taken by the cat to escape in successive trials is represented by the height of the curve; the successive trials are laid off along the horizontal base-line. (From Thorndike.)

and down until the act is well learned; whereupon the time becomes fairly regular. A learning curve of the time required in successive trials by one young cat to escape from a box kept closed by a single bolt attached to a wire loop is shown in Figure 14.

In the figure the twenty-four separate trials are represented by equal distances laid off along the horizontal axis;

and the time in twenty-second units is laid off on the vertical axis. Note the jagged appearance of the learning curve in the earlier trials as the time is first longer and then shorter; and the smoother appearance of the performance line as the cat learns the trick. This graph is fairly typical of animal performance in situations like the one described, and is a good instance of what is generally called "trial-and-error" learning. Such learning begins as a varied hit-or-miss process and continues as such until the successful response is hit upon, as we say, "by accident." After this, elimination of the unsuccessful responses begins, together with a gradual building-in of the successful reactions. The cat whose performance is shown in Figure 14, for example, was evidently learning in a slow and painstaking way to reduce its useless activities; and at the same time the successful response of pulling the wire loop was becoming more and more firmly established.

In his experiments with dogs, Thorndike used puzzle boxes of the same sort as those used with cats. However, he used only three dogs, whose state of hunger was not as great as that of the cats, and hence the results of these experiments are not directly comparable with those just described. Despite this fact, the trend of results is much the same in the two experiments. The dogs, like the cats, used the method of trial and error in seeking to escape, but on the whole their learning curves tended to be smoother, indicating better observation, a more planful attack, perhaps, and a somewhat higher level of intelligence. That dogs learn more quickly than cats, and somewhat less quickly than monkeys or raccoons, seems to be the consensus of investigators who have worked with these animals. However, as pointed out by Warden and Warner,[1] the inferiority of the dog to the raccoon or even the monkey is not certain, since in many of the tests

[1] Warden, C. J., and Warner, L. H., *Sensory Capacities and Intelligence of Dogs, with a Report on the Ability of the Noted Dog Fellow to*

the dog is at a decided disadvantage because his paws cannot so easily manipulate mechanical devices as can the digits of the raccoon or monkey.

(4)

Experiments much like those described on dogs and cats were also carried out by Thorndike upon three small South American monkeys. These monkeys were tested to see how readily they could learn to operate simple mechanical devices so as to get into or out of boxes. In addition, they were taught to manipulate a simple mechanism by means of which food could be thrown into their cage. The results of these tests are interesting and quite definite. In almost every instance the monkeys quickly learned the trick—often at an astonishing rate, far surpassing in skill and speed of acquisition both the dog and the cat. The superiority of the monkey in tests of this sort is probably to be expected, however, since, as Thorndike points out, they have better vision than dogs or cats and this, plus the fact that they have fingers, would enable them to manipulate simple contrivances more easily than other animals. Beside these natural advantages, monkeys are more active and more curious than other animals, and are quicker to play with and manipulate movable objects.

(5)

In spite of the evident superiority of the monkeys over the other animals both in speed and permanence of learning, they exhibit, says Thorndike, no real understanding of, nor "insight" into, the problem. This is still more surely true of the other animals. In fact, in none of his experiments did Thorndike find any clear evidence that the animal ever "thinks its way out," i.e., observes relations clearly, uses "ideas," or makes inferences and comparisons. Perhaps this result came out most clearly in a series of experiments which involved choice and discrimination on the part of the animal. The monkeys had formed the habit of coming down to the bottom of the cage from their accustomed place near the top whenever the experimenter approached with food. Thorndike decided to use this habit as a basis upon which to build up habits of discrimination in the following way. Whenever the experimenter picked up food with his left hand, the monkey was fed; but when he picked it up with his right hand, the monkey was never fed. At another time food was given when a certain sentence was repeated, and withheld when another was said; or food was given at one visual signal (a large letter or geometrical figure), and withheld at another. The problem set the animal was to see whether, after having learned to discriminate between the food and the non-food signals, he would get the general idea: *one stimulus means food, the other does not.* Evidence of such insight or understanding into the situation might be expected to show itself if, after several discriminations of the kind described, the monkey perceived a new relation almost instantly. On the other hand, if there were no clear abstraction of the principle of choice required, the monkey might be expected to take each discrimination as a new task to be solved by trial and error. This would, of course, show up in the large number of trials needed. The results of these tests were not entirely unambiguous, but their general implication seems clear. Despite the fact that the monkeys learned the separate tasks very quickly, apparently they never formed a clear concept of what was essentially involved in *all* of the tasks in terms of which their future behavior could be governed.

This failure to infer or abstract the essential facts involved in a discriminatory act is shown more clearly, perhaps, in the case of a kitten tested by Thorndike. This animal had formed the habit of climbing up the wire netting of its cage whenever the experimenter approached. At one verbal signal ("I must feed those cats") the kitten was always fed, at another signal ("I will not feed them") it was never fed. The object of the test was to see how long it would take the cat to learn that one signal meant food and the other did not— that is, to discriminate one stimulus from the other. After a total of 380 trials, the cat finally learned that one signal was different from the other. Thorndike remarked, apropos of this experiment, that it "shows beautifully the animal method of acquisition. If at any stage the animal could have isolated the two ideas of the two sense-impressions, and felt them together in comparison, this long and tedious process would have been unnecessary."

(6)

Another line of evidence cited by Thorndike as opposed to the thesis that animals think or reason is the fact that there are no sudden vertical drops in the learning curves of his cats, dogs, and monkeys. Sudden drops usually indicate that the learner has got the trick—seen the connections or relations—and henceforth might be expected to do it correctly whenever the situation presents itself. Instead of this sudden insight, what we usually find is a gradual sloughing-off of excess and useless movements (see Figures 12 and 14), with no clear evidence that the animal observed just how he got out or made use of this observation in future trials.

Thorndike's view that animals learn almost entirely by trial and error and have little insight into the problem at hand has recently been attacked by the German psychologist, Koffka (1924), who belongs to the school of *Gestalt* psychology. Köhler (1925), another member of the *Gestalt* school, in his studies of learning in the chimpanzee found many instances of quick learning which, he says, indicate that the ape suddenly grasped the relations involved in the problem.[2] According to Thorndike, such quick learning (which presumably involves insight) is to be expected only when the task is "very simple, very obvious, and very clearly defined"; whenever the problem is at all complex, the animal's behavior, he thinks, may be fairly described as "stupid." In Koffka's view, on the contrary, the animal exhibits insight or intelligence whenever it is possible for it to grasp the problem; stupid errors, he says, occur when the task seems simple to us, but is almost surely not at all simple to the cat or chick. Koffka argues further that Thorndike's puzzle boxes set before the animals tasks so difficult (for the animal) that trial-and-error learning was the only kind possible. Despite the difficulty involved in these tasks, Koffka points out instances in Thorndike's own data of sudden vertical drops in the learning curve which, he thinks, indicate insight into the problem.

Koffka's argument for intelligent learning in animals cannot be reproduced in brief space, and should be read entire by the student.[3] It is an exceedingly keen and searching criticism of the mechanistic view which holds that animals always learn stupidly in a hit-or-miss fashion without any real comprehension of the situation or of the relations involved.

If it seems probable that Thorndike overemphasized the aimlessness of animal learning, partly, no doubt, as a result of his particular set-up, it is certainly just as probable that the insight shown by Köhler's apes is also the result of the *kind* of problem set. Köhler's chimpanzees were assigned

[2] See Chap. 11, pp. 256-259.
[3] *The Growth of the Mind* (1924), pp. 163-174.

very different tasks from those required of Thorndike's monkeys and cats, and for this reason the two sets of results are not directly comparable. For one thing, the chimpanzees were given much freedom, while Thorndike's animals were nearly always confined. Examples of the kind of tasks set the chimpanzees are (1) securing a banana suspended from the ceiling of a cage by piling up boxes one on another; (2) reaching for and pulling into the cage a banana placed outside by ingeniously hooking together two sticks. Many other tasks involving ropes, sticks, and the piling-up of boxes were set before the monkeys (see Chapter 11). In such situations sudden learning might very well take place, if the animals are intelligent to begin with (as Köhler's chimpanzees undoubtedly were) and if the task is not too different from the kind of thing which the animals habitually do. As Sandiford (1928) has pointed out, too, all of the learning is not shown in the fluctuations of the learning curve. A sudden drop in the curve may be preceded by a long trial-and-error process which is not represented, as when a man suddenly "sees the point," after a long, tedious, and bungling effort at solution. The chimpanzee who suddenly does a trick which he could not do before has not necessarily seen through it in a sudden burst of comprehension. Many tentative trials and errors not shown in the learning curve nor seen by the experimenter may precede the solution.

(7)

The statement that animals show little evidence of learning through imitation usually provokes astonishment and strong protest from champions of animal intelligence, accustomed to discourse at length upon the marvelous performances of their pets. Yet Thorndike's results point strongly to this conclusion. When a cat, for instance, which had not learned to get out of a puzzle box was allowed to observe another trained cat, it made no difference whatever in the first cat's behavior. Nor did it make any difference when an untrained cat was placed in the box with a trained cat and allowed to escape when the second cat opened the door of the cage. The untrained cat still used the old hit-or-miss method as before; there was not the slightest evidence that learning had been speeded up through imitation. This same result was obtained in similar experiments with dogs and chicks. Even monkeys who had failed in their efforts to operate some simple mechanism were unable to do it after having seen a monkey or the experimenter do the trick many times. In one case a monkey was shown fifteen consecutive times how to open a box which contained food (the door was held shut by a simple lever). At the end of this training period, the monkey's efforts did not differ essentially from his previous attempts before tuition. In summing up his observations on imitation, Thorndike writes, "Throughout all the time that I had my monkeys under observation I never noticed in their general behavior any act which seemed due to genuine imitation of me or the other persons about."

One may well inquire—if these observations are accepted —why monkeys are so generally believed to be accomplished imitators. Thorndike's answer is that monkeys, being active, curious, and possessed of a repertoire of movements much like ours, will inevitably do many things which seem almost human. He writes, "If you put two toothpicks on a dish, take one and put it in your mouth, a monkey will do the same, not because he profits by your example, but because he instinctively puts nearly all small objects in his mouth. Because of their general activity their instinctive impulses to grab, drop, bite, rub, carry, move about, turn over, etc., any novel object within their reach, their constant movement and assumption of all sorts of postures, the monkeys perform many acts like our own and simulate imitation to a far greater extent than other mammals."

It should be added before leaving this topic that M. E. Haggerty (1910) has made some observations on learning in anthropoid apes which seem at first glance opposed to Thorndike's conclusions. One ape having learned to get food out of a long pipe by pushing it out with a stick, another animal was set to watch him do the trick. When the second animal was allowed to try alone, he at once took the stick and put it into the pipe, but *pulled* (instead of pushed) the food in to himself. This is hardly imitation in the ordinary sense of reproduction of another's actions, but is rather intelligent observation. Haggerty made only a few tests, and since his two animals were orang-outangs (highly intelligent manlike apes) his observations are hardly in conflict with Thorndike's statements regarding the lack of imitation in lower orders.

(8)

Thorndike has laid down five principles which serve to characterize animal learning as he observed it. These are as follows:

1. Multiple Response, or varied reaction to the same external situation. This simply means that the animal brings to bear all of the instinctive and learned responses of which it is capable when faced by a new problem which it does not fully understand. It is the principle of trial-and-error learning.

2. Set, Attitude, or *Disposition*. Set, or attitude, is the internal "drive" or condition which predisposes the animal to a particular kind of behavior rather than some other kind. A hungry cat, for example, will try to escape from a puzzle box if food is outside, but a well-fed cat is usually content to remain quiet unless much frightened or disturbed.

3. Partial or Piecemeal Activity. As learning proceeds, the animal gradually eliminates useless and unsuccessful movements and confines its activities to those objects or details which have hitherto proved to be of value. From a random and aimless activity, the animal's efforts become more restricted, partial, and piecemeal.

4. Assimilation or Analogy means that an animal when put into a new and strange situation will draw upon movements which have been employed in like or somewhat like situations.

5. Associative Shifting. This principle is now generally known as that of the "conditioned response." It means that, in time, the animal will shift his response from the general situation, box or maze, to some element or detail of the total which possesses value, or from the original stimulus to some fact associated with it. Ordinary animal tricks by the score furnish illustrations of this principle. The cat taught first to come when a saucer of milk is held in the hand will after a few times respond to the sight of the empty saucer or to the person who does the feeding. In like manner a dog or monkey can be taught to sit up and beg when a command only is given; while it is said that bears are taught to dance to music by being placed upon hot grills while music is played. Shifting of response from one stimulus to another, or from the total situation to some part of it, enormously expands the animal's range of responses. This increase in range of response is of fundamental importance in human as well as in animal learning (see further pages 97-100).

One of the most striking instances of seemingly intelligent learning in an animal, which is explainable in terms of associative shifting or the conditioned response, is that of the famous German horse, Clever Hans. In 1901 Hans, a five-year-old horse, was trained by his owner Herr von Osten to answer questions and solve problems. A letter system was constructed on a numbered chart to enable Hans to answer questions; if the letter *m*, for example, occurred in the fourth vertical column and the second horizontal row of the chart, four taps with the left hoof and two with the right meant *m*. In solving numerical problems, taps with the right hoof meant units and taps with the left hoof meant tens. Thus 53 was represented by five taps with the left hoof and three with the right. By means of these schemes, Hans was able to solve problems and answer questions ordinarily requiring considerable intelligence. The wide interest aroused in Hans's performance led finally to his being examined at successive times by two commissions. A psychologist on the second commission named Pfungst apparently solved the mystery of Hans's answers. He showed that the horse responded to involuntary "cues" or signals given by his trainer, such as slight (approving) movements of the head, changes in facial expression, and the like. Thus if the answer to a problem were 68, Hans would count rapidly with his left hoof until some small (and probably unintentional) signal from his trainer warned him to stop and begin with the other hoof. The trainer, therefore, was the substitute stimulus to which the clever horse responded.

Hans was later acquired by another owner and became one of the group of famous Elberfeld horses. One of these horses, an Arabian named Muhammed, was reputed to be able to extract square and cube root beside performing the simpler arithmetic operations of addition, subtraction, multiplication, and division. No satisfactory proof seems to have been brought forward to show that these horses were responding to cues, but such seems undoubtedly to have been the case. As Washburn (1926) points out, these horses learned too quickly to permit of any real understanding of the problem; they took no longer to solve hard problems than easy ones; often they would begin tapping without even glancing at the problem set up before them. Again, the kind of mistakes made are not those of an intelligent calculator: common errors were reversals of figures such as 36 for 63, or errors of one unit such as 26 for 25. These errors might easily happen if the horse temporarily confused the left and right hoof or failed to stop tapping quite soon enough. All of the evidence, then, is decidedly against the opinion that performances (such as these) of clever animals really indicate mathematical genius or intelligence of a high order. Such "stunts" do show, however, that animals are extremely clever in picking up very slight cues and signals not readily observed by onlookers, who, of course, are not watching out for them.

All of the principles outlined in this section apply with but little modification to human learning. When placed in a totally new situation or faced by a complex and little-understood problem, the behavior of a man will, at first, differ very little from that of a dog, cat, or monkey. His activity is largely of the trial-and-error type, as he draws upon the reservoir of his past experiences for a possible solution of his immediate difficulty. After a time, however, differences appear which are usually sufficiently great to provide a distinct gap between the things which men and animals *can* learn and the *rates* at which they acquire them. Very soon in their learning, often at the very beginning, men begin to reason or think, i.e., to use ideas and verbal formulations. Alternatives are accepted or rejected symbolically, rather than by concrete trial; principles are perceived and applied; insight into the problem is gained.

A good illustration of human learning in situations which are roughly analogous to Thorndike's puzzle boxes is to be found in the experiments of H. A. Ruger (1910). Ruger set out to discover how quickly and by what method men and women learn to solve difficult Chinese ring puzzles. His learning curves at the beginning look very much like those of Thorndike's cats, dogs, and chicks; but instead of the irregular rise and fall observed in animal learning curves, sudden drops often appear later on which, according to the subjects' reports, occurred when insight was had into the mechanical features or principles of the puzzle. Such sudden drops were rare in the learning curves of Thorndike's animals. Since animals have no language, presumably they do not reason or think things out symbolically as man does. The ability to formulate general principles, evolve concepts, and educe relations of a symbolic kind would thus seem to be strictly a human accomplishment.

(9)

Out of his experiments with animals grew Thorndike's two fundamental laws of learning, *the law of exercise* and *the law of effect*. The law of exercise, which is often called the law of habit-formation, has two parts, one of which is the complement of the other. The first part, *the law of use,* may be simply stated as follows: When a given situation is frequently followed by a certain response or group of responses, the bond or linkage between the two becomes stronger through the exercise so obtained. The opposite of the law of use is the *law of disuse:* When a given situation is rarely followed by a certain response, the association is weakened, its degree of weakness depending upon the amount of neglect. The law of use is clearly shown in the learning curves of Figures 9 and 11. When it has once learned the knack of escaping from the box or pen, the movements of the chick or cat become faster and smoother the more often they are repeated.

Numerous applications of the law of exercise to human learning will at once come to mind. Learning to skate, to drive an automobile, and to run a typewriter are matters of getting the right movements in their proper sequence *first,* and then rehearsing them until they run off rapidly, smoothly, and accurately. This is true also of the more mental performances. Thus in order to learn well a French vocabulary, a poem, or a set of mathematical formulas, it is necessary to repeat (exercise) the elements in their right order regularly and often.

Under the law of exercise belong several sub-laws or corollaries which readily follow from it. These are the *law of frequency,* the *law of recency,* and the *law of vividness, intensity, or interest.* The law of frequency emphasizes the cumulative effect of repetition or repeated learning. Improvement in a given function is usually fairly rapid at first as a result of continued exercise and effort. Sooner or later, however, the physiological limit is reached, beyond which additional repetitions have little beneficial effect. This is as true of learning poetry or the multiplication table as it is of learning to skate or dance; continued application is necessary up to a certain point, but after that it is probably of little value (see Chapter 3, page 58).

The *law of recency* refers to the commonly observed fact that performances recently learned or practised are smoother and less subject to error than those unpractised for some time. Most busy adults, for instance, have completely forgotten the algebra and Latin learned in high school or college (unless they happen to be teachers); but they remember the necessary details of their business or profession. The negative side of the law of recency is covered by the law of disuse. Activities once learned but not recently practised tend to deteriorate with the passing of time (see Chapter 3, pages 63-4).

The *law of vividness or intensity* means that active and interested activity is more beneficial than passive and perfunctory repetition. If the learner sets out vigorously and with determination to learn a given task, if he has, as William James puts it, "the will to learn," he will progress more rapidly than if he simply sits passively, hoping that somehow the desired information will sink in. The law of vividness will explain why a boy learns his Scout Manual and the fine points of baseball more quickly than he learns to play the piano or recite his Sunday-school lesson.

All of these principles of learning are well illustrated in modern advertising. Over and over again (frequency and recency) by newspaper, magazine, and flashing electric sign (vividness), we are told about the merits of some particular cigarette or tooth-paste. As a result of this bombardment, most of us have become familiar with the names and slogans of many articles and "brands" and this very familiarity predisposes us to the purchase of these products. In the schoolroom, too, the operation of these laws may be readily observed. For example, there must be drill and repetition (frequency); constant review and recitation (recency); and finally, the attempt is made to relate the subject-matter of mathematics or literature in as many ways as possible to the everyday needs and interests of the student (vividness).

(10)

The *law of effect* may be stated most simply, perhaps, as follows: When a response or series of responses leads to success or to a satisfying state of affairs, the connection between the situation and this response is strengthened, while other responses not so satisfying (i.e., annoying) are weakened and hence rendered less probable of recurrence. The law of effect is really prior to the law of exercise, since it explains *how* the successful response came to be selected in the first place. This is clearly evident in these instances of animal learning which we have cited. When a cat, for example, in learning to escape from a puzzle box, makes a variety of responses most of which are useless, one might expect from the law of exercise alone that *all* of these responses would be equally bound up with the situation "trying to escape from the puzzle box." Hence, all would tend to be repeated. Instead of this, however, the successful response, namely, pulling the loop or turning the button of the cage, soon gets the upper hand, while the useless responses are dropped out. Reference should be made again to Figures 12 and 14. Note how the escape of the cat or chick becomes faster and smoother as the animal goes more and more promptly to the proper exit. The successful response—that is to say, the one which leads to food or comrades—once having been made, exercise soon enables it to supplant the non-satisfying reactions. Gates (1927) has given a striking illustration of the law of effect which is quoted here with some adaptation. Suppose, he says, that five cats have been taught to come to the call "kitty, kitty." Now, suppose later on that, on being called, cat no. 1 is given food and is petted; cat no. 2 is petted only; cat no. 3 is totally disregarded; cat no. 4 is sprinkled with water; and cat no. 5 is douched heavily with water. What will happen the next time these cats are called? The answer is easy. Cat no. 1 will come quickly and promptly when called; cat no. 2 will probably come, but not so promptly; cat no. 3 may come, also, but still less promptly; cat no. 4 may try it once more, but if sprinkled again will surely give it up; cat no. 5 will not only fail to come, but (if he is an intelligent cat) will run in the opposite direction. Here the end-effect—what happens to the cat—is the primary factor in guiding behavior.

Thorndike's law of effect has not escaped criticism at the hands of other experimenters. The most frequent objection seems to hinge on the difficulty in seeing just how the satisfaction which comes *after* the successful response could possibly work backward so as to "stamp in" this one response or make it more probable than some other. This problem is really *the* fundamental problem of learning, since it deals with the basic question of why we retain some responses and drop out others. It has excited investigators for thirty years or more, and has been subjected to analysis from many points of view.[4] A simple practical explanation of much learning is that the successful response (the one which is retained) and the resulting satisfaction often occur together, or so nearly together as to be essentially part of the same process. The successful movements and the satisfaction which they bring are so closely associated—in time or space or through their relatively greater intensity—that the successful movement comes to "mean" or "stand for" the satisfying effect. The substitution of one response for another and the linking-up of the second or substitute response with the original situation through repetition is simply the principle of the conditioned response over again. In many cases, therefore, the conditioned response and the laws of exercise and effect are really two ways of describing the same phenomena. Of the alternate descriptions, that of the conditioned response is perhaps the more comprehensive and general.

(11)

If satisfying states are simply taken in general to mean those which lead to positive approach-behavior, and annoying states are those which predispose to avoidance and retreat, the law of effect would seem to be adequate to cover nearly all learning as we find it in a practical and understandable way, i.e., to explain why some responses are re-

[4] For a review of various attempts at solution, see F. A. Perrin and D. B. Klein's *Psychology, Its Methods and Principles* (1926), pp. 218-243.

tained and some are not. If the results of our behavior are pain, punishment, social disapproval, regret, and failure generally, certainly the acts which lead up to such annoying states are rarely repeated by the normal person. On the other hand, responses which bring food, comfort, kindly treatment, praise, and success will most probably be repeated and through exercise become more rapid and more certain. In those cases in which learning takes place where there is no observable satisfaction, but even indifference or actual annoyance, it is often true that behavior of the opposite sort would be still more dissatisfying. The boy who dutifully practises his music lesson often has an ulterior motive which is not wholly inconsistent with the law of effect. And it is probable, too, that the life of a martyr is not entirely devoid of satisfaction.

It often happens, of course, that the end-result, i.e., the effect, while providing self-satisfaction to the individual concerned, is actually injurious, or is socially disapproved or morally hurtful. Numerous examples could be brought forward to illustrate this situation. If a baby is fed or caressed whenever it cries; if the small boy is given money or candy whenever he whines or teases; and if the bully is applauded and feared by the other members of his group, such unfortunate behavior, because satisfying, will tend to persist. To change or alter it, the end-effect must be made unsatisfying. Social disapproval, the withholding of something valued or desired by the child, mild punishment, or the substitution of new interests at once satisfying and more healthful, are common methods employed. Prizes, medals, the honor-roll, and other forms of approbation are some of the traditional ways in which the school has utilized the law of effect. The modern school has set as its ideal the making of the results of industry and application seem worth while in themselves to the child. To reach this end, it strives to get the desired responses and then through exercise to build them in. This is the fundamental problem in the psychology of learning, and it involves essentially the laws of exercise and effect.

Suggested Readings

1. Thorndike's own account of his animal studies will be found most conveniently in his *Animal Intelligence: Experimental Studies,* 1911 edition. For his laws of exercise and effect, see Thorndike, E. L., *Educational Psychology, Briefer Course* (1914).
2. For a short account of the history of animal psychology, see C. J. Warden's *A Short Outline of Comparative Psychology* (1927).
3. W. Köhler's *The Mentality of Apes* (1925) contains an interesting description of the author's experiments with chimpanzees.
4. A clear discussion of the laws of learning will be found in P. Sandiford's *Educational Psychology* (1928). For the educational applications of the laws of learning, see A. M. Jordan's *Educational Psychology* (1928), Chapter V.

Chapter 6

THORNDIKE AND WOODWORTH'S EXPERIMENT ON THE TRANSFER OF TRAINING AND ITS INFLUENCE UPON THE DOCTRINE OF FORMAL DISCIPLINE

(1)

THE doctrine of formal discipline is the time-honored view that by hard study and application the fiber of the mind becomes toughened like a muscle, and that, as a direct result, one's "powers" of attention, memory, reasoning, and the like are markedly strengthened and increased. Advocates of this belief will contend that a boy's "reasoning ability," if thoroughly trained by the solving of numerous originals in geometry, is thereby better prepared to handle the knotty problems of business and professional life later on. In other words, the transfer of training from one activity to another, or the spread of improvement, is conceived to be broad and general. Opposed to this concept of general mind training inherent in the idea of formal discipline is the view that transfer of acquired skill or special training is relatively specific and narrow; that training, for example, in the duties of a department store salesman will carry over or benefit another activity or pursuit only in so far as there is a similarity of method or material between the two. For many years a controversy, which is still very much alive, has raged between these two opposing views.

Historically the doctrine of formal discipline owes its origin and its present-day survival to two well-intrenched beliefs. The first is the view that mind is made up of numerous distinct powers or faculties—the so-called "faculty psychology"; the second is the idea that discipline is the essential function and even the main duty of education. According to faculty psychology, mind is analogous to an intricate machine, the various parts of which correspond to the faculties of observation, memory, reasoning, judgment, volition, and the like. Experiences are the raw material fed into this mind-machine; here they are weighed and estimated by the faculty of judgment, arranged in logical sequence by the faculty of reasoning, and stored away by the faculty of memory. With training and long practice the mind takes on strength, agility, and quickness, and these characteristics are generally exhibited in all sorts of situations.

The second belief, that of the disciplinary function of education, grows directly out of faculty psychology. It is deeply rooted, too, in the moralistic view that whatever is difficult, by virtue of that fact alone, is valuable in the training of the child's mind. This view is still widely prevalent to-day among school people, although it is showing some signs of weakening. It has long been a tradition that among school studies Latin and mathematics are especially valuable in training the powers of concentration, reasoning, and precision. It is interesting to trace the growth of this belief in the disciplinary value of Latin. For many years Latin was taught as a very necessary subject for priests and men of learning; later on it was studied for its cultural value in contradistinction to the often despised language of the common people. To-day, when its chief use seems to be in furnishing inscriptions for monuments and in decorating college diplomas, its value has become largely disciplinary. Thus, its value in disciplining the mind seems to have grown greater and greater as its utility became less and less. Much the same thing is true of certain branches of mathematics. Thousands of high school boys and girls study geometry to-day, although an almost negligible per cent of them will ever use it in later life. Its retention in the curriculum is based upon its alleged value in training the mind in precision, in judgment, and in logical reasoning.

As we noted above, the view is still widespread among educators that an individual has a mind which possesses certain powers, and that these can be trained and disciplined only by hard and not always interesting tasks. The following quotations,[1] some of which are not more than two decades old, will show how strong and orthodox is the belief in the superior disciplinary value of certain subjects. This doctrine, it must be remembered, is based implicitly, if not explicitly, upon the faculty psychology.

"The study of the Latin language itself does eminently discipline the faculties and secure to a greater degree than that of the other subjects we have discussed, the formation and growth of those mental qualities which are the best preparation for the business of life—whether that business is to consist in making fresh mental acquisitions or in directing the powers thus strengthened and matured, to professional and other pursuits."—*Lectures on Education,* by Joseph Payne, Vol. I, page 260.

"The most valuable thing in the way of discipline which comes from the study of a foreign language is its influence in improving the pupil's command of his own. Of course this means the improvement in general judgment and discrimination which is evinced by a finer linguistic sense."—*Methods of Teaching the Modern Languages,* by E. H. Babbitt page 126.

The value of the study of German "lies in the scientific study of the language itself, in the consequent training of the reasoning, of the powers of observation, comparison and

---

[1] The first four are taken from E. L. Thorndike's *Educational Psychology* (1913), Vol. II, pp. 360-361. For the fifth, I am indebted to Professor Pintner.

synthesis; in short, in the upbuilding and strengthening of the scientific intellect."—*Methods of Teaching Modern Languages,* by Calvin Thomas, page 26.

"We speak of the disciplinary studies . . . having in our thought the mathematics of arithmetic, elementary algebra, and geometry, the Latin-Greek texts and grammars, the elements of English or of French or of German. . . The mind takes fiber, facility, strength, adaptability, certainty of touch, from handling them, when the teacher knows his art and their power. The college . . . should give . . . elasticity of faculty and breadth of vision, so that they shall have a surplus of mind to expend."—Woodrow Wilson, in *Science,* November 7, 1902.

"A knowledge of the foreign languages contributes in an unusual degree to the making of internationally minded, broad thinking, intellectually resourceful and contented citizens."—Morgan, B. Q., *The Place of Modern Foreign Languages in the American High School,* School and Society, Feb. 28, 1928.

(2)

The modern view of mental organization holds, in opposition to the faculty doctrine outlined above, that what we loosely call "mind" consists of more or less closely connected behavior tendencies, and that transfer of improvement as a result of special training takes place almost exclusively among related activities. Activities may be related through similarities in form or in procedure and method, or through identities in content or material. Thus a knowledge of Latin will undoubtedly aid one to learn Spanish more easily, while a knowledge of mathmatics is indispensable in engineering or physics. Moreover, experience gained as a consulting chemist with one concern will usually enable a man the more easily to perform his duties with another firm. Added to this fairly specific transfer, there is almost certainly some general carry-over growing out of such broad factors as a common language, definite rules of study, habits of neatness, care, and thoroughness, quickness in reading and writing, and the like. But such general transfer is very much smaller than that assumed by formal discipline.

The evidence against formal discipline and the faculty psychology comes from (1) everyday observation, (2) from physiology, and (3 and chiefly) from experiment. In the first place, we all believe in a certain amount of transfer—but in a certain amount only. The able lawyer is made a judge, and the active young executive becomes a general manager. But the engineer is not made health officer, nor is a minister or physician put in charge of building bridges. In other words, common sense tells us that special training cannot possibly prepare a man for all sorts of vocations nor make him an expert in all branches of knowledge. In fact, striking instances of the opposite are found. All too often the eminent scientist gives opinions on theology which are simply banal, while the highly trained mathematician is rarely more logical or rational in selecting an automobile than is his less gifted neighbor. In other words, there is little evidence from everyday life of general mind training.

The pseudo-science of phrenology is closely related to faculty psychology on the physiological side. Phrenology taught that the different faculties of the mind have "seats" in specific parts of the brain, and that their respective developments can be estimated from the "bumps" or prominences on the skull. Phrenology is no longer taken seriously by scientific men, but, like palmistry and graphology, has descended to the level of a parlor amusement. Physiologists who have studied the brain and the nervous system have found no evidence of nervous centers corresponding to the alleged phrenological faculties. They have been able to map out on the cortex general sensory and motor areas, a visual area, an auditory area, and an area for taste and smell. But no centers for such faculties as judgment, observation, volition, fear-of-God, or concentration have ever been found. To the present-day psychologist the term *concentration*, for instance, instead of meaning a power or faculty, is simply a name to describe responses which are alike in being marked by a high degree of intensity. Such responses may fall into many categories, from concentration upon a symphony to concentration upon a boxing match. In short, what a man concentrates upon is dependent upon his age, education, special interests, and training, not upon a mysterious "power of concentration" which exists *per se*.

The experimental attack upon the question of general versus specific transfer of improvement has been made by psychologists interested in the theoretical problem of mental organization as well as by those interested in the educational aspects of the transfer problem. Upon both of these questions the laboratory studies of transfer have thrown much light.

(3)

The first experiment upon the problem of transfer was reported by William James in about 1890. James measured the time required by himself and four students to memorize selections from Victor Hugo's poem the *Satyr*, before and after training with other passages of poetry, for example, lines from *Paradise Lost* or from certain of the German poets. After memorizing a given passage from Hugo, each subject spent about twenty minutes per day for a month attempting to train his memory with other selections, after which he again memorized passages from the *Satyr*. On these final tests, three of the subjects showed slight improvement over their first records—averaging about 1½ per cent—but the other two were slightly worse than before training. This experiment of James was inadequate in method and inconclusive in result, but it possesses historical significance, since it started the experimental attack upon the problem of the extent of transfer through special practice. A later and better controlled experiment by W. F. Dearborn (1910) on the same topic of memory training should be mentioned in this connection. Dearborn found transfer of from 50 to 0 per cent as a result of special practice with material of a somewhat like nature. This percentage of transfer was by no means as great, however, as the improvement shown in learning the material upon which Dearborn's subjects specifically practised.

The most significant of the early attacks on the problem of transfer was a series of three studies by E. L. Thorndike and R. S. Woodworth (1901) in the field of discrimination and perception. These experiments furnished the first really exact and quantitative evidence against the doctrine of formal discipline. The influence of the training received in one kind of perception upon efficiency in other related activities was investigated by practising five to six subjects (1) in estimating the areas of various geometric figures, the lengths of lines, value of weights, and so forth; and (2) in observing designated words or letters on a printed page. In the first series of experiments—those on sensory discrimination—Thorndike and Woodworth trained their subjects in the ability to estimate the areas of rectangles and other geometrical figures. Before the training or practice period, and again afterward, the subjects were tested for their accuracy in estimating the areas of many other figures, e.g., rectangles, circles, triangles, and trapezoids. Some of these figures were different in shape but similar in size to those of the training period, others similar in shape but different in size, and still others different in both size and shape. From the records before and after practice the effect of the intervening training period upon the accuracy of discrimination was then determined. If we let $I\,T$ = initial test; $T\,P$ = training period;

and F T = the final test, we can represent the experiment diagrammatically as follow:

$$I T — T P — F T$$

During the training period (T P) of the principal discrimination experiment, the subjects practised in estimating the areas of rectangles of ten to 100 square centimeters in size, in every case carefully checking the accuracy of their results until they had acquired marked proficiency at this task. The improvement, as measured by tests given before and after this training period, made in estimating areas of the same size as these rectangles, but of different shape, was about 44 per cent as large as the improvement shown in the T P, namely, in estimating areas different in size but of the same shape. When the subjects were tested with figures of the same shape but somewhat larger in size (e.g., rectangles of 140 to 300 square centimeters) than those used in the training series, the improvement was only 30 per cent as great as in the T P. Very probably this low figure is partly a result of confusion and interference due to the similarity in shape of the rectangles in the two series. For areas different in shape and larger in size (140 to 400 square centimeters), the improvement in accuracy was 52 per cent as great as in the training series.

Thorndike and Woodworth next trained their subjects in estimating the lengths of lines .5 to 1.5 inches long until an improvement of about 25 per cent was noted. This training period produced little or no improvement in the estimation of lines six to twelve inches long as shown by tests given before and after the practice period. Nor did the training with six-inch to twelve-inch lines lead to any improvement in estimating lines fifteen to twenty-four inches long.

In another sensory field, that of tactual and kinesthetic discrimination, improvement to about the same degree as

Photograph by Bachrach

ROBERT S. WOODWORTH

(1869–   )

with geometrical figures was noted as a result of previous training in closely similar functions. The subjects were tested this time for their accuracy in estimating weights of 120 to 1,800 grams. They were then trained in estimating weights of twenty to 120 grams; and then retested with the first set of weights in order to measure the effect of the intervening practice period. The improvement in the F T over the I T was about 40 per cent of that which appeared in the T P, indicating that transfer, while evident, was by no means considerable.

Thorndike and Woodworth's second series of experiments, those with language, are especially valuable because of their implications for educational practice; that is, because they parallel fairly closely the kind of work done in school from which much transfer had been confidently expected. In these experiments, which dealt with the perception of words and letters, the training period consisted in the rapid cancellation of every word on a printed page containing both *e* and *s*. Before and after this training, the subjects were tested for their ability to perceive and cancel words containing *a* and *t*, *s* and *p*, *l* and *o*, and the like. In another experiment the subjects were tested for their ability to perceive and cancel certain parts of speech, e.g., verbs and adjectives, as well as words of a certain length, and misspelled words. They were then trained in like material and again retested. Improvement in finding and cancelling two letters—as shown by tests given before and after training—was about 25 per cent as great as the accuracy achieved in the training period itself. Efficiency in finding and marking verbs and prepositions was improved from 20 to 25 per cent in speed, and often three times as much in accuracy, as a result of training with analogous material. But although the ability to perceive and mark other parts of speech as a result of this training in some instances showed an increase in speed, there was often a great decrease in accuracy. Here again interference rather than transfer of improvement seems to have been the rule.

The result of Thorndike and Woodworth's experiments indicated clearly that even in performances superficially much alike there may often be not only comparatively little transfer of improvement, but instead considerable interference or negative transfer. Such transfer as appeared our authors attribute to the carry-over of specific methods and rules of procedure, or to similarity in the trained and tested material. One subject, for example, discovered in himself a tendency to overestimate small areas, and allowed for this in his later judgments. Another found that too much interest in the subject-matter of the selection cancelled slowed him up, and that too close attention to the particular letters cancelled led to interference when other letters were marked. In general, attitudes of confidence, familiarity with the task, and improvement in methods of attack seem also to have been transferred.

Thorndike and Woodworth's findings gave little encouragement to a belief in a general observational ability, or in a faculty of perception for dealing with language which, once trained, raises thereafter the whole level of performance in such abilities. On the contrary, their results suggested strongly that the amount of transfer from one activity to another depends chiefly upon the degree of community among, or the overlapping of, their elements. Obviously, this conclusion, if established for other material, would make any broad spread of improvement an impossibility; as it stands, it is diametrically opposed to the idea of formal discipline.

(4)

Thorndike and Woodworth's experiments delivered a broadside against formal discipline—at least in its extreme form—from which it never fully recovered. Scores of experiments on transfer since carried out, although differing much as to method of attack and activity selected for study, have on the whole corroborated these early results. Practically all later studies agree that transfer as the result of special practice is far from general, and that, for the most part, it is confined to closely related capacities.

The largest degree of transfer seems to be found in studies of animal maze-learning, the least in studies of the disciplinary or transfer value of school subjects. One typical investigation from each of these fields will be cited by way of illustration. A careful and well-controlled experiment of transfer in maze-learning, in which both rats and humans were subjects, was carried out at the University of Chicago by L. W. Webb (1917). Webb employed six square mazes as learning problems for his animals. In order definitely to favor positive transfer, two of these mazes, A and B, were closely similar as to turns and blind alleys, while the other four, C, D, E, and F, were dissimilar in this respect in order to favor negative transfer. When a group of rats had learned maze A, transfer was measured by seeing how much more quickly these trained rats could learn the other mazes than comparable control groups which had had no previous practice in A. Records were secured in terms of number of trials, errors made, and time required to learn. In every instance, Webb found positive transfer from maze A to the other five mazes, the greatest carry-over being from maze A to maze B wherein the patterns were most similar. The effect of practice was shown in a decided tendency to enter blind alleys less frequently. Increase in the efficiency of learning the other mazes as a result of practice in A varied from 19 to 77 per cent for the trials required; from 20 to 95 per cent for errors; and from 29 to 90 per cent for time. The greatest transfer occurred in the first five trials with the second maze.

Webb obtained substantially the same results, i.e., consistently positive transfer, with his human subjects, who were trained with four pencil mazes.

Webb's results are probably to be attributed in no small part to the fact that maze situations require the learning of a fairly simple and somewhat artificial motor habit, and that mazes—even the most dissimilar ones—are more alike than the learning tasks ordinarily confronting rats or humans outside of the laboratory. The fact that transfer of practice is concentrated mainly in the first five trials on the second maze is especially significant. It suggests that what is carried over from maze A to the other mazes is a general familiarity with the situation to be learned, plus feelings of certainty and confidence, perhaps, which enable the learner (rat or human) to get off to a "running start." Of course, it need hardly be pointed out that even very extensive transfer in simple motor tasks can have little effect in bolstering up the concept of mental faculties or the disciplinary value of intellectual tasks. However, transfer even from maze A to maze B fell considerably below 100 per cent, the average of results by the three criteria being about 82 per cent.

(5)

One of the most comprehensive recent studies on the subject of transfer in school subjects was carried out by Thorndike in 1924. In this experiment, which Sandiford speaks of as a crucial test of the transfer value of special practice, Thorndike investigated the effect upon intellectual achievement of a year's work in various high school subjects, such as Latin, mathematics, and history. The subjects were 8,564 high school students in grades 10, 11, and 12. As a preliminary or initial test (I T) all pupils were given Form A of the *Tests of Selective and Relational Thinking,* published by the Institute of Educational Research, Teachers College, Columbia University.[2] After one year of school work these students were given Form B of the same tests as a final test (F T). The two forms A and B are equivalent, being of approximately equal difficulty. The training period (T P) was supplied by one regular year of schooling in from four to five studies. The gain in final score over initial score (F T — I T) was taken to be a joint product of growth plus the influence or transfer effect of the subjects studied. To separate out the differential effect of each school subject, Thorndike employed the following plan. All pupils whose programs included, let us say, English, geometry, history, and Latin were matched for initial score in the tests with pupils whose programs included English, geometry, history, and some other subject than Latin, say physics. These two groups, being equal in initial ability, and having taken the same subjects throughout the year, except for Latin in one group and physics in the other, any difference in gain at the end of the year would be the result, presumably, of the differential or transfer effect of the two compared subjects. To cite an example, if the average gain in the final test of the Latin Group were 25 points, and the average gain of the Physics Group 15 points, then since the two groups were equal at the start, the training effect from Latin is, on the average, ten points greater than that from physics. The transfer effect of the other school studies was calculated in the same way. The amount which each contributed to the final score was computed by balancing programs alike except for the one variable study in each case. Of course, various combinations of studies had to be made owing to the wide diversity of programs, so that the task of determining differential gains was

[2] This "battery" included those tests usually found in group tests of general intelligence, e.g., arithmetic, opposites, number series completion, analogies, sentence completion, etc. There were fifteen tests in all.

by no means so simple as our illustration might suggest. The example given, however, will serve as a simplified description of the method. To determine the carry-over of a study as compared with simple growth during the year, equated groups with programs containing studies *ABCD,* for instance, and studies *ABCDX* were compared. This gives the effect of study *X* against non-*X,* growth being the same for both groups of students.

The results of this extensive investigation were later checked in another study of 5,000 pupils (1927). The implications of these two experiments for formal discipline are extremely important, and the specific findings are probably at variance with what many of us might have been led to expect. As far as the different studies are concerned, mathematics, including bookkeeping and arithmetic, proved to have the greatest training effect, with general science, physics, and chemistry close seconds. Latin was inferior to mathematics and science, about equal to French, and superior to economics, sewing, stenography, manual training, and dramatic art. In general, these last-named studies showed negative transfer—a loss in final score rather than a gain. Undoubtedly the traditional view that Latin is the subject *par excellence* for training one to reason or think is hardly borne out by these findings.

While fairly consistent differences appeared between school subjects, the transfer effect of even the best subjects was astonishingly small. Apparently, the gain made by a pupil during the year depends far more upon his native ability, as shown by a high initial score on the tests, than upon the transfer value of a particular study. This is clearly shown by the fact that, while the highest 1 per cent in initial general ability gained about twenty points in the final test after a year's work in high school, the lowest 1 per cent gained only one and one-half points. This was irrespective of the subjects studied. In commenting upon these facts Thorndike writes:

"The expectation of any large difference in general improvement of the mind from one study rather than another seems doomed to disappointment. The chief reason why good thinkers seem superficially to have been made such by having taken certain school studies, is that good thinkers have taken such studies, becoming better by the inherent tendency of the good to gain more than the poor from any study. When the good thinkers studied Greek and Latin, these studies seemed to make good thinking. Now that the good thinkers study Physics and Trigonometry, these seem to make good thinkers. If the abler pupils should all study Physical Education and Dramatic Art, these subjects would seem to make good thinkers. These were, indeed, a large function of the program of studies for the best thinkers the world has produced, the Athenian Greeks. After positive correlation of gain with initial ability is allowed for, the balance in favor of any study is certainly not large. Disciplinary values may be real and deserve weight in the curriculum, but the weights should be reasonable."

We may summarize briefly the present-day opinion of psychologists on the problem of how transfer takes place as follows: Improvement in one function, as a result of the exercise of another, depends (1) upon the identity of elements, either as to material or as to method, between the capacities measured; or (2) upon the carry-over of attitudes or methods or techniques of attack which are fairly generalized. The first view is substantially that of Thorndike and Woodworth previously stated; the second, that of generalized experience, was first advanced by Judd, and is sometimes taken to be an alternative—and opposed—explanation of transfer. It seems doubtful, however, whether there is really any opposition between the two views, though there is a difference in emphasis. The value of Latin as an aid in learning French depends upon the identical elements in the two languages as well as upon the similarity in general form and syntax which they possess in common with English. It seems hardly probable that common attitudes or techniques are abstracted from a variety of experiences unless there are common bonds (identical elements) running through them all. The most common bond is language; others are everyday information, similarity of method or procedure, and plan of attack. Such connections as these probably supply the identical elements as well as the more abstract procedures which lead to transfer. It is hardly necessary to add that both of these views of the mechanism of transfer are directly opposed to the faculty view of mental organization.

(6)

Many of the early experiments on the transfer of improvement from practice were faulty because of the experimenter's failure to check the results obtained from special training against the results secured from a control group. A control group, which takes the initial test and the final test, but not the training, enables one to separate out, from the transfer effect due to special training, the carry-over due to mere repetition of the final test. The control group technique— often called the *method of equivalent groups*—is so generally employed to-day in transfer experiments, as well as in many other experimental problems in psychology, that it seems worth while for us to consider it in some greater detail. The first step in the method of equivalent groups is to equate the two (or more) groups employed on the basis of one or more variable factors, such, for example, as age, sex, or general intelligence. Often the groups are equated in terms of the specific function, e.g., memory or reaction time, upon which the influence of the experimental factor or E F (in transfer experiments this is special practice) is to be studied. In equating groups, the usual method is to match or pair off the subjects so that the two groups will have the same or nearly the same average initial score (I T) and the same variability around this average. After the groups are equated, the E F is applied to one—the experimental group—and at the conclusion of this training period both groups are given the final test (F T), which is usually an alternate form of the I T. The difference in gain of the experimental group over the control gives a measure of the effect of the E F, *minus* the practice effect of simply repeating the test. That is to say, the control group enables us to separate out the practice effect due to mere repetition of the I T, from the effect of the E F *plus* the repetition of the I T. We may diagram the whole process simply as follows:

$$\text{Experimental group:} \quad I\,T - E\,F - F\,T = C_1$$
$$\text{Control group:} \quad I\,T \text{————} F\,T = C_2$$
$$C_1 - C_2 = \text{the effect of the E F}$$

A recent experiment by Gates [3] illustrates clearly the method of equivalent groups as applied to transfer problems and is quoted here as a concrete example of the method. Gates was interested in finding out to what extent a simple function, i.e., digit span, could be improved as the result of intensive practice and how permanent such improvement would be. A group of kindergarten children four to six years old were subjects. From this group two equated groups were made up by matching each child with another child as nearly as possible in the following traits: sex, age, mental age, I Q, scholastic maturity as estimated by teachers, memory for digits presented orally, for letters presented orally, for un-

[3] *An Experimental Study of the Nature of Improvement Resulting from Practice in a Mental Function,* Journal of Educational Psychology (1925), 16, 583-592.

related words presented orally, for geometric figures, for pictures, and for names. How well the two groups were matched may be judged from the following table:

TABLE XIV

Traits	Number	Age	Mental age	I Q	Memory for digits	Memory for letters	Memory for unrelated words	Memory for related words	Memory for geometrical figures	Memory for pictures	Memory for names
Experimental group	16	5.1	6.31	122	4.33	3.64	3.86	14.0	4.3	5.3	7.5
Control group	16	5.1	6.35	123	4.33	3.71	4.07	13.7	4.0	5.7	7.0

The experimental factor was intensive practice in immediate memory for digits. For seventy-eight days the children in the experimental or practice group were given daily drill in learning groups of digits, the control group, meanwhile, receiving no training. At the end of the practice period when both groups were retested (F T) for digit span, the practice group had progressed from an average span of 4.33 digits (see Table XIV) to an average of 6.40, a gain of 2.07 digits. The control group, on the other hand, had increased its average from 4.33 to 5.06, a gain of .73 digit. The difference between 2.07 and .73 gives the effect of the intervening practice upon this simple memory function. Gates writes: "In the Stanford-Binet Scale, 4 digits is placed at year 4, and 6 at year 10. The practice group, then, advanced during a period of 4.5 months during which they practiced 78 days, an amount equal to that which the average untrained child advances in approximately 6 years."

Is this comparatively enormous gain the result of some real improvement in retentivity, or of a stimulated rate of growth of neural connections, or can it be attributed simply to an improvement in the technique of memorizing, better methods and the like? To answer this question, Gates allowed four and a half months to pass, and then retested fourteen members of each group—all that could be located. The result was quite conclusive. On this retest, the average memory span of the practised group was 4.36 digits, that of the control group 4.41 digits: the two groups were again equal as they were at the beginning of the study. Improvement, although quite large immediately after training, had resulted in no permanent benefit. This result indicates clearly, as Gates points out, that the large increase in score brought about by the seventy-eight days of intensive practice was probably due almost entirely to the acquisition of special techniques, familiarity with the task in hand, adaptation to the examiner's voice and signals, loss of anxiety, better habits of attention, and the devising of simple schemes of grouping, getting combinations, and the like. Obviously these techniques, though temporarily highly effective, did not remain as permanent acquisitions.

The method of equivalent groups has been widely used in numerous psychological problems and has proved to be exceedingly valuable in the study of the effects of various experimental factors. Apart from the E F of special training in transfer experiments, the incentive value of praise versus blame, the effects of various drugs upon mental activity, visual versus auditory presentation, and positive versus negative suggestion may be mentioned as a few of the many problems which have been investigated by this method.

Suggested Readings

1. The experimental work on transfer of training is scattered through many psychological and educational journals and over many years. The following general references give convenient summaries of most of the important investigations along with elementary discussions

and evaluations: A. M. Jordan's *Educational Psychology* (1928), Chapter VII; A. I. Gates's *Psychology for Students of Education* (1923), Chapter XV; and S. S. Colvin's *The Learning Process* (1914), Chapters XIV and XV.

Chapter 7

WATSON'S EXPERIMENTAL STUDIES OF THE BEHAVIOR OF THE HUMAN INFANT

(1)

PRIOR to the studies (from 1917 to 1920) of John B. Watson and his co-workers upon the growth and behavior of the human infant, little actual experimental work had been done in this highly interesting field. There were, to be sure, several excellent biographies of individual children, notably those by Darwin (1877) and Miss Shinn (1907); but owing to the resistance and the objections of many people, parents in particular, to any "experiments" upon the human young, few systematically controlled observations on the appearance and development of behavior patterns had been made on large numbers of children from which reliable conclusions could be drawn. Watson's pioneer studies, carried out upon many young children at the Harriet Lane Hospital in Baltimore, did much to remedy this neglected state of affairs and to emphasize the need and importance of further work. A large share of the interest in the study of the young child which we see exhibited so widely to-day in the establishment of institutes of child welfare and nursery schools had its origin in these early experiments of Watson and his students.

Despite the recognized value of this work, however, John B. Watson is best known to-day not as a child psychologist, but as the "founder" and champion of the strictly mechanistic type of psychology known as behaviorism. Watson received the Ph.D. degree in psychology from the University of Chicago in 1903 with a dissertation in the field of animal psychology. The next year he went to Johns Hopkins University, where he became professor of experimental psychology in 1908 at the age of thirty years. Watson brought to Johns Hopkins a strong interest in animal experimentation and a growing belief in the practicability of extending to man the objective methods used with so much success in animal work. One of his primary objects, in fact, in initiating the experiments with children described in this chapter was to exemplify the value of objective and behavioristic methods in genetic studies of the human young.

In general Watson's method was to observe infant activity from birth onward; to catalogue the fundamental reflexive and instinctive tendencies as well as the unlearned emotional expressions as they appear; and to discover how early habits develop from these innate modes of behavior. Careful note was made of the times at which children begin to reach for, manipulate, and handle objects; sit alone, crawl, and walk. What objects and situations babies are afraid of, angered by, and delighted with were also listed, and the genesis of these emotions studied. Information was secured not simply by observing behavior, but by arranging situations and trying them out on the children as well. Such records furnish exact and definite data on the old and much-discussed question of whether a person inherits specific fears of animals and objects, or whether such fears are learned. They have proved to be extremely useful in giving a genetic or growth picture of the developing human infant, and in enabling us to detect and remedy habit-deficiencies and perverse emotional attachments at an early age. Eventually, too, studies such as these will aid us better to guide and direct older children toward the kind of education and kind of vocation for which their talents best fit them.

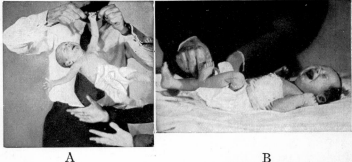

A   B

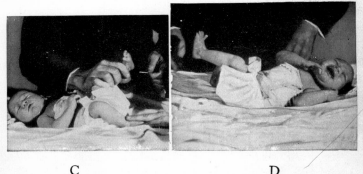

C   D

FIGURE 15: SHOWING SOME INFANT REFLEXES.

A is the grasping reflex of a child 12 days old. B shows the defensive reflex of left foot to slight pinch on inner surface of right knee. C is stimulation for the Babinski reflex. The blunt end of a match is rubbed across the sole of the foot. The result is shown in D. The great toe shows extension, the small toes "fanning" or flexion. (This is a very variable reflex so far as pattern is concerned.) From J. B. Watson's *Psychology from the Standpoint of a Behaviorist*, 2nd edition (J. B. Lippincott Company, 1924), Fig. 56.

(2)

The earliest reflex noted by M. G. Blanton (1917), working under Watson's direction, was sneezing, which may occur even before the so-called birth-cry. Hiccoughing, yawning, and, of course, crying also appear very shortly after birth. Besides the birth-cry which is apparently entirely reflexive and comes with the first gasping intake of air by the new-born infant, Mrs. Blanton differentiates crying due to (1) hunger, (2) injury and rough treatment, and (3) fatigue or lack of exercise. It is interesting that the regular flow of tears does not ordinarily appear until the child is about a month old. Sucking which includes tongue, lip, and cheek movements and is followed by swallowing can be demonstrated in the first hour after birth. The reflexes of elimination occur shortly after birth, and sometimes even before birth. Smiling, which comes somewhat later—usually not before the fourth or fifth day—is also unlearned behavior. If the child is comfortable and well fed, smiling may be elicited by light touches on the body, stroking the skin, or gently rocking. Apparently the child does not learn to smile until it is at least one month old. Mary Cover Jones (1926) in a study of 185 babies, found that conditioned or learned smiling, i.e., smiling when the experimenter smiles or talks baby-talk, rarely appears before the child is thirty to forty days old. Gesell (1928) reports smiling in response to social stimulation at about ninety days.

One of the earliest motor activities to appear in the human infant is that of grasping (Figure 15, A). A baby's fingers will readily close upon a stick, pencil, finger, or any small object, and, clinging to this like a small monkey, the child can easily be lifted. All but about 2 per cent of normal children can support their own weight in this way, the time during which they hang suspended varying from a fraction of a second to as long as a minute. This activity, which is entirely innate or unlearned, appears shortly after birth and drops out when the child is about four months old, although it sometimes persists for a longer time. Once it disappears, it apparently never returns. Watson suggests that the late disappearance of this reflex may indicate abnormally slow development; but at just what age the line should be drawn has not as yet been determined definitely. If the experimenter presses with his finger upon the chin of the new-born child, the coördination of the two arms into a single defense movement is diffuse and poor. After four or five days, however, coördinated movements of the two arms appear with fair regularity.[1] Figure 15, B shows the defense reflex of a baby to a slight pinch on the inner surface of one knee. Note that the opposite leg is drawn up as though to push away the annoying stimulus.

With the waning of the grasping reflex, the child begins to reach; this involves extending the hands for an object, seizing it, and (usually) carrying it to the mouth. At about the same time, too, (five months) the baby begins actively to employ its thumb, which hitherto has been well-nigh useless, in opposition to its other four fingers. Watson tested for reaching activity by holding a stick of candy directly in front of the child and allowing him to try and get it. If he grasped it, he was allowed to taste or suck it. A five-months-old baby will reach not only for candy but, in general, for any small object held close by. If the object reached for hurts or gives pain, the child will soon learn not to reach for that particular thing. Several scorches from a candle, for example, and the baby, even at an early age, learns to let lighted candles alone when they come within his reach. A somewhat surprising result obtained from this study of reach-

[1] Sherman, M. and I. C., *Sensori-motor Responses in Infants,* Journal of Comparative Psychology (1925), 5, 53-68.

ng is the discovery that the child does not reach for objects more than two feet away. This, of course, is quite
contrary to the poetic notion that the young child will reach
for the moon or for any distant object.

As we all know, most adults are right-handed, although
quite a respectable minority use the left as the preferred
hand. Is the preference for the right hand innate or hereditary, or is it a learned response? The answer we give to this
question is of more than theoretical interest. If handedness
is inborn, it is probably safer to let a child use his preferred
hand—whether right or left—rather than to try and cause
him to change, as there is some evidence that stammering
and other emotional disturbances often occur when a left-
handed child is forced later on to change over to his right
hand.[2] But if handedness is entirely a matter of chance or
of early habit-formation, then, since the great majority of
people are right-handed, it would certainly seem best to teach
all children from the beginning to use the right hand in
preference to the left. Watson investigated this question of
handedness in several ways which illustrate so clearly the
experimental techniques used in child study that they will be
described rather fully.

1. First, a comparison was made of the length of time
during which twenty very young children could hang from a
bar supporting their own weight either by the right hand
alone or by the left hand alone. The tests were begun at
birth and continued for the first ten days of the child's life.
Results showed that children hang, on the average, as long
with the left as with the right hand: i.e., no innate preference in this activity, at least, was apparent (see Figure 15,
A for illustration).

2. Next the amount of random slashing movements made
by the baby with its right and its left arms was measured.

[2] Terman, L. M., *Hygiene of the School Child* (1914), 345-346.

The record of such voluntary activity as appeared was kept by means of a small "work adder," a device which when operated caused a notched wheel to revolve in one direction, thereby winding up a weight attached by a cord to a drum and giving a record of work done. One end of the adder cord was fastened to the child's wrist, the other to the weight. Two adders were used so that records from both arms could be taken simultaneously. This experiment, which occupied about five minutes, showed that almost identical amounts of work were done by the right and left arms, thus indicating that neither arm (and neither hand) is favored in gross slashing movements of this kind.

3. In the third test, children from five to twelve months old were examined to see which hand was used first in reaching for objects. Twenty babies were tested once a week, ten to twenty trials being given to each. Generally a stick of candy or a candle served as the test object. This was brought in slowly toward the baby on a level with its eyes, and exactly in the middle line squarely between the baby's two hands. Usually reaching occurred when the object was about two feet away. A careful record was kept of which hand was used for reaching, or, if both hands were used, as sometimes happened, which touched the object first. No marked preference for either hand appeared in this test, sometimes the baby used the right and again the left hand more often.

4. As a final test, measurements were made of the length of the right and left forearms, wrists, palms, and fingers. No significant differences were found between the right and left measurements of 100 babies.

These studies of handedness suggest strongly the absence of any inborn preference for either hand. If this be the true state of affairs, it is probable that we shall never know how preference for the right hand originated in man, and it would make little practical difference if we did. Certainly the desire of parents that their children shall not be "different" is of major importance to-day in fitting the growing boy and girl into the right-hand mold. At an early age the boy is taught to shake hands with his right hand, take off his hat with his right hand, and write with his right hand; later on he finds that tools, baseball gloves, and golf-clubs favor the right-hander. Much the same thing is true for girls. Probably this early forcing toward right-handedness plus convenience and social pressure are strong enough, even if left-handedness were native for some individuals, to make all but the most stubborn left-handers conform.

(3)

Grasping of objects depends upon hand-eye coördinations, and because of this it is important to know when eye movements become coördinated and which movements are first to appear. One method of studying eye movements is to place the baby on its back in a dark room with the head held gently in place by an assistant. Just above the baby's head a perimeter is then placed. This contrivance, which looks like the half of a hoop, carries a small light. The baby's head being the center of the circle of which the perimeter is the semicircumference, the light when moved is always the same distance from the baby's eyes. Now by moving the light to the right or left, the "following" movements of the baby's eyes can be studied. Watson found that the "roving" movements of the eyes are poorly coördinated at birth. Sherman (1925), who has verified these observations on ninety-six babies ranging from one hour to twelve days old, adds that after thirty to forty hours coördination is fairly good. The first coördinated following movements with true fixation are those in which the baby's eyes turn to the left or right. Somewhat later (after fifty to eighty days) upward and downward movements appear; and the baby is able to follow the light when it is moved in a circle when he is two to three months old. At about the same age, too, blinking, brought about by passing the hand between the child's face and a source of light occurs. This reflex is extremely useful in protecting the eye from injury, and belongs to the general class of movements known as "protective reflexes."

(4)

An important sign of development in the young child is the ability to sit alone, for, like reaching, it shows that the baby is gradually learning how to use its own body. At three months and a half, says Watson, the infant may sit unsupported for as long as two minutes. M. C. Jones, on the basis of more observations than Watson, puts the first appearance of sitting alone at five months, Gesell at six to eight months. (The discrepancy here is apparently the result of setting up different criteria for "sitting alone.") By the age of six months the child will sit alone twice as long as at three months, and will play with its toes, pull at its clothing, and strike the bed upon which it is sitting. After sitting alone, the first step in the locomotion series is crawling, from which standing and walking develop. Many infants can support themselves in the standing position by holding on to some object as early as the eighth or ninth month. The age at which a child begins to walk depends upon its health, its weight, and whether it has had any frights or injuries from falls. Walking may appear at one year of age or even earlier. After the first step has been taken, actual skill in learning to walk is contingent upon the increase in body strength and growth, as well as upon the praise and encouragement received from the parents.

As the sphere of his interests enlarges, the normal child seeks voluntarily to increase his means of getting what he wants.

Tickle the sole of a baby's foot or stroke it gently with the blunt point of a pencil and the big toe will turn upward in a fanning or extension movement, while the other toes are turned down (flexion movement). This reaction, which is entirely unlearned, is called the Babinski reflex, and is found in practically all infants (Figure 15, C and D). Sherman (1925) reports that in 90 per cent of the cases examined by him, extension at the first stimulus was followed quickly by flexion at the next stimulus. He regards the failure of the second movement to appear to be evidence of poor functional or neural development. The Babinski reflex usually disappears between the sixth and twelfth months of the child's life. It is of considerable clinical value, since its presence indicates, apparently, a lack of complete development in the nervous system. Hence if the reflex persists longer than one year the supposition is that the baby is not developing normally. When found in adults the Babinski reflex is a sign of pathological or diseased condition.

(5)

Tests of physiological development and motor control like those just described are often used to determine whether or not a baby is normal for his age. Such tests are usually grouped into graded series or scales from which norms or developmental standards have been formulated. A good illustration of such a scale is Kuhlman's revision and extension of the Binet-Simon tests.[3] Terman's Stanford Revision, it will be recalled (see Chapter 1, page 16), like Binet's original scale, does not extend below three years. Kuhlman devised

[3] *A Handbook of Mental Tests* (1922).

and standardized tests for three months, six months, twelve months, eighteen months, and two years, in addition to tests for the age-range covered by Binet (three to fifteen years). These early tests are attempts, for the most part, to discover whether the child possesses the normal reflexes, as well as the motor, sensori-motor, and language activities normal for his age. The average child of three months should, according to Kuhlman, be able (1) to carry his hand or an object to his mouth; (2) to react "with a marked 'start' or wink" to a sudden sound, such as a clap of the hands, or the snap of a small telegraphic "snapper"; (3) to fixate a light or bright object and follow it readily with his eyes in a coördinated movement; (4) to turn his eyes (or head and eyes) voluntarily toward a light or bright object somewhat out of the direct line of vision; and (5) to wink when an object, such as a hat or a book, is suddenly brought in toward his eyes. Tests for the other age-levels below three years are described in detail in Kuhlman's manual. To illustrate with a few examples, the normal child of six months should be able, among other things, to sit alone, use his thumb in opposition to his four fingers, and reach for seen objects; at twelve months he should be able to repeat two or three syllables, mark with a pencil on paper, and discriminate among several objects such as a ball, rattle, and block; at eighteen months he should feed himself with a spoon, understand simple questions, and show interest in and recognize familiar objects in large colored pictures; at two years he should be able to obey simple commands, copy a circle, imitate simple movements, and recognize objects in a picture, such as a dog or a man. According to his successes and failures with these tests, the mental age of the baby can be calculated in the same way as that of an older child.

An interesting set of performance tests for the young child

is the Merrill-Palmer series of tests drawn up and standardized by Rachel Stutsman (1926) under the direction of Dr.
Helen T. Woolley. These tests (there are ninety-three in
all) are grouped into six-month intervals from eighteen
months to six years; that is, the first group of eleven tests
is for children eighteen to twenty-four months old; the second group (ten tests) for children twenty-four to thirty
months old; and so on. The mental age of the child is calculated from the total number of tests in the series which
he is able to pass. To illustrate the kind of performances
called for, the average child of two to two and one-half
years is expected to be able to repeat four simple words (e.g.,
kittie, ball); to recognize himself in the mirror; fit sixteen
cubes into a box in 125 seconds or less; put pegs into a
board; pull a stick attached to a string in toward himself,
using one or both hands; arrange four cubes—of different
sizes all open at one face—into the form of a "nest," each
cube being fitted into the one next larger in size; answer
six out of ten simple questions, e.g., "What does a kittie
say?" "What is this (chair)?"; cut paper with scissors;
and repeat simple word-groups, such as "see the pretty
dollie." As is evident, these tests measure the child's ability
to recognize and manipulate the objects of his environment
in a sensible, if elementary and simple, fashion.

A variety of simple performance tests, much used with
younger children, is shown in Figure 16. These tests all
measure, in a general way, the child's muscular development
and hand-eye coördination. They gauge, too, his perception
of form and shape, and knowledge of common everyday
things. The Wallin Peg Boards (A and B) set before the
child the task of fitting the six round pegs in A and the six
square pegs in B into the holes in the board. These are very
easy tests and can be done by normal children from eighteen
months to two years of age. They are often used as tests

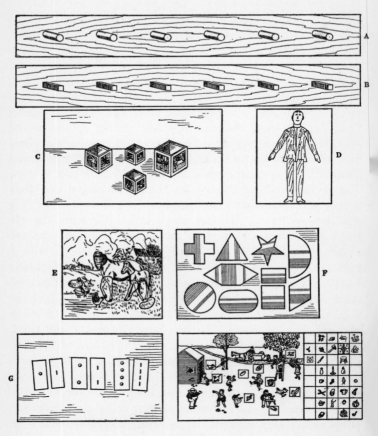

FIG. 16

SOME PERFORMANCE TESTS MUCH USED WITH YOUNG CHILDREN

A and B are Wallin Peg Boards; C, the Nest of Cubes Test; D, Pintner's Manikin Test; E, the Mare and Foal Test; F, the Sequin Form Board; G, the Decroly Button Test; H, the Healy Picture Completion Test, No. 1.

of the feeble-minded and the low-grade. The Nest of Cubes Test (C) has been described above. Each cube is to be fitted into the one next larger in size. The average child of two to two and one-half years should do this test in four minutes or less. In D, Pintner's Manikin Test, the child is required to fit the arms, legs, and head pieces, which are separate, onto the trunk to form a man. This test is rarely done correctly by children under eight years of age. The Mare and Foal Test (E) sets the task of fitting certain cut-out pieces into their correct locations. The normal three-year-old takes five minutes or less to do this test. The Sequin Form-Board Test (F) is the best known of the many form-board tests. The average child of three years can fit the blocks into their proper places in about two minutes. The Button Test (G) was devised by the Belgian psychologist, Decroly. The six strips are of flannelette, three inches by six inches, and are arranged in pairs. The first pair consists of a strip with a button sewed on it and a second strip in which a buttonhole has been worked to fit the button. The next pair of strips contains two buttons and two button-holes, respectively, and the third pair four buttons and four button-holes. The buttoning and unbuttoning process is first demonstrated to the child, who is then encouraged to try it. A normal child of two and one-half years can usually do one button, a child of three years, two buttons. H, the Picture Completion Test, No. 1, of Healy, is usable with children from about five to twelve years of age. The child is called upon to fill in certain cut-out portions in the picture with appropriate blocks selected from a set supplied by the examiner. There are more blocks than are needed to complete the picture, so that a real choice must be made. The test is first explained and demonstrated to the child. The score is computed from the number of correct placements. Of the tests shown in Figure 16, A,B,C,D,E,F, and G are used in the Merrill-Palmer series; D,E,F, and H are a part of the Pintner-Paterson Scale of Performance Tests.

Gesell (1925), in his studies of the pre-school child at the Psycho-Clinic of Yale University, has devised a fairly complete schedule of tests and observations to be employed with children from about one month to six years of age. Four fields of behavior activities are sampled: (1) *Motor behavior,* which deals with muscular capacity, coördination, locomotion, and the use of hands and arms, etc.; (2) *language* involving vocalization, word comprehension, speech, and conversation; (3) *personal-social behavior* as exhibited in reactions to persons, initiative, play, social experience, and information; and (4) *adaptive behavior,* concerned with hand-eye coördination, imitation, discrimination, ability to make proper adjustments to a given situation, and sensible control. Gesell's schedule is not a test in the sense that it is concerned primarily with determining the mental age. It is rather a summary and a diagnosis of the child's developmental status based on physical and psychological examinations as well as upon clinical observation.

(6)

As a result of many observations carried out on very young children, Watson reached the conclusion that there are only three fundamental emotions, fear, anger (or rage), and love. These primary emotional patterns, he says, appear at birth or shortly thereafter. Watson's method of testing for native emotions was to bring the child into the laboratory, present stimuli which are known to produce emotions in adults, and note carefully the child's typical reactions. In every case, an effort was made to describe the emotion in terms of its characteristic pattern, and to define it strictly in terms of the situation which called it out.

Photograph by Nickolas Muray, N. Y.

JOHN B. WATSON

(1878–   )

What stimuli, for example, will call out the emotion of fear in the very young child? After working with various stimuli, Watson discovered that invariably *loud noises, pain* or *injury,* and the *sudden loss of support* cause the infant to catch its breath, clutch with its hands, pucker its lips, and often cry. These responses constitute the pattern of what Watson called a "fear-reaction" (see further page 235). No other stimuli brought out fear so regularly and definitely; for instance, these very young children were found to have no native fear of the dark, of animals, of people, or of the thousand and one things of which children are supposed to be "naturally" afraid.

To bring out the emotional response of rage or extreme anger Watson found it sufficient to hamper or restrict the infant's movements in some way. Hold the child's head lightly between the hands, or restrain the movements of his arms or legs, and he will exhibit the behavior which is called rage. This "pattern" consists in a stiffening of the body, crying or screaming, and struggling to escape. If the first attempts are unsuccessful, the child will hold its breath or scream until it becomes blue with rage.

In very young children the emotion of love, as Watson defines it, is characterized by smiling, gurgling, and cooing. Sometimes the child moves its arms and legs rapidly, and sometimes it lies very still, the picture of contentment. The stimuli for love responses are stroking of the skin, tickling, patting, and rocking. When the child becomes older, it will hold out its arms to be taken by the adult.

As stated above, these three emotions, fear, rage, and love, are believed by Watson to be the only definite and clear-cut patterns in what is loosely called emotional behavior (see pages 234-5 later). In searching for other situations and objects which might call out these fundamental responses, Watson decided to carry out several tests on older children, i.e., those varying in age from about four months to one year. All of the children examined had been brought up in the hospital and had never seen any of the animals or other objects used in the tests.

First, the child was brought into the laboratory and allowed to sit upon the lap of its mother or an attendant. Various animals were then presented and the baby's reactions noted. When a very lively black cat purred near by, the baby showed no fear; nor did he show any fear of a pigeon, a rabbit, or a white rat. These were all reached for, one baby trying to put the rabbit's ears into her mouth. In addition to the tests in the laboratory, each child was taken to the zoo and allowed to get quite close to the animals. The result was the same as before: not the slightest fear was shown.

(7)

The tests cited above are highly interesting and at first sight almost unbelievable. If originally a baby shows fear only when confronted by a loud noise or when threatened with loss of support or when actually injured, how does it come about that older children and many adults are afraid of so many things: the dark, snakes, dogs, bugs, cats, and far more innocuous stimuli? The answer given by Watson is that they have *learned* to fear these things, and that the method by which such fears have been learned is the familiar conditioned response (see Chapter 4). A conditioned response, as we know, is behavior called out by some stimulus other than that to which it was originally bound. Strike a dog with a stick and yell "Go away," and it is probable that at a later time the dog will not wait to be struck, but will run when he sees the stick, or even when he hears your voice. This is a simple illustration of a conditioned response. Fear and running away are brought out in the dog by stimuli, sight of the stick or yell, originally powerless to produce these specific reactions. In the same fashion, the fear of lightning is very probably aroused in the young child by the fact that lightning and thunder (loud noise-original stimulus for fear) usually occur together. Many examples of the same kind are cited elsewhere (see pages 96, 117-19).

Watson decided to see whether he could build up a conditioned fear in the laboratory. His subject was a boy, Albert B., eleven months old, and possessed of a stolid and phlegmatic disposition. First, it was determined by actual test that Albert was not in the least afraid of furry animals, such as the rabbit and the white rat. Put them within his reach and he immediately grasped them and played with them. His reaction, however, to a loud noise made by striking a steel bar with a hammer was distinctly one of fear. He would pucker up his lips, throw up his arms, and begin to cry; then turn over on his side away from the noise and make off as rapidly as he could. The problem which Watson set was this: Can an animal be substituted for the loud noise and thus become a fear-object? The experimental set-up was as follows: First, the white rat was presented to Albert. At once he reached for it, and as soon as he touched it, the steel bar was struck a heavy blow just behind the child's head. The fear reaction immediately appeared. The next time the child reached for the rat the noise was repeated with the same result—fear was distinctly shown. Seven days later the child eyed the rat warily when it was presented, refusing to touch it. When the rat touched the baby's hand, the hand was quickly withdrawn, but the child did not cry. It was clearly apparent, however, that the child, while not quite afraid, was not favorably inclined toward the rat. No fear response at all was shown by Albert toward other objects, such as building blocks, which had not been presented together with the noise. Three more joint presentations of rat plus noise were now given, which were sufficient to produce unmistakable signs of fear when the rat was later presented alone. Two more joint stimulations, and the instant the rat appeared on the scene the baby began to cry and to crawl away as fast as he could. Five days later the child was still afraid of the rat.

In order to discover whether this conditioned fear had spread to other objects, Watson then tested Albert with a rabbit, a dog, a fur coat, and cotton wool. To all of these the child was sharply negative: either he cried or crawled away or both; in every case he refused to play with the objects. None of these things, it must be remembered, had been presented along with the loud noise. Yet because of their similarity, the fear reaction had been "transferred" to all of them. But no fear was exhibited whatsoever to building blocks, the conditioned fear apparently having spread only to furry objects. Watson did not attempt to build up any rage reactions experimentally, evidently because of the danger involved in dealing with such reactions; nor did he condition any love reactions in the laboratory. Conditioned or learned rage reactions are often seen, however, as for instance when a child goes into a temper-tantrum or screaming fit in order to get candy or some other desired object, or to gain his ends. We are all familiar, too, with the ease with which a child's love reactions can be transferred from mother to nurse or to grandmother, depending upon which one provides food, petting, and comfort.

(8)

Such experiments as those described in Section (7) are distinctly valuable in showing how useless and even harmful emotional responses to many innocent situations may arise. The discovery of just what causes lie behind such behavior and the formulation of methods of treating and eradicating them is a major problem for the child psychologist. If, working backward, we are able to uncover the reason why a child is afraid of a dog or a dark hallway, or why he is thrown into a tantrum by a seemingly innocent circumstance, we are certainly in a better position to clear the matter up. Much unhappiness could undoubtedly be prevented if harmful habits could be broken up or "reconditioned" in childhood as soon as they appear.[4]

Several experimental studies of the best methods of eliminating or reconditioning harmful habits have recently been undertaken, largely as an outgrowth of the work we have described. Among the most interesting of these is the study of unnatural fears in childhood carried out by Mary Cover Jones (1924) under the guidance and with the advice of Dr. Watson. About seventy children in all, from three to seven months old, were the subjects. These children were all being maintained in an institution for the temporary care of children; they were from fairly good homes and were of normal intellect as determined by individual mental examinations. Children who showed marked fear of snakes, rats, rabbits, frogs, "scare" faces (masks), loud sounds, and so on were selected for study. The main object was the removal of these useless and hampering forms of behavior. The following descriptions will serve to illustrate the methods employed by Mrs. Jones.

1. The Method of Elimination through Disuse. This method is grounded in the common opinion that a childish fear will gradually wear itself out, if the child is shielded from the fear-inspiring object. This may be true when the interval extends over long periods of time during which

[4] See Watson, J. B., *The Psychological Care of the Infant and Child* (1928).

the child grows and enlarges his experiences; but it did not work very well in Jones's tests, which extended over several weeks and even months. At best, ignoring a fear, or shielding the child from fear-objects would seem to be a rather stupid plan. Fears cannot all be so treated, nor can the child be shielded all of its life.

2. The Method of Verbal Appeal. It is a common assumption of many parents that a child can usually be reasoned with or talked out of his fears, of say, snakes or dogs; that by telling stories woven around the fear-object, showing pictures, and the like, the child's curiosity and interest will be sufficiently aroused to overcome his fear. Mrs. Jones tried this plan with a five-year-old girl who exhibited marked fear of a rabbit. Picture-books of "Peter Rabbit," toy rabbits, and stories were used to create interest in real rabbits. At the end of a week of such treatment, however, the child's fear of the real rabbit was as strong as before. Apparently verbal assurances are not sufficient defense against a strong fear urge. Here actions not only speak louder than words, they speak more truthfully.

3. The Method of Negative Adaptation. Negative adaptation in plain language means that familiarity breeds contempt. The idea behind this method is that the child will finally become indifferent or used to snakes, bugs, or even "ghosts" in a dark room, if such situations are encountered often enough. This assumption seems fairly well founded. In several instances Mrs. Jones found that a child, originally very much frightened by a white rat, became at least tolerant, if not exactly friendly, when the animal was often seen around. This method would seem to be valuable if used intelligently—i.e., if the stimulations are not too frequent nor too drastic.

4. The Method of Repression. Children's fears are often repressed or temporarily hidden under the surface when they are ridiculed by other children or by adults. Little boys, particularly, of around four or five and even younger will often make a brave show, their desire not to be eclipsed or made to feel inferior serving for the time to overcome their real feelings. But the repression of a fear in this way is dangerous business, as the remedy may turn out to be worse than the original ailment. Mrs. Jones found that instead of being lost, a fear was often more strongly entrenched as a result of social ridicule and teasing.

5. *The Method of Distraction.* This method, much used by mothers in everyday child upbringing, consists in presenting an object or other stimulus so pronouncedly positive in appeal that the child's attention is temporarily, at least, distracted from the fear-object. Mrs. Jones found that a child's fear of a frog or rabbit could be somewhat lessened by placing toys and other desirable playthings near the animals. Verbal distractions, too, such as soothings, calling the animal by name, pointing out characteristics of the "bunny" or "hop-toad" proved useful in inducing the child to forget his fear in his new interest. But, as Mrs. Jones remarks, the presence of an adult (who does the distracting) introduces a variable factor so that it is impossible to tell how much of the child's confidence is due to the reliance and trust which is placed in the protection of the grown-up. At best, in such cases, the fear is only temporarily lightened and is not completely overcome.

6. *The Method of Direct Conditioning.* In this method, which has already been outlined in Section (6) above, an attempt is made to associate with the fear-object some definite stimulus which is known to be capable of calling out a positive or pleasant response. The hope is that in time the fear-object will bring out a positive rather than a negative reaction. In several experiments, Mrs. Jones used food as the positive stimulus-object to overcome a specific fear of

animals, e.g., a rabbit. The procedure was to put the rabbit upon the table, on which the child's food had been placed, at a sufficient distance not to interfere with the child's eating, but close enough to keep the animal well in sight. At first the child ate with a wary eye on the rabbit; and for several days this continued with nothing happening. Gradually the animal was moved closer and closer to the food until finally tolerance changed to indifference and even to the positive response of reaching and stroking the rabbit. While very successful in many cases, this method requires the most careful handling. If fear of the animal or other object is very intense, it may produce a negative response to the food, or such violent crying and screaming as to make the child ill. If care and patience are exercised, however, it would seem to be the most effective method of removing useless and hampering fears.

7. *The Method of Social Stimulus.* Mrs. Jones reports several cases in which this method was used successfully. When a child discovers that other children—as well as grown-ups—are not frightened at the sight of dogs, rabbits, bugs, and so on, curiosity and self-assertion are often power-ful enough to uncondition his fear without more to do. To some extent this is true also of adults, unless the fear be deeply ingrained as the result of some intense experience; or else serves some ulterior purpose. Girls, for instance, are no more afraid of small animals and bugs than boys up to the period of adolescence. When the "grown-up" period is reached, girls find that it is considered "feminine" and rather commendable by the young males if they scream and show fright at such objects; and so a fear, partly feigned, is developed. If an adult is in earnest about ridding himself of a foolish and useless fear, the original cause must first be found and a period of reëducation instituted until the fear-stimulus becomes no longer effective.

Of the seven methods outlined in this section, undoubtedly the most practical are direct conditioning and social stimulation. While sometimes effective alone, verbal appeal, elimination through disuse, negative adaptation, repression, and distraction are probably most valuable when employed together with the other techniques. Which method to employ will depend upon the kind of fear and its intensity, as well as upon the child's general health, intelligence, and environmental background. Work on problems such as these is going on in many laboratories throughout the country. Watson's studies marked the beginning of the present widespread activity and interest in the problems of the preschool child.

Suggested Readings

1. An interesting account of the behavioristic view of the instincts and emotions may be found in J. B. Watson's *Psychology from the Standpoint of the Behaviorist,* 2d edition (1924), Chapters VI and VII.
2. M. and I. C. Sherman's *The Process of Human Behavior* (1929) contains many important recent experiments with infants.
3. For methods of reconditioning harmful habits in children, see J. B. Watson's *Psychological Care of the Infant and Child* (1928), and M. C. Jones's *The Elimination of Children's Fears,* Journal of Experimental Psychology (1924), 7, 382-390.

Chapter 8

GALTON AND THE MEASUREMENT OF INDIVIDUAL DIFFERENCES

(1)

THE eminent English scientist Sir Francis Galton (1822-1911) is probably best known to psychologists as the pioneer student of heredity and mental imagery, and as the first investigator to apply statistical methods systematically to the problem of differences between individuals and among groups. Galton was not a psychologist in the professional sense, as he never held an academic appointment, nor did he confine himself to work upon definitely psychological problems. His interests were wide and varied. According to Terman (pages 24-25), he showed the marks of genius in early childhood, and his later versatility, originality, and active interest in problems of all sorts bear out this early promise. Galton was the founder of the eugenics movement; he established one of the very first laboratories (in 1884) wherein mental and physical tests—mostly of the sensori-motor variety—were given for a small fee; and he initiated, as already stated, the statistical study of individual differences.

The psychology of individual differences or "differential psychology" deals in general with the variations and differences between individuals and between groups in mental traits and performances. In a broad sense, individual differences are the result of the two opposed but at the same time closely interwoven forces of heredity and environment,

urtesy of The Science Press, New York

FRANCIS GALTON

(1822–1911)

or, more simply, nature and nurture. Under the head of nature we may list such factors as immediate ancestry, race, sex, and age; under nurture must be included all of the social, educational, cultural, and other extrinsic agencies which affect the individual from birth until death.

One of the most valuable techniques which has been developed for the study of individual differences is that of correlation, the fundamental notions of which were discovered by Galton and used by him in his studies of the inheritance of traits. Correlation is a mathematical method which enables one to secure a quantitative statement of the degree of relationship existing among the many measures of physical and mental traits which can be obtained from individuals and groups. Degree of relationship is expressed by the coefficient of correlation, a ratio denoted by the letter r. This ratio may vary from 1.00 (perfect relationship) through .00 (no relationship) to —1.00 (perfect inverse relationship). Its meaning may be demonstrated most simply, perhaps, from such a diagram as that shown in Figure 17. This table is taken from Galton's *Natural Inheritance* (1889), page 208, and represents graphically the relation between the heights of "mid-parents" and their adult offspring. Galton obtained the mid-parent heights by multiplying the mother's height by 1.08 and averaging this value with that of the father. The same correction was also applied to the heights of the female offspring, in order to give the lesser female heights equal weight with those of the males. As each mid-parent is counted separately with each offspring (of which there may be several), the table shows many more offspring (928) than mid-parents (204). The average height for both mid-parents and offspring is close to 68¼ inches, and the horizontal and vertical lines drawn through the diagram have been located at this point in each distribution of heights. The value of this "scatter diagram" or correlation

Height of Mid-parents in inches	Heights of Adult Children in Inches														Total Number of		Median Height of Offspring for given Mid-parent Height
	Below 62.2	62.2	63.2	64.2	65.2	66.2	67.2	68.2	69.2	70.2	71.2	72.2	73.2	Above	Adult Offspg.	Mid-parents	
Above 72.5												1	3		4	4	—
72.5								1	2	1	2	7	2	4	19	6	72.2
71.5					1	3	4	3	5	10	4	9	2	2	43	11	69.9
70.5	1		1		1	1	3	12	18	14	7	4	3	3	68	22	69.5
69.5			1	16	4	17	27	20	33	25	20	11	4	5	183	41	68.9
68.5	1		7	11	16	25	31	34	48	21	18	4	3		219	49	68.2
67.5		3	5	14	15	36	38	28	38	19	11	4			211	33	67.6
66.5		3	3	5	2	17	17	14	13	4					78	20	67.2
65.5	1		9	5	7	11	11	7	7	5	2	1			66	12	66.7
64.5	1	1	4	4	1	5	5		2						23	5	65.8
Below	1		2	4	1	2	2	1	1						14	1	—
Totals	5	7	32	59	48	117	138	120	167	99	64	41	17	14	928	204	

FIG. 17

DIAGRAM TO SHOW THE CORRELATION BETWEEN THE HEIGHTS OF MID-PARENTS AND OFFSPRING, AND THE TENDENCY FOR ADULT OFFSPRING TO "REGRESS" TOWARDS THE MEAN HEIGHT

The horizontal and vertical lines on the chart have been drawn through the means of the two distributions. The oblique line through their intersection shows the tendency for tall parents to have tall children and for short parents to have short children. The last column in the diagram indicates that offspring are somewhat shorter than tall parents and somewhat taller than short parents. (From Galton.)

table in showing relationship will be easily grasped from an illustration. Note the entry 34 near the center of the diagram. This entry is opposite the 68.5-inch entry in the mid-parent column of heights and below the 68.2-inch entry in the offspring row of heights. This means that these thirty-four adult offspring with an average height of 68.2 inches possessed mid-parents whose average or mean height was 68.5 inches. The other entries are interpreted in exactly the same way. Now consider the oblique line drawn across the diagram from the upper right-hand corner to the lower left-hand corner. This line represents the trend of median (roughly average) heights of offspring corresponding to the mid-parent heights given in the first column. The calculated median heights of the offspring which serve to locate this line are given in the last column of the diagram. If now the median height of each group of offspring is compared with the mid-parent height in the same row, it will be seen by reading down the column that the adult offspring are on the average slightly *below* their mid-parents in height, e.g., 72.2 < 72.5, 69.9 < 71.5, 69.5 < 70.5, and so on until the mean is reached. After the mean, the offspring tend to be slightly *above* their mid-parents in height, e.g., 65.8 > 64.5, 66.7 ⁀ 65.5, and so on. This tendency of the heights of offspring to deviate away from the heights of their parents and back toward the mean height of both parents and adult children (68¼ inches) was called by Galton the Law of Filial Regression. This law is the expression of a natural tendency to protect the race from extremes. It will readily be seen that unless some such principle held true—if tall parents tended to have still taller children and short parents still shorter children—we should soon have a race of giants on the one hand and of dwarfs on the other. Undoubtedly the Law of Filial Regression must hold in a general way for mental traits as well as for physical characteristics; its operation is exhibited in the relatively infrequent appearance of freaks at either extreme of the mental ability scale.

In addition to the tendency for the heights of adult offspring to vary away from the heights of their parents and regress back towards the mean, it is evident from Figure 17 that the entries are clustered in the upper right-hand and the lower left-hand sections of the diagram. This means that tall mid-parents tend in general to have tall children and short parents to have short offspring; or, in other words, the heights of parent and offspring tend to be related. The best single measure of this relationship, i.e., of the tendency of two traits to vary together, is the coefficient of correlation. Galton first used the symbol r as a measure of the regression or reversion of offspring away from the parents and back toward the mean of the whole group, as described in Figure 17. The symbol r is still used to denote the coefficient of correlation, although the idea of regression is no longer necessarily implied by it. The mathematical derivation of r was made by Karl Pearson, one of Galton's early followers and the foremost living English statistician. The calculation of r is somewhat involved, and since it is described in detail in many elementary textbooks on statistics,[1] it will be unnecessary for our purpose to outline it here. Since Galton's time, literally hundreds of correlations have been calculated, so that the relationship of most of the physical traits and many of the mental ones is now fairly well established. To Galton belongs the credit of having first shown that quantitative relationships between abilities can be calculated, and of having demonstrated the value of correlation.

[1] See H. E. Garrett, *Statistics in Psychology and Education* (1926), Chap. III, or K. J. Holzinger, *Statistical Methods for Students in Education* (1928), Chap. IX.

(2)

In studying the problem of individual differences, it is well-nigh impossible to investigate the rôle of native factors apart from a host of social influences sometimes very difficult to evaluate. This follows from the fact that intrinsic agencies such as immediate ancestry (heredity), sex, and race always operate in some definite environmental setting. Because of this, the following discussion, although devoted primarily to a treatment of native determinants, will not lose sight of such conditioning factors as those of custom, training, and tradition.

In his *Hereditary Genius,* first published in 1869 and later in 1892, Galton attacked specifically the question of the inheritance of conspicuous ability or talent. This was the first statistical study of the effect of immediate inheritance upon achievement. Galton selected for study 977 eminent British men, each of whom he judged would rank as one man in 4,000 in ability. These selections were based upon a survey of the man's accomplishments, upon his biography, and upon all other available information. Among those included in the 977 were judges, statesmen, premiers of England from around 1768 to 1868, commanders, literary and scientific men, poets, artists, and clergymen. Galton's method was to inquire whether these men had more eminent relatives—fathers, brothers, sons, uncles, and others—than would be expected of any average 977 men selected from the general population. His findings showed that his selected group of 977 had close relatives equally as eminent as themselves as follows: 89 fathers, 114 brothers, 129 sons, or 332 in all as against a probable number of only 1. Moreover, this same group had 203 equally eminent grandfathers, grandsons, uncles, and nephews, as against a probable number of 3. The probabilities of 1 and 3 here stated mean simply that the statistical chances are 1 and 3, respectively, that an average group of 977 men will have eminent relatives up to Galton's standard of 1 in 4,000. In another study of the inheritance of artistic ability, Galton found that in thirty families wherein both parents were artistic, 64 per cent of the children were artistic, while in 150 families wherein neither parent was artistic, only 21 per cent of the offspring showed artistic ability. Other studies of related individuals showed a tendency for traits to be found in a like degree in parents and offspring. Galton took these data to imply the great superiority of heredity over environment. Even the best environment, he contended, is unable to raise a man to a position of eminence unless he possesses natural gifts of a high order.

The statistical studies begun by Galton were extended and increased in scope by Karl Pearson, Galton's disciple and, since 1911, Galton Professor of Eugenics at the University of London. In one typical study, Pearson (1904) had about 2,000 brothers and sisters rated by their teachers for intelligence, vivacity, conscientiousness, popularity, temper, self-consciousness, assertiveness and handwriting. In each of these characteristics, except handwriting and temper, the individual rated was described simply as falling into the upper or lower group with respect to the given trait. Correlations for all eight traits averaged .52 between brother and brother, .51 between sister and sister, and .52 between brother and sister. Pearson had discovered that the correlation between such attributes as eye-color, hair-color, height, and length of forearm, over which environment can have little if any effect, also averaged from .50 to .55 for siblings (i.e., brothers and sisters). From these results he argued that since the relationship of physical traits must be due to heredity, and since these characteristics are no more highly related than mental traits, the correlation of the latter must also be basically the result of hereditary influences. He writes: "We are forced, I think literally forced, to the conclusion that the physical and psychical characters in man are inherited within broad lines in the same manner and with the same intensity." Pearson also found that resemblance in mental traits between parent and child is expressed by an r of .50.

Despite the authority which these statistical studies carry with them because of the eminence of their authors, several difficulties arise in accepting their results as indicating beyond question the predominant influence of heredity over environment upon achievement. The first and most obvious difficulty is the error of unfair selection. Galton's choice of eminent men was almost inevitably affected by subjective factors such as personal bias and preferences as well as by the relatively greater accessibility of data on some men than on others. It is extremely doubtful whether eminence as a statesman, in which political and social conditions play so large a rôle, can be equated to eminence as an artist or as a man of science. Again, it is doubtful whether a man's true worth can be correctly judged from the length of his biography or from what his contemporaries think of him. And it is unnecessary to add that we do not know just what part social factors and family tradition, wealth, education, and opportunity played in determining the eminence of Galton's selected group. The error of unfair selection is almost certainly present, too, in Pearson's ratings. For one thing, the teachers who did the rating knew that the investigation was designed to discover whether children of the same parents resemble each other, and hence they very probably were looking for resemblances more often than not. Moreover, pairs of siblings were rated against each other rather than separately on all the traits, thus giving ample opportunity for likes and dislikes to come into play. Finally,

Pearson's twofold classification of traits was extremely rough, making chance errors highly probable.

Still another difficulty which regularly arises in studies of this kind wherein the questionnaire method—invented by Galton—is used, or wherein ratings are required, has been often pointed out by Thorndike. This is the so-called "halo" effect, which means simply that when an individual is rated for intelligence, say, and then for a number of other traits, such, for instance, as reliability, honesty, and courtesy, it is next to impossible to prevent his first rating or ratings from unduly influencing the others. An oft-quoted illustration of halo is that of Rugg (1921), who cites the case of an American officer in the World War who, although one of the most intelligent men in his group as measured by army Alpha, was regularly rated low for intelligence by his fellow-officers because he was so thoroughly disliked. Suggestion, inertia, misunderstanding, the vagueness of the traits to be rated, not to mention prejudice and envy, are influential forces in producing a halo effect. Beside the unknown amount of halo in Pearson's ratings, it seems evident too that such characteristics as temper, popularity, vivacity, and handwriting must depend to a large degree upon health, home conditions, training and degree of stimulation. It is impossible, then, to say just how much of Pearson's fraternal correlation of .50 in mental traits is the result of native and how much of environmental factors.

(3)

In spite of the obvious limitations of this early work, later studies strongly suggest that, if not entirely correct in attributing his fraternal r of .50 to heredity, Pearson was certainly entirely right in emphasizing the greater potency of heredity over environment. One of the most extensive of recent investigations bearing on this topic is Terman's study of gifted children (1925), mentioned briefly elsewhere (page 23) as evidence that high intelligence is probably inherited. It will be remembered that a gifted child in Terman's sense means a child with an I Q of 130 or above. In Terman's main experimental group of 644 children, seventy-three families contributed two gifted children, and nine families contributed three or more. The number of families in which two bright children were found was more than 1,200 times the number which chance alone would allow. Nearly one fourth of the members of the Hall of Fame were related to this group, while many of their parents and near relatives hold or have held major political offices, college presidencies, professorships, and important business positions.

The 27th Yearbook of the National Society for the Study of Education (1928) contains many valuable studies of the relative importance of nature and nurture. H. E. Jones, for instance, reports a study of 105 families containing 317 children, all of whom had been born and reared in rural sections of New England. The general intelligence of parents and adult offspring was measured by the army Alpha, that of the younger children by the Stanford Revision of the Binet tests. The sample selected for study was particularly good, since environmental conditions, education, home training, amusements, and church influences were closely similar for all members of the group. Moreover, all of the individuals tested were native-born whites of old American (mostly British) stock and only English was spoken in their homes. Correlations between brothers and sisters were found by Jones to be .49; between father and child, .51; and between mother and child, .55. These results are very similar—almost identical in fact—with those of Pearson. Working with a group of more than 1,000 siblings, all high school students, Thorndike (in this same volume) reports a correlation of .60 between sibling scores on a battery of tests designed to measure general ability. Thorndike remarks that if Pearson's coefficient of .50—.52 for siblings in physical traits is accepted as giving the undiluted native or inherited resemblance, then the effect of the environment is to raise the sibling correlation from .52 to .60. Provided that .52 really represents true native resemblance, this result assigns an exceedingly meager influence to environment.

Two very extensive studies, both from the 27th Yearbook, bearing upon the influences of immediate ancestry and nurture should at least be mentioned before leaving this topic. The first deals chiefly with the influence of environment upon the intelligence of children. It was conducted by F. N. Freeman, K. J. Holzinger, and others at the University of Chicago. The second deals especially with the relative effects of nature and nurture upon intelligence. It was carried out by Barbara S. Burks at Stanford University under the general supervision of L. M. Terman. Both studies make use of foster children, and accept the Stanford Revision as their standard measure of general intelligence. Foster children were selected for study because their foster homes are usually superior to their heredity. This gives the investigator the opportunity of seeing whether such children will show an I Q corresponding to their heredity, or whether their superior environment will operate to increase their I Q. In the Chicago study it was found that children who were tested on being placed in foster homes had gained on the average seven points in I Q when retested after about four years of residence. Children placed in superior homes (the status of the home was measured by certain rating devices) gained about ten points of I Q; those in below-average homes, about five points. The Stanford study found an average gain of five to six points of I Q as a result of residence in good foster homes. Both of these studies agree, therefore, that an average home environment may raise the I Q five to six points, while a superior home may increase it still more. Unfortunately this conclusion is not entirely certain, owing to the many uncontrolled factors which enter into the choice of a foster child, the uncertainty of the heredity of many of the foster children, and the difficulty in establishing with exactitude the cultural status of the foster home. Certainly, however, the weight of evidence inclines to the conclusion that environment has remarkably little effect upon general intelligence.

(4)

The most direct way of evaluating the influence of immediate ancestry is through the study of twins, since twins represent the nearest approach to identical heredity. Here again Galton was the pioneer. In his *Inquiries into the Human Faculty* (1883) he gives an interesting narrative account of his study of twin resemblance. Galton collected data on about eighty pairs of twins from teachers, friends, parents, and the twins themselves. These reports are in the nature of stories, anecdotes, and the like, for the most part stressing the prevalent idea that twins are much more alike in mental characteristics than siblings. Galton's records have little scientific validity, in spite of their historical interest, as reports collected from untrained observers are invariably colored by all sorts of temperamental and emotional inferences. It should be noted, however, that Galton did distinguish between fraternal and non-fraternal twins. Fraternal or non-identical twins are really the result of multiple births and develop from two fertilized ova. They may be both of the same sex or of the opposite sex. Non-fraternal or identical twins are probably developed from a single ovum and are always of the same sex. Their resemblance is striking, and it is often difficult to tell them apart.

Thorndike's study in 1905 was the first quantitative study of mental resemblance in twins. He measured fifty pairs of twins on six mental tests, comparing the correlation between their scores with the correlation of siblings on the same tests. The r's for the twins ranged from .70 to .80 with a mean at .78, while the r's for siblings averaged around .30. Thorndike next divided his twins into younger twins (nine to eleven years) and older twins (twelve to fourteen years) and computed correlations among his six tests for the two groups separately. The average r for the younger twins was .83, for the older twins .70, indicating that older twins are no more alike than younger twins in the functions measured by the tests. Thorndike argues that if resemblances between twin-pairs in mental ability are the result of common training and common surroundings in school and home, the older twins should be more alike than the younger, especially in those traits much influenced by training. Since his results show the opposite to be true, he concludes that the chances decidedly favor common heredity as the cause of twin resemblance.

Many careful studies of twins have been made since Thorndike's study with more cases, better technique, and better tests; but the results are not far different from his findings. Merriman (1924) found the r between I Q (Stanford-Binet) for forty-seven twins five to nine years old to be .81; for fifty-eight twins ten to sixteen years old, .76. Lauterbach (1925) using twenty-one tests and 210 twin pairs, found that like-sex twins (probably non-fraternal or identical) are much more alike in both physical and mental characteristics than unlike-sex twins (probably fraternal or non-identical), the latter being scarcely more alike than siblings. The average r for seven mental tests was for like-sex twins .67, for unlike-sex twins .41. Hildreth (1925), using many measurements, finds the average correlation for twins to be approximately .75, for siblings about .50. All in all, these studies of twins indicate quite definitely (1) that twins are in general more alike than siblings; and (2) that identical twins are more alike than non-identical. The difference between the r's for mental traits of around .50 (for siblings) and .75 (for twins) may be reasonably attributed to the more nearly identical inheritance of the twin-pairs.

To summarize briefly what has been said in the last three sections, it may be repeated that most careful investigators are convinced that native factors—heredity in general—are far more potent than environmental agencies in fixing both the initial amount of an individual's aptitudes and the extent to which these may be developed. But no one would dispute the fact that no matter how great a child's potential ability, it cannot express itself adequately unless such environmental factors as disease, cruel treatment, and deprivation from normal contacts are definitely negligible or are not present at all.

(5)

Competent investigators who have studied the question of differences in ability between the sexes are convinced that on the whole such differences are small; and that, when they exist, are probably to be attributed to a complex of temperamental and social factors rather than to innate or hereditary differences in capacity for achievement. The very different training given men and women until very recent times; the attitude of both men and women toward women entering business or the professions; the traditional idea of what constitutes a man's work and of what constitutes a woman's—all of these things have so colored the whole question of sex differences in mental capacity that an unbiased conclusion is extremely hard to reach. Still another complication results from the exclusive rôle of woman as mother and nurse of her offspring. One of the earliest studies of sex differences in ability was conducted by Helen Thompson at the University of Chicago in 1903. A variety of tests were employed, including measures of motor ability, sensory acuity and discrimination, and intellectual ability, the whole battery requiring between fifteen and twenty hours to administer. The subjects were twenty-five men and twenty-five women college undergraduates, between the ages of twenty and twenty-five years with a few exceptions. The results of these tests may be summarized briefly as follows: In motor tests of speed and accuracy of movement, except in speed and accuracy of sorting cards according to color, the men did slightly better than the women; in sensory tests of smell, taste, pitch discrimination, and accuracy in judging weights, there were no differences; in tests of rote memory, the women were slightly better than the men; in quickness in solving "ingenuity" problems, the men were slightly ahead. It must be emphasized that in nearly every case the overlapping was very great and the differences extremely small, most of them being unreliable. In no case did the poorest member of one group score higher than the best of the other. In short, the differences *within* either group were very much greater than the differences *between* typical members of the two groups: the gap between a high-ranking man and a low-ranking man was much greater than the gap between the average man and the average woman. Thompson's groups were highly selected, and their small size limits considerably the general applicability of her findings.

Pearson (1904) in his study of the resemblances of sibs, mentioned before, had brothers and sisters rated by their teachers for such attributes as athletic aptitude, intelligence, shyness, good temper, and conscientiousness. As already pointed out, Pearson's results are open to the errors of bias and misunderstanding likely to affect all ratings, but despite this their trend in general is probably fairly indicative of any marked differences between brothers and sisters. According to Pearson's findings, boys are more athletic than girls, more noisy, more self-conscious, and quicker-tempered; girls are more inclined to be shy and are more conscientious. Boys and girls were about equally intelligent as judged by their teachers.

Hundreds of studies of sex differences have been made for all sorts of traits since these early studies. It would be impossible to describe all of them briefly, and in many cases not worth while. In general, differences reported between the sexes have been small and often directly contradictory. We shall try to summarize what appear to be the major and more reliable findings under the following heads: differences in physical characteristics; differences in sensory traits; differences in motor and mechanical abilities; differences in mental and emotional traits. It must always be remembered in what follows that, when one sex is said to be "better" in some performance than the other, the meaning intended is better on the average. In no trait is there an absence of overlapping of male and female.

1. Sex Differences in Physical Traits. Until puberty at least, girls have been found to be more advanced than boys of the same age in height, weight, dentition, and anatomical and physiological maturity. The brain of the female is smaller than that of the male, but in proportion to the weight of the body it is heavier. Women have a faster heartbeat than men, and their simple reflexes are usually faster. Men have larger muscles than women, and excel them in feats of endurance and physical strength.

2. Sex Differences in Sensory Traits. Tests in this field have usually given small and often contradictory results. There are probably no real differences between women and men in visual and auditory acuity and discrimination. Women are consistently faster than men in discriminating differences among colors and in quickness of perception. Men judge differences in weight somewhat better than women and stand pain better.

3. Sex Differences in Motor and Mechanical Traits. Women are consistently faster than men in cancellation tests. There are no real differences in simple motor functions such as tapping and tracing. Boys are nearly always better than girls in performance tests of a manipulative sort, in form-board tests, and in tracing mazes. They are also superior in tests of mechanical construction, mechanical aptitude, and knowledge of mechanical things. Much of this difference is undoubtedly the result of training and the early cultivation of very different interests. Boys are given mechanical toys and bicycles, girls dolls and wearing apparel, and such things soon come to be identified as belonging properly to the male or to the female sex.

4. Sex Differences in Mental and Emotional Traits. Most studies agree in reporting women as better than men in nearly all tests of memory. Girls almost always do better than boys on vocabulary tests, as well as on tests involving language usage and verbal association. Terman found girls slightly better than boys on the Stanford-Binet at each age up to fourteen, a result which may be due to the large verbal content of the test. Boys are fairly consistently better in tests involving numbers and spatial concepts (of a geometric sort), and in arithmetic reasoning tests. Men usually do better than women on general information tests, owing partly no doubt to their greater opportunity for contacts in their business and professional lives. In group intelligence tests there are no reliable differences in favor of either sex; the superiority of high school boys over high school girls sometimes reported is probably to be explained by the fact that high school boys form a more highly selected group than high school girls. If stupid boys drop out of school earlier and more often than stupid girls, the boys who survive high school will be, on the average, somewhat better than the girls. Girls are definitely and regularly better than boys in school work. This has been explained as due to the slower physical development of the boys, to the greater docility of the girls, and to various temperamental factors. In selecting his potential geniuses, Terman found that 54.7 per cent were boys and 45.3 per cent girls. The occurrence of more very bright boys than very bright girls has been commented upon by several investigators, and has been attributed by some to the reputed greater variability of the male sex in mental traits. Greater variability in males would mean that men range higher (and of course lower, too) on a scale of intellectual ability even when the average man and the average woman are about equally endowed. Greater variability would account for the greater number of male geniuses, and for the greater achievement of men in general. This is a very neat explanation, but since equally competent investigators dispute the evidence for greater variability in the male, the issue is by no means settled.

Studies of sex differences in emotional and temperamental traits have given few definite and consistent results. Women are reported to be more interested in persons and personal problems, men in activities and mechanical things. Studies of sex differences in free association indicate a tendency for women's associations to run more to personal ornament and to concrete and individual problems; while men's associations exhibit rather an interest in business relations, money-making, and general and abstract matters. Differences in conversation and in preferences for books and pictures reflect so many things besides the sex of the observer that any differences found are scarcely to be attributed to it alone. Women have been reported to be more impulsive than men; more introverted; less given to exercising foresight; but such statements are little more than opinions.

Most of the studies of sex differences are open to one or both of the following criticisms: (1) the samples are often very small and many times are selected by different criteria; and (2) many of the tests used to measure abilities are unreliable statistically, and the meaning of their scores is uncertain. To say, for instance, that boys are superior to girls in "logical reasoning" means little unless one knows the test from the results of which this conclusion was drawn. The only general conclusion that one may draw from the mass of available data is that women are usually better in tests of language, verbal usage, vocabulary, and memory; that men are generally better in tests of arithmetic reasoning, in performance and manipulative tests, and in the ability to deal with spatial concepts of a geometric sort. Whatever the considerations may be (and conceivably they could be many) which guide parents and educators in planning separate courses of study for boys and girls, certainly the assumption of marked differences in mental ability need play no important part in them.

(6)

The study of individual differences which arise from remote ancestry or racial extraction is complicated even more than the question of sex differences by prejudice, bias, preconceived notions of superiority and inferiority, and special pleading. There is difficulty, too, in defining just what is meant by a "race," because of the great admixture which has gone on all over the world. If, as some anthropologists hold, the white peoples of Europe can be divided into three great racial groups, Nordic, Alpine, and Mediterranean, on the basis of differences in eye-color and hair-color, stature, head shape, and other anatomical characterstics, then almost every national group is a compound of all three of these strains. The modern British, for instance, are Scandinavian Nordic, Norman-French Alpine, and Old Celtic Mediterranean, one or the other strain being dominant depending upon the section of the country selected for study. The modern Germans and Italians are equally as mixed a people, the German being largely Nordic and Alpine, the Italian Alpine and Mediterranean. Probably the Swedes represent as pure a strain as any, being very largely Nordic.

Opinions on race differences vary all the way from a firm belief in the native superiority of certain groups (usually including one's own) to the diametrically opposed view that there are really no hereditary racial differences, such diversities as appear being the result of wide differences in culture, kind of education and training, traditions, customs, relative isolation from other groups, and climatic and geographical factors. Galton was a firm believer in race differences in native capacity; and it was to improve his own race that he initiated the eugenics movements in 1883. Galton concluded, as a result of his observations and study of the history and accomplishments of the different races, reports of travelers, and other data, that the Negro is two grades in mental capacity below the modern Englishman, who in turn is two grades below the ancient Athenian Greek. Galton's scale of intellectual ability contained sixteen steps and ranged from very high to extremely low capacity.

Both Galton's conclusions and his scale have been criticized, the latter on the score that it is arbitrary and subjective, the former on the score that it is not justifiable to compare races on the basis of the number of famous men produced, or in terms of apparent progress; since, for one thing, it is hard to define progress; and for another, social conditions and climatic and geographical locations cannot be equated. Granted that this is undeniably true, it would seem nevertheless that *wide* variations in accomplishment and in the building-up of an ordered civilized life must go deeper than the effects produced by environment and culture. Probably no one would contend seriously that the Australian Bushman has shown the same capacity for achievement as the present inhabitants of that country, or that African tribes have shown the same aptitude for scientific invention as, say, the modern Germans. In other words, Galton's contention that there are native differences in intellectual capacity between races far removed from each other on a scale of accomplishment would certainly seem to be justified. As Thorndike aptly remarks: "Common observation of the African and the European, for example, decides that the latter is superior in intellect, enterprise, and self-reliance . . . two races need not be equally gifted because each is equally well adapted to its environment, if the second race has by superior enterprise sought out or created a more exacting but also more remunerative environment . . . The Bushman may count all that he needs to count but to put oneself in a position that needs algebra and calculus may itself be a symptom of superiority . . . The very fact that a certain test seems unfair to the Bushman may be evidence of his inferiority."

Wide divergences in culture and attainment between races are not so difficult to explain. The real trouble arises in deciding to what causes we may attribute small and variable differences in mental measurements between two racial groups. So far, there is no way of isolating native factors

from those of training and environment, and it may well be
that no method of doing this satisfactorily will ever be
found. Differences in language offer a considerable obstacle,
as well as tests which mean one thing to one group and
another and different thing to another group. Culture and
convention—habits of thought and action and manner of
living—vary widely, and their influences are next to impossible to evaluate. This is well illustrated by Boas's example of an Italian child who in a picture-completion test
put a crucifix over the door of a house from which the
chimney was missing.[2] In this child's experience a crucifix
was more necessary to a house than a chimney; and hence
his response, in view of his background, was an intelligent
one, albeit "wrong" from the point of view of the test.

Hundreds of studies have been made in an effort to evaluate the influence of racial extraction upon achievement.
Without attempting to discuss more than a fraction of these,
we shall try in the next few paragraphs to give those results
which seem to be most reliably established. Studies of primitive peoples, as in the pioneer study of Woodworth made
at the St. Louis Exposition in 1904, indicate that these
races do not differ markedly from the modern white European or American in keenness of vision, in hearing, in sensitivity to pain and pressure, or in delicacy of skin and
muscle senses. Form-board tests (see page 14), designed
to gauge intellectual activity of a simple and rudimentary
sort, brought out no reliable differences between whites
and many less cultured folk such as Eskimos, Indians,
Filipinos, and Singhalese; but the Negrito and the Pygmy
(African tribes of small stature and extremely low culture)
did no better than low-grade or even imbecile whites. Since
the feeble-minded white differs least from the normal in

[2] Picture-completion tests are drawings in which something left out is
to be added by the child.

STUDENTS LIBRARY
CONCORDIA TEACHERS COLLEGE
RIVER FOREST, ILLINOIS

physical characteristics and motor abilities and most in language and verbal usage (represented by the stock tests of general intelligence), this result makes it appear probable that the intellectual gap between the civilized white and these primitive folk is distinctly wide.

In America a great many studies have been made of the performance of the Negro on mental tests, and as a result of these the inferiority of the Negro to the white in mental ability has been frequently asserted. It is extremely hard, however, to tell how much of the Negro's apparent inferiority should be attributed to his lower social status, usually inferior training, and lack of opportunity for wide contacts. The fact that the Negro soldier scored on the average lower than the white on both language and non-language tests has been discussed elsewhere and some of the difficulties in accepting this finding at face value have been indicated (pages 40-41). Mayo (1915), in a study of negro high school students in New York city, found that on the average they remain in school longer than the white; they average about seven months older than white students judged to be of approximately the same social status; and they are somewhat inferior in school work, only about 30 per cent doing as well as or better than the average white student. Mayo's negro students were more stringently selected than his white students, as only the more ambitious and able negroes, usually, remain in high school; hence the inferiority of the negroes is probably even greater than his figures indicate. Ferguson (1916) administered a number of mental tests to white and negro students in three Southern cities in an effort to study abilities less complicated by social factors than school marks. On these tests the negroes returned performances about three-fourths as good as those of the whites. When classified as to skin-color, those negroes with apparently the highest degree of white blood approximated most closely to the white score. On the whole, it is hard to see how differences in selection or in social status can account for all of the difference found in these studies, although it might very well account for part of it. In two later studies, A. H. Arlitt (1921) and D. Sunne (1924) have found fairly consistent differences in mental performance in favor of the whites over the negroes about as large as those of Ferguson and Mayo. Arlitt stresses particularly the necessity for taking account of social status. When white and negro children are really equated for social status, she says, the superiority of the white is much reduced. For example, she found that within the white group only there was a gap in I Q of thirty-three points between those children from very superior and those from very inferior social surroundings. This is a wider intellectual gap than that between whites and negroes, but it must be noted that even the "inferior" and "very inferior" whites are slightly ahead of the negroes.

On the whole, one must admit that the negro measures consistently below the white on tests designed to gauge mental ability. Whether these differences are chiefly native or chiefly environmental, we cannot at present say, but a reasonable view is that native differences play some part. This does not alter the fact, of course, that because of the overlapping of test scores, many negroes return scores much better than those of whites whose scores are average or above average.

There have been a few studies of temperamental differences between negroes and whites. In one study J. H. McFadden and J. F. Dashiell (1923) found small and unreliable differences on the Downey Will-Temperament Test, a test designed to measure temperamental and impulsive traits. A. L. Crane (1923) has attempted to compare experimentally the fear reactions of negroes and whites in a laboratory situation. His test consisted in measuring the ability to inhibit the withdrawal of the hand from an apparatus when a weight appeared to be falling upon it. Although each subject had been assured that no harm would come to him, many were unable, despite this fact, to keep from pulling the hand away. Crane found among the whites fewer complete withdrawals than among the negroes, but a greater *tendency* to withdraw as shown by small tentative movements, twitchings of the arm muscles, and sudden catchings of the breath. He concludes that negroes are more given to sudden and overt impulsive reactions, the whites being more inhibited, and less liable to react violently.

Various studies of the American Indian and the Mexican indicate that they generally score lower than the white on both verbal and non-verbal tests. There is fairly reliable evidence that mixed-blood Indians are superior to full-bloods (W. S. Hunter and E. Sommermier, 1922), just as mulattoes are in general superior in mental test performances to pure negroes. A part, at least, of the Indians' inferiority in mental tests has been shown by Klineberg (1928) to be temperamental, the result of a very different attitude toward life, as well as different ideas of what is important and valuable. Indians, for instance, while much slower than white children on Klineberg's tests (mostly form-board performance tests) were consistently more accurate, the need for speed making no appeal to them. Orientals, Japanese and Chinese, who have been tested in America are little if at all inferior to the native whites, given equal opportunity for education and contacts with American life.

The comparative showings of various European national groups on the army "combined scale" has been presented elsewhere (page 42). Differences in selection, in language, in customs, and in education and outlook prevent any definite decision as to the superiority or inferiority of a given national group. Though reliable statistically, the differences in performance on the "combined scale" are actually small. Many studies of the children of foreign-born parents in New York City and elsewhere agree fairly well that Italian and Polish children born in the United States test consistently below the native-born white, and that the Jewish child is not far below and is often considerably above the performance of the native white. In his main group of gifted children (see page 23), Terman found that about 10 per cent were of Jewish extraction—nearly twice the number to be expected from the proportion of Jews in the cities covered by his survey. The largest per cent of Terman's group was of British and Scotch extraction, the percentage of Latin blood being very low. This finding agrees in the main with the army results, but again we cannot be sure that Terman's selections represent samplings from the same intellectual strata of the foreign countries from which the forbears of these children came.

Probably the most salutary impression which a reader can carry away from a survey of the studies of racial groups is a better appreciation of the difficulties encountered, and of the practical impossibility of reaching a result which can definitely be attributed to racial origin alone. We stress again differences in language, in customs, in culture, in attitude, in schooling, and in social, economic, and geographic conditions. Also, the difficulty in securing comparable samples and in evaluating the meaning of test differences cannot be overemphasized. It is possible that true differences between races as such will never be found, but only differences between racial groups, or groups of somewhat different racial origin. Future workers will do well to avoid false comparisons and unjustified inferences from unreliable tests, from tests which measure very narrow functions, and from very small groups.

(7)

No discussion of individual differences would be complete without at least some account of Galton's work on mental imagery. In his studies of the presence and amount of imagery, Galton used his now famous "breakfast table" questionnaire, in which each subject was asked to call up a picture of his breakfast table as it appeared in the morning and to report whether the objects seemed well defined, natural, and comparable in vividness with the actual objects. Many of Galton's subjects were scientific and scholarly men, who to his surprise reported an almost total absence of visual images. Other subjects, however, gave very different accounts, several reporting that the objects on the table appeared in retrospect to be as real as though they were actually present before the eyes. Galton accounts for the feeble visual imagery of scientific men as a group in the following way: "My own conclusion is that an over-ready perception of sharp mental pictures is antagonistic to the habits of highly generalized and abstract thought, especially when the steps of reasoning are carried on by words as symbols, and that if the faculty of seeing the pictures was ever possessed by men who think hard, it is very apt to be lost by disuse."

Although Galton seemed to believe that a lack of imagery is largely a result of one's training and his manner of thinking and working, he found considerable evidence that this trait is at least partly hereditary. Thus, he found that it tends to run in families; it is stronger in the female than in the male; also it is stronger in younger than in older persons. Imagery, according to Galton, is not correlated with eminence as a painter or as an imaginative writer. Great individual differences exist in kind and amount of mental imagery.

The study of individual differences, though as yet in its

infancy, has progressed far beyond Galton's pioneer work. It was Galton's invention and use of statistical techniques, however, and his genius in seeing problems that gave the impetus and showed the way to later workers. To quote E. G. Boring, Galton was "the father (in large part) of mental measurement of individual differences with respect to traits, . . . and the originator of the questionnaire and the theory of eugenics." As a pioneer in these various fields, Galton's place in the history of modern psychology seems assured.

Suggested Readings

1. For a good account of some of the difficulties encountered and pitfalls to be avoided in studying individual differences, see R. S. Ellis's *The Psychology of Individual Differences* (1928), Chapter I.
2. A. T. Poffenberger's *Applied Psychology* (1927), Chapter II, contains a comprehensive discussion of the influence of heredity upon achievement.
3. For an account of Galton's work and place in psychology, see E. G. Boring's *A History of Experimental Psychology* (1929), pages 467-478.

Chapter 9

CATTELL'S STUDIES IN THE MEASUREMENT OF REACTION TIME

(1)

ONE of the most obvious and direct ways in which the mental processes of perception, discrimination, and choice may be subjected to quantitative study is to measure the time it takes an individual to respond to a given object or stimulus, or to perceive and report upon the likenesses of or differences between several stimuli. Because of this, many experiments in the psychological laboratory have been concerned with the measurement of time of response, or *reaction time,* i.e., with the accurate recording of the time intervening between the application of a stimulus, the sound of a buzzer, say, and the objective response of the subject, e.g., lifting the finger from an electric key. The primary interest of many experimenters has been in the establishment of reaction time norms for various kinds of stimuli, viz., lights, sounds, and touches, and in studying individual differences in the time of reaction to such stimuli. Others have studied the effect of different stimulus conditions—the subject meanwhile being kept relatively "constant"—by changing the quality, intensity, or duration of the stimulus; or by stimulating different parts of the body, and, in the case of light, for example, comparing the effect of stimulating the retina at the fovea, and at varying distances from this central point.[1] Still other workers have investigated the effect of varying the condition of the subject, meanwhile keeping the

[1] Poffenberger, A. T., *Reaction Time to Retinal Stimulation* (1912), Archives of Psychology, 23.

JAMES MCKEEN CATTELL

(1860–1944)

task relatively constant. In this way can be measured the effect of drugs, fatigue, practice, incentive and punishment, and other factors upon the reaction time of the individual.

In America much of the interest in reaction time in psychology may be traced to the work and influence of James McKeen Cattell. Cattell was one of the first American students to take his doctor's degree in Wundt's laboratory at the University of Leipzig. This laboratory was established in 1879, and was the first psychological laboratory in the world. Cattell's dissertation was printed in English in 1886 under the title *The Time Taken Up by Cerebral Operations*, and was immediately followed by other important reaction time studies. During his thirty years as Professor of Psychology at Columbia University, Cattell and his students published many investigations on the measurement of the mental processes. Many of these studies will be described later on in this chapter. For the present, let us consider the influences which prepared the way for the interest of psychologists in the time measurements of mental phenomena.

(2)

The reaction time experiment has a long and interesting history. A story which dates back to 1796 tells of an unlucky assistant in the astronomical observatory at Greenwich, England, who lost his job because he persistently read the passages of stars across the meridian with too large an error; his reaction time or "personal equation" was abnormally long. The first publication of the results of comparative tests showing fairly large and persistent individual differences in recording the transits of stars was made by the German astronomer, Bessel, in 1822, too late, unfortunately, to save the slow-reacting assistant mentioned above. In 1850 Helmholtz, the great physiologist, used the reaction time method to measure the speed of nerve conduction. Working with the motor nerve of the frog, Helmholtz stimulated a nerve attached to a muscle at a point some distance from the reacting muscle. The time intervening between the application of this stimulus and the movement in the muscle was recorded, as was also the shorter time-interval elapsing between the application of a stimulus nearer the muscle and the appearance of movement. The difference between these two reaction times gives the time taken by the impulse in traveling along the nerve between the two points of stimulation. For the frog Helmholtz reported the speed of motor nerve conduction to be 27 meters (about 89 feet) per second; in man he calculated the speed of motor nerve conduction by the same method to be about twice as great.

Helmholtz also applied his method to the measurement of sensory nerve conduction. He assumed that if two points on the same sensory nerve, one, say, on the foot, and one on the upper leg, were stimulated in succession, the response in both cases being the same, the difference in reaction time would be a measure of the time taken by the impulse in crossing the nerve length between the two stimulated points. The results of these experiments, however, were so variable that his determinations were highly uncertain. No doubt the main reasons for this variability are the many influences, both facilitating and inhibiting, which the impulse must undergo in passing through the nerve centers in the brain and cord.

The many investigations which followed those of Helmholtz gave results for the most part widely divergent from his results and from each other. Finally, in 1893, Cattell and Dolley published their research *On Reaction Times and the Velocity of the Nervous Impulse,* the most thorough investigation into the problem of nervous conduction in man by the reaction time method. Cattell and Dolley applied electrical stimuli at two points on the median nerve of the arm thirty centimeters apart, and at two points on the posterior tibial nerve of the leg fifty centimeters apart. The reaction move-ment was the same for all stimuli. Large variations were found in the velocities of the sensory impulse as so measured, the times being 31 meters per second for one observer, and 65 meters per second for another. Considerable variability, as well, was encountered in each observer. These results led Cattell and Dolley to suggest that the differences in reaction time found must be due, not to differences in the speed of the nervous impulse, but to the variability of the central con-nections involved, as well as to qualitative differences in the sensations aroused at the different points of stimulation. This explanation was substantiated by the interesting finding that either hand will react more quickly when it, rather than the other hand, is stimulated. According to these authors, this obviously means that some sensori-motor connections, owing possibly to innate linkages and more probably to practice, are more closely knit than others, so that the reaction time varies even when the *same* length of nerve fiber is traversed. Because of these complications in the central connections, Cattell and Dolley concluded that the velocity of the nervous impulse cannot be adequately measured by reaction time methods. It might be added in ending this section that physi-ologists using other and improved methods have determined the speed of the nerve impulse in the human to be around 120 meters (about 394 feet) per second,[2] much faster than the times found by the early investigators who used reaction time methods. The speed of the sensory nerve process is probably about the same as that of the motor.

(3)

The first studies of the psychological factors influencing simple as well as complex reactions were those of Donders and De Jaeger in 1865. In the simple reaction experiment

[2] See Herrick, C. J., *An Introduction to Neurology* (1921), pp. 103-104.

as now set up in the laboratory, the subject knows beforehand what stimulus he will receive, as for example, a flash of light or a sound. His instructions, usually, are to make a single prescribed movement, such as lifting the finger from an electric key as quickly as possible when the stimulus is given. After practice, the simple reaction becomes highly automatic and almost reflexive. In the discriminative reaction experiment, as devised by Donders, two stimuli (e.g., two notes of different pitch or two differently colored lights) are employed, and the subject is instructed to react to the one and remain quiet to the other. When, in addition to the two stimuli, the subject is given *two* reaction keys, and is instructed to react with the *right hand* if one stimulus appears and with the *left* if the other appears, we have, according to Donders, both "discrimination" and "choice."

Donders, as well as other early workers, believed that by subtracting the simple from the discriminative reaction time, discrimination times could be obtained; and that likewise, by subtracting discrimination reaction time from discrimination plus choice, "will" or "choice" times could be secured. This procedure is called elimination by subtraction. It assumes that a complex response is in reality a simple response plus certain added central processes, the time of which may be determined by subtracting the time of the simple reaction.

Cattell, as early as 1885, criticized the view that a discriminative reaction may be analyzed into a simple reaction plus some more or less constant will time or perception time. He accepted these subtracted times as nothing more than valid measures of the increased complexity of the total process, or of the increased difficulty of the task. Other investigators also questioned elimination by subtraction as a method, notably Erdmann and Dodge (1898), and Ach (1905). The latter, especially, argued that the different preparation of the subject for a simple and a discriminative reaction made the two very different psychologically. When faced by several stimuli, or given the choice of several responses, the *situation,* said Ach, is very different from that in the simple reaction time experiment. As a result a different attitude is set up in the subject, so that the whole process is different and not merely the *central* part of it. Moreover, as was urged by other experimenters, there is no introspective evidence that, when one mental process is superadded to another, the first retains its identity unchanged.

Cattell's view of what happens in reaction time experiments is very different from that of Donders, and also from the explanation advanced by Wundt. At the ready signal, he said, the subject, in making a simple reaction, concentrates his attention upon the stimulus which is to appear, e.g., a red light, or an electric shock, and upon the finger which is to react; hence the nervous pathways between the eye or skin → brain → finger are especially well prepared or open when the stimulus comes. In the discriminative or choice experiment, naturally more switches and more pathways must be "set" because of the increased complexity of the situation. This introduces an element of suspense or indecision which in turn necessitates greater preparation and makes for a longer reaction time. Wundt had regarded the whole reaction process as analyzable psychologically into (a) perception of the stimulus, (b) apperception (Wundt's term for the recognition or clear perception of the stimulus), and (c) will, or the release of the impulse to react. This analysis, said Cattell, while descriptive, is highly artificial. Apperception, or the clear recognition of the stimulus, comes if at all *after* the reaction has been made, while will exists simply in the preparation for movement and becomes less and less a factor as the reactions grow more and more automatic.

In justice to Wundt it should be said that, while his

analysis was probably more elaborate than is necessary to describe the somewhat artificial laboratory experiments on reaction time, it does fit quite well the unprepared reactions of everyday life. Suppose, for instance, that a child runs in front of an oncoming street-car, and that the motorman cuts off his current and applies his brakes just in time to prevent an accident. Here, in Wundt's terms, we have perception of the child on the tracks, apperception of the danger in the situation, and will, or the release of impulses which stop the car. But these psychological processes cannot be analyzed out in any such clear-cut fashion in the simple laboratory situation of lifting a finger from an electric key as soon as one hears a sound or sees a light; nor do they appear as separate and distinct processes when reactions become habitual and automatic as they are for experienced street-car motormen.

(4)

We have seen that the simple reaction time experiment measures the time-interval between a single and oft-repeated stimulus and a prescribed and constant response. In the usual laboratory set-up, the subject sits with his forefinger depressing an electric key; and at the appearance of the stimulus he reacts by lifting his finger from the key as quickly as possible. Various methods have been employed in the laboratory for measuring the time-intervals between stimulus and response. All of these make use of a chronoscope or some other time-measuring device. The Hipp chronoscope, an instrument which measures in units of .001 second [3] has perhaps been most widely used in the past by

[3] .001 sec. is usually represented by 1σ in psychological literature. Thus, 100σ and .1 sec. are the same. Unfortunately, the sign σ is a bad choice, because of its widespread use in statistics to denote the standard deviation. A better time-unit is milliseconds, or ms.; 1 ms. $= .001$ sec., and 100 ms. $= .100$ sec.

psychologists (see Figure 18). Apparatus for checking the accuracy of the Hipp chronoscope, as well as many improvements in the instrument itself, have been made by Cattell

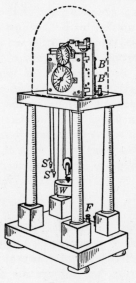

FIG. 18

THE HIPP CHRONOSCOPE

The clockwork of this chronoscope is driven by the weight, W, which is raised by a key fitting into the center of the lower dial. The chronoscope is started by pulling S' and stopped by pulling S''. The two recording dials are divided into hundredth parts. The hand on the upper dial revolves ten times every second, each division on the dial corresponding to a thousandth part of a second or 1σ. The hand on the lower dial revolves once every ten seconds, each division on the dial corresponding to one-tenth of a second or 100σ. Reaction time is calculated from both dials, the units and tens from the lower and the hundredths and thousandths from the upper dial. The speed of the dial hands is controlled by a small steel tongue which is accurately tuned to vibrate 1,000 times per second. B' and B'' are electromagnets which control the starting and stopping of the dial hands. F is a binding-post. Various control instruments have been devised to check the accuracy of the readings given by his chronoscope.

and his students. The Bergstrom (a pendulum) chronoscope, and the Dunlap chronoscope, a more recently devised instrument, are also widely used, the latter having almost displaced the Hipp in reaction time work. A diagram showing the complete set-up of a Dunlap chronoscope is shown in Figure 19. In addition to instrumental measurements, graphic records of reaction time may also be secured by using an electrically driven tuning-fork and a smoked drum

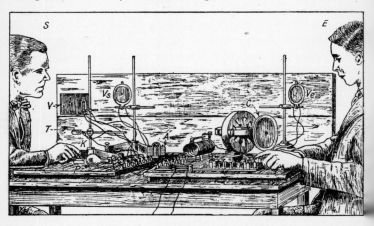

FIG. 19

SET-UP FOR A DUNLAP CHRONOSCOPE

C is the chronoscope with its dial turned toward the experimenter, *E*. When *E* presents the stimuli, which may be tactual (pressure on the skin), auditory (a sound), or visual (a light), the subject, *S*, responds by releasing the telegraph key, *K*, or pressing upon the bulb, *P*. *E* may present a problem verbally or ask a question by speaking into the voice key, *Ve*. *S* replies by speaking into the voice key, *Vs*. Voice keys are much used in measuring reaction time when either the stimulus or the response is spoken. They are delicate circular membranes which vibrate to a sound, thus temporarily breaking an electric circuit. (From Dashiell, J. F., *Fundamentals of Objective Psychology*, 1928, p. 45.)

apparatus. A tuning-fork which vibrates 100 times a second, say, is set to mark off a time-line on a revolving drum. Beneath this time-line the appearance of the stimulus and the subject's response are recorded by means of electric markers. The graphic method is accurate and is often used as a check on other methods; but it is too slow and cumbersome for practical work.

All of the apparatus described above may be used in the measurement of complex as well as simple reactions. Experiments in complex reaction time may be set up either through the addition of extra stimuli, or through the employment of more than one response. Thus, in the Donders discrimination reaction experiment previously described, either of two stimuli was presented, to only one of which the subject was instructed to react. The obvious disadvantage of this set-up is that records are obtained in only about one half of the trials. In Donder's discrimination and choice experiment, two stimuli were employed and two responses, the subject reacting with the right hand if the one stimulus appeared, and with the left hand if the other appeared. Henmon, one of Cattell's early students, simplified and improved this procedure by an arrangement in which two stimuli were always presented side by side. The subject was instructed to react to a previously designated stimulus with his *right* hand if it appeared to the right of the other, and with his *left* hand if it appeared to the left of the other. As will be readily surmised, reaction time is considerably slower when the conditions are so complicated than when only one stimulus and one response are employed (see page 217).

Reaction time is still longer in the associative type of response. Here the stimuli may be words (or lists of words) to which the subject is to react with the first word which comes to mind (free association); or, the subject may be instructed to give the opposites of the stimulus words, or responses bearing some other designated relation, e.g., part-whole, adjective-noun, verb-object (controlled association). The color-naming and form-naming tests illustrate other varieties of controlled association. The usual method in associative reaction is to take the total time required by the subject to give the correct responses to a list of words and then determine his average reaction time for each word. The one-fifth second stop-watch is usually considered to be accurate enough for reactions of this kind; for finer work, a one-hundredth second electric stop-watch may be employed.

(5)

There are many conditions which influence directly the speed of reaction besides the complexity of the stimulus-response situation. Most of these factors have been studied at one time or another by Cattell and his students, as well as by many others, and some of the more important findings will be considered in this section.

1. Sense Organ. In the first place, the reaction time varies with the particular sense organ stimulated. Cattell reported the simple reaction time to light to be about 150 σ, with some variability (8-10 σ), and the simple reaction time to sound to be about 120 σ. The simple reaction times to stimuli applied to the different sense organs, as determined by many investigators, are summarized as follows:

Type of stimulation	*Reaction time*
Visual	.150 sec.- .200 sec.
Auditory	.120 - .160
Tactual	.110 - .160
Olfactory	.200 - .800
Gustatory	.300 -1.000
Pain	.400 -1.000
Temperature	
cold about	.150
warm about	.180

The slow reaction time to taste and smell is probably owing to the chemical nature of these senses and to the difficulty in getting stimuli directly to them. The "free nerve endings" of the pain sense are fairly close to the surface, but are relatively slow to react. The fact that hot and cold stimuli must act by conducting heat or cold into the skin to the sensory end organs will obviously slow up the reaction time to such stimuli.

The part of the sense organ stimulated makes a difference in reaction time also. Poffenberger (1912), a student of Cattell, found for example that when the retina is stimulated with a light beam at points to the right and left of the fovea, the reaction time is longer than it is at the fovea and becomes longer and longer as the stimulus is moved out from the central point to the periphery. Reaction time is faster to stimuli applied to the hand than to stimuli applied to the forehead or foot, as a result probably of closer nerve center connections in the first instance.

2. *Intensity, Size, and Duration of the Stimulus.* Cattell studied the influence of all three of these factors upon reaction time as early as 1886, but more accurate work was done later by Froeberg (1907), under his direction. Working with graded light intensities (light reflected from gray and white paper), Froeberg found that the reaction time increased, but very slowly, as the intensity of the light decreased. When reaction time to a given medium intensity, for example, was 191 σ, the reaction to a stimulus one-half as bright was increased by 3 σ; while the reaction to a stimulus one-tenth as bright was increased by 17 σ. The same general result was found when the size (area of a square surface reflecting light) and the duration of the stimuli were decreased. The reaction time increased in both cases, but somewhat more slowly for duration changes than for size changes. Froeberg found also that the reaction time to

sound increased fairly rapidly when the intensity of the sound was diminished.

3. The Foreperiod and the Reacting Movement. The foreperiod, that is, the time-interval between the signal "Ready" and the presentation of the stimulus, is quite important in reaction time work. During the foreperiod, the subject "gets set," so to speak, prepared to react to the expected stimulus as quickly as possible. If the foreperiod is short, i.e., less than one second, the subject may be caught before he is entirely ready, and in consequence react more slowly than usual; if the foreperiod is long, say ten seconds or more, the subject is liable to lose his "edge" and again react too slowly. Cattell (1886) placed the optimum foreperiod close to one second. This interval, he said, is about as long as the nerve centers can be kept in a state of preparedness; longer times (up to fifteen seconds) were found to increase the reaction time as well as the variability of response. Other investigators placed the best foreperiod at from two to three seconds. Breitwieser (1911), working in Cattell's laboratory with improved technique and more subjects, found the optimum foreperiod to be between two and four seconds, with, however, some individual differences. This determination has been verified by Woodrow (1914), who found two seconds also to be the most favorable foreperiod.

The influence of the reacting movement upon time of response has already been touched upon. Either hand, for instance, responds more quickly to a stimulus applied to it than to one applied to the other hand. It has been shown, too, that releasing rather than depressing the reaction key gives a less variable response. In a careful study of the movements of the hand in reacting to a stimulus, carried out in the Yale laboratory in 1905 by Judd, McAllister, and Steele, it was discovered that the hand does not maintain a steady pressure on the reacting key during the foreperiod.

On the contrary, there is a fluctuation from stronger to weaker pressure, the key sometimes being completely released to give a "premature" reaction. Whenever degree of readiness to react has reached a high point, the response may easily be premature, as when a runner springs from his mark before the signal is given. The Yale experimenters found, too, that often the first reactions of unpractised subjects show a quick depression of the key before it is released. This counter-movement takes time and consequently slows up the reaction. With practice it tends to be inhibited in favor of the correct release movement.

4. *Practice, Attention, Distraction, and Fatigue.* Practice, according to Cattell, has little effect upon time of response after the first few trials, in which the subject's reactions often vary markedly. The effect of distractions, such as the beating of a metronome, or the performance of mental addition during the experiment he found also to be relatively slight provided the subjects were highly practised. For the first type of distraction the reaction time may increase from 2 to 10 σ, for the second from about 20 to 30 σ. Woodrow (1914-1916) has investigated with much thoroughness the rôle of attention and practice in reaction time. He found reaction time to vary considerably with the amount of attention given the task. Degree of attention was measured by the prolongation in reaction time brought about by introducing foreperiods of varying lengths. For stimuli of "moderate" intensity, Woodrow reports the subject's attention to be less affected for touch than for sound or light. J. E. Evans (1916), using flashing lights, noises, and touch stimuli as distractions, found that these extraneous factors increased the reaction time markedly at first, but that their influence was much lessened with training. Both trained and untrained observers were affected by the distractions, however, the greatest disturbance occurring when both the distraction

and the stimulus to which the subject was instructed to respond affected the same sense organ. Cassel and Dallenbach (1918) found also that, in general, distractions tend to lengthen reaction time, the increase for two observers ranging from 3 σ to 37 σ. Fatigue, strangely enough, has an almost negligible effect upon reaction time. In his own case, Cattell found his reaction time to decrease very slightly even after a day of continuous reacting.

5. *Incentives, Punishment, Drugs, and Age.* The effect of incentive—encouragement or mild praise—upon reaction time is to increase it about 8 σ.[4] Negative incentive, or punishment, as for example giving the subject an electric shock if he fails to react within a given time, speeds up the reaction time 20 σ or more. Drugs have a variable effect upon reaction time. Coffee and tea appear to shorten it; small doses of alcohol first shorten and then lengthen it; morphine, ether, and chloroform usually lengthen it. As might be surmised, time of response is slower and more variable in old age.

(6)

In addition to the factors discussed in the last section, there is still another determinant in reaction time experiments which has excited much controversy, and which is important enough to be considered at some length. This has to do with the direction of the subject's attention, or his attitude during the experiment. Several early workers on reaction time in Germany, notably Lange, in 1888, observed that when the subject in a simple reaction time experiment directed his attention specifically toward the awaited stimulus, his time of response was considerably longer than when he fixed his attention upon the movement

[4] Johannson, A. M., *The Influence of Incentive and Punishment upon Reaction Time* (1922), Archives of Psychology, 54.

to be made. Lange called the first kind of reaction "sensorial," and the second "muscular," or "motor." The first type of response, he said, is always longer than the second, the difference being as much as 100 σ. The distinction between sensorial, or sensory, responses and motor responses was accepted by most contemporaries of Lange as valid, although the differences found were not always as great as those found by him.

Lange's Attention Theory, as this view was called, was challenged by Baldwin's (1895) and Flournoy's (1896) Type Theory. These two workers found among their subjects some whose motor reactions were faster than their sensory reactions and others who gave quicker sensory reactions than motor reactions. They suggested, accordingly, that individuals are natively sensory, motor, or indifferent in type, and that each type reacts at his best when allowed to follow his natural inclination. Thus, while accepting the distinction between sensory and motor responses, Baldwin and Flournoy reached a very different conclusion with regard to the differences in speed between the two types from that of Lange and his group.

Still a third explanation of the difference between sensory and motor responses has been given in terms of practice and habituation. This was the view advanced by Cattell in 1892 and by Angell and Moore in 1896. Cattell had found no reliable differences between the sensory and motor types of reaction in the case of practised observers. Whether a new subject is sensory or motor at the start, he said, is largely a matter of the instructions given, accidental direction of attention, and previous training; after practice, there is little or no difference between the two attitudes. Later work, done by Breitwieser, under Cattell's direction, tended to confirm this view. Breitwieser first took a long series of reactions in some of which his subjects were verbally instructed to give sensory, and in others motor, responses. Following these experiments. Breitwieser forced the attitude of his subjects into the sensory or motor category by means of the following ingenious arrangement. To insure a sensory attitude, he presented sometimes the one and sometimes the other of two closely similar stimuli, and required his subjects, after reacting, to report which of the two had been given. This necessitated close attention to the stimulus. To make sure that the reaction was of the motor type, Breitwieser used a reaction key which varied somewhat in the resistance which it offered to the subject's reacting finger. The subject was instructed, after responding, to tell which of the two resistances (the greater or less) had been employed. Here, clearly enough, it was the reacting movement which needed special attention. Finally, in order to guarantee a neutral, or indifferent attitude, the subject was instructed to report after each reaction *both* on the key pressure *and* the differences in the stimuli.

Breitwieser's results indicated in general a very slight advantage—averaging about 20 σ—for the verbally instructed motor over the verbally instructed sensory reactions. He found little difference between those sensory responses in which the subject was verbally instructed to attend to the stimulus, or forced to attend. However, the verbally instructed motor responses were much faster (in fact, the fastest of all) than those motor reactions in which the subject was required to report upon the key pressure. When the subject was instructed to report *both* upon key pressure and stimulus difference, his reaction time was the slowest of all, the time being almost as great as that in a discriminative reaction.

The upshot of the whole controversy would seem to be (1) that there is a real distinction between the sensory and motor attitudes; (2) that untrained subjects are probably for the most part sensory at the start, becoming motor as the novelty wears off and the need for close attention to the stimulus becomes less; and (3) that the motor, being the more highly practised attitude, is the faster type of response.

(7)

Cattell was interested not only in the study and analysis of the factors influencing simple reaction time; he did extensive work as well on the more elaborate discriminative and associative reactions. He found, for example, wide variations in the time it takes persons to multiply two numbers presented at the same time, and that one can name objects or pictures in his own language more readily than in a foreign tongue. All this seems fairly obvious, and is probably no more than one might expect. But many other findings are by no means so evident. Thus, Cattell found that when a word indicating a part of an object is the stimulus, e.g., *roof,* it takes longer to give the name of the whole object, e.g., *house,* than to give the part when the whole is presented, e.g., *pencil—point.* Also, it is easier to go from a special to a more general class, e.g., *cat—animal,* than in the reverse direction. Opposites give the quickest reaction times, but these vary greatly, the differences here, as in the other cases, being due largely to differences in familiarity, training, and frequency of usage.

In other experiments with words and language, Cattell found that while the reaction time to a single word exposed alone is about 360 σ, this time is reduced to 200 σ per word when a series of words is exposed together. He found also that a higher speed of reading per word is secured when two words instead of one are presented; three instead of two, and so on up to four or five. These results, taken together with experiments made with the tachistoscope in which it has been demonstrated that one can group as many as two or three words together in an instant of exposure, indicate quite clearly the great importance of *overlapping* in efficient verbal response. They show, too, that an individual's re-action to a phrase or sentence composed of several words is not simply the sum total of his time reactions to the separate words, but is rather the response to a group of words taken as a larger unit. This suggests clearly that growth in reading ability, as well as in many other highly skilled performances, must be due to the fact that reactions are made to larger and larger groups of discrete impressions as wholes. Re-sponses in larger units enter into the performance of the skilled typist or telegrapher as well as into that of the highly trained musician playing from score. For his experi-ments with language, Cattell devised a lip key and a voice key, both of which were distinct improvements on similar devices used by others in recording oral responses.

The last series of experiments which we shall describe is that in which a new psychophysical method, the "discrimi-nation time method," was employed. This method was de-vised by Cattell in 1902, and is based upon the assumption that differences in sensation are equal when it takes the same time to perceive them; since, in general, the smaller the difference, the longer the time necessary to perceive and react to it. The most important study by the discrimination time method is that of Henmon (1906). Henmon's method (see page 207) was to present two stimuli simultaneously. Two keys were used, the subject being instructed to react to one of the two stimuli (which one was previously desig-nated) with the right hand if it appeared on the right, and with the left hand if it appeared on the left. For example, suppose red and blue are the two stimuli, and the subject has been instructed to react to red. Under these conditions, when the stimuli are presented the subject must react with his right hand when the red is to the right of the blue, and with his left hand when the red is to the left. Some of Henmon's results with colors appear below.

Colors to be discriminated	Discrimination time
White and black	.197 sec.
Red and green	.203
Red and blue	.212
Red and yellow	.217
Red and orange (mixed with 25% red)	.252
Red and orange (mixed with 75% red)	.271

It is clear that the smaller the qualitative differences between the two colors, the longer the reaction time. Using small differences in pitch Henmon obtained much the same results:

Differences in pitch (in vibrations)	Reaction time
16	.290 secs.
12	.299
8	.311
4	.334

When the subject was instructed to react to the *shorter* of two lines, shown side by side, the following reaction times were obtained:

To discriminate a line of 10 mm. from one of 13 mm.		.296 sec.
10	12	.305
10	11½	.313
10	11	.334
10	10½	.345

These results show that the smaller the difference between the two stimuli, whether in vibration rate or in millimeters, the longer the reaction time to the difference.

Henmon's findings may be interpreted to mean (1) that the mental processes of apprehension and discrimination must proceed further when differences are decreased; and (2) that the preliminary adjustment for the movement is less and less adequate as the difference between the two stimuli becomes smaller and smaller. Both of these conditions serve to explain the lengthened reaction time. If we are justified in the assumption that differences are equal, for perception, when the times required to discriminate them are equal, it appears from Henmon's results that tones eight vibrations apart differ *perceptually* to about the same degree as lines differing by one and one-half millimeters (ten and eleven and a half millimeters).

(8)

It should be evident, even from the brief sketch which has been given, that the study of reaction time has passed through many phases and has excited many and various interests. Reaction time is measured to-day not so much for the purpose of analyzing its determinants or of finding "choice" or "will" times, but rather as a means of attacking practical problems of behavior. For example, the reaction time experiment may be employed for measuring the difficulty of a task in an objective way, or as an index of an individual's efficiency under different conditions. Or, it may be taken as a means of comparing individuals under the same conditions, or the same individual under different conditions; that is to say, the establishment of individual differences may be the primary interest. Again, the speed of a person's simple or discriminative responses may be compared with his quickness in solving problems or in performing other intellectual tasks to see whether a given individual may be characterized as generally quick or generally slow intellectually. In a study of this kind, Lemmon (1927) found that good memory for words, numbers and the like, tends to be somewhat related to speed of simple reaction, while the learning of verbal and other abstract relations tends to go along with quickness of discriminative reaction. However, few persons can be fairly described as possessing a definite speed-level at which they habitually work; differences in familiarity with the tasks to be done, degree of previous practice, interest, and incentive play too large a rôle. For these reasons a bookkeeper who is ordinarily very slow may, after long practice, or with sufficient incentive, surpass in mental calculation—addition, say—an individual much faster in other respects.

In vocational selection, as well as in the diagnosis of aptitudes, the reaction time of the individual is often an important factor. It is apparent, for instance, that the time required by a chauffeur or a motorman to apply his brakes at a given signal, a colored light, for example, or to react quickly in an emergency is of the greatest practical value. Ingenious devices for testing the reaction time of prospective drivers of automobiles or of street-cars have been devised by psychologists. Wechsler (1926), for instance, has constructed a dummy automobile, with steering-wheel, brakes, clutch, and so on, which is used in testing candidates applying to be taxi chauffeurs. The candidate is instructed to depress his clutch and apply his brakes at the flash of a yellow light on a board placed before him; at the appearance of other colored lights he is told to react in various ways with appropriate hand and foot movements. Time of reaction and errors (wrong responses) are carefully recorded. After actual road experience it was found that, while men with the slowest reaction times had the most accidents, the fastest reacting men also had a large number of accidents. The failure of the very fast men to avoid accidents is attributed by Wechsler to the fact that very quick men are liable to take chances through overconfidence and hence risk mishap. It is significant that the number of errors, or wrong responses, proved to be a better criterion than simple speed of response in separating high-accident men from those who have few accidents. High-accident men consistently made more errors than low-accident men.

One study in which reaction time was employed in tests of prospective motormen may also be cited briefly as an example of the work in this field. Shellow (1926) measured the time required by street-car motormen to react with the appropriate movements upon the appearance of a light signal. Time of reaction and errors, wrong responses and omissions (failure to react to signals), were recorded. Two groups of men were found to make the best operators, those who react very quickly but who have a fairly high error score (mostly omissions) and those who react slowly but make practically no errors. If a man reacts slowly and also makes errors, he is a poor prospect as a motorman.

It will be recognized that many of these problems have arisen since the early reaction time work of Cattell to meet new conditions and to satisfy new demands. Despite this fact, most of them have their origin in the early interest of psychologists in general, and of Cattell in particular, in the objective study of the time relations of human performance.

Suggested Readings

1. A brief but comprehensive account of Cattell's work on reaction time will be found in E. G. Boring's *A History of Experimental Psychology* (1929), pp. 522-525.
2. Studies on reaction time by Cattell's students, Froeberg, Breitwieser, Poffenberger, Evans, and others not mentioned in this chapter may be found in the Archives of Psychology.
3. A full discussion of reaction time and its importance in experimental psychology is given in Chapter VI of Ladd and Woodworth's *Elements of Physiological Psychology* (1911). Some of this material will doubtless prove to be difficult for the beginning student.

Chapter 10

EXPERIMENTAL STUDIES OF EMOTIONAL REACTIONS: THE WORK OF CANNON AND OTHERS

(1)

THE experimental study of the emotions offers some of the most fascinating and at the same time elusive problems for research in psychology. The widespread interest of psychologists in the topic is seen in the number of experimental studies recently made or now in progress; while the difficulties encountered in them are attested to by their wide diversity in results. The reasons for this are not hard to find. Emotions tend to dissipate when examined introspectively and to lose their color and intensity when recalled. It is difficult, too, to get genuine emotional states under laboratory conditions; and furthermore, numerous technical difficulties arise in the attempt to measure complex physiological changes in order to square these off against the subject's verbal report of his felt emotions. If anything, however, such difficulties as these have acted as a spur rather than as a check to experimental investigation.

The importance of the emotions in behavior has long been recognized by psychologists, but it is only recently that they have come to realize keenly that the success or failure of an individual in academic, professional, or industrial life is contingent upon emotional balance as much as, if not more than, upon intellectual ability. The stimulus to investigation, therefore, has come from practical as well as from theoretical considerations.

What do we mean by an emotional response? Why does it arise, and upon what factors does it depend? Historically, it appears that nearly all writers on the emotions have in some way connected up emotional behavior or states with the viscera—heart, stomach, lungs, and other internal organs. The ancient Greek philosophers located the seat of the emotions in the heart or abdomen. Such expressions as "hard-hearted," "spleeny," "to eat one's heart out," "bowels of mercy," and the like show the influence of these concepts, which have survived in common speech to our day. Several views of the emotions seem to be fairly well defined to-day, with, however, many varieties and modifications. The first of these regards the emotions as chiefly mental or conscious phenemena, accompanied, to be sure, by organic and circulatory changes, but not dependent upon these. The difference between a man running a race and one running away from a mad dog lies, according to this view, not in the physiological activities of the two, which are closely alike, but rather in their very diverse mental states. A second view considers an emotion to be the subject's conscious awareness of the organic and physiological processes going on in his own body. This is the famous James-Lange theory of the emotions, proposed by William James in 1884 and independently by the Danish physiologist C. Lange in 1885. In the average man's view, a person cries when he is sorry and laughs when he is happy or joyful. Commenting upon this common-sense view, James wrote: "My thesis on the contrary, is that the bodily changes follow directly the *Perception* of the exciting facts, and that our feeling of the same changes as they occur IS the emotion." "We feel sorry," he says, "because we cry, angry because we strike, afraid because we tremble." This view, because of the eminence of its authors, has exerted much influence upon the thinking of later workers.

A third view of the emotions stresses the part played by

visceral and skeletal muscles as well as glandular changes, but places considerable emphasis, too, upon the conscious processes involved. Woodworth best represents this position. An emotion, he says, is a "stirred up state of the organism" in which there is an impulse or conscious attitude toward some given definite activity. First comes the stimulus, then the tendency, impulse or motor set, e.g., to escape or fight, which is followed by physiological changes. These organic elements are biologically valuable in that they prepare the animal or the human the better to run or fight, as the case may be. Feats of strength and endurance—the run from Marathon to Athens, unbelievable deeds on the football field, heroic actions in the face of danger—all illustrate the value of an emotion in reinforcing the dominant drive and giving impetus to behavior. The factor which, according to this view, marks one emotion off from another is the set or impulse, which is, of course, governed by the situation. Watson, as an ultra-behaviorist, represents still a fourth view. Consciousness is completely ignored. We have done all that we can scientifically, he says, when we have described emotional behavior as we see it. Emotions are simply complex reaction patterns, the difference between anger and joy, say, being simply the difference in the way the body reacts. The difference in the individual's mental state is of no consequence, or at best is of value simply as a verbal report of how he feels.

(2)

From these different, and to some degree contradictory, points of view, various problems involving the physical basis, the isolation, or the measurement of emotions have been attacked by psychologists. The following groups of problems are fairly typical of the experimental work in this field. Although by no means exhaustive, they will help to center the discussion and make it more concrete. First are those studies which deal with the physical basis of emotions and the physiological changes in emotional states. What rôle do the brain and the nervous system play in emotion? Can an emotion exist apart from the body changes—flushing of the skin, rapid heart-beat and breathing, clenched fists, and so on—usually associated with it? In another group are experiments which have sought to discover whether emotions can be measured by instruments; whether there are any fairly definite and recognizable emotional patterns; and whether emotions can be differentiated on the basis of the physiological changes corresponding to the subjective emotional states reported by the subject. Still other experiments have been planned to see how well one can judge an emotional state from the verbal expressions or the total body response of the person stimulated; and whether emotional states are highly correlated, i.e., whether a person who reacts in a highly emotional way to one stimulus will tend to react with equal intensity to other stimuli. Finally, there are the attempts to reach and resolve emotional difficulties (complexes) by ferreting out the cause of the original upset in the subject's history. This list will serve at least to illustrate how wide and varied has been the experimental attack upon the subject.

In general two methods have been employed by psychologists in investigating emotions: *the method of expression* and the *method of impression*. The method of expression is the more widely employed, largely because it is more objective. What it seeks to do is to record and measure the bodily changes which accompany emotional states, putting little or no emphasis upon introspective reports. The method of impression, on the other hand, studies emotions introspectively or, better, retrospectively. The subject, for instance, tells which of two color combinations he prefers, or which of two musical selections has moved him most. Again, after an emotional experience, the subject may be asked to report upon his thoughts and feelings; were there conflicts, feelings of embarrassment, or anger? When and how did they appear? Sometimes the emphasis is on one method and sometimes on the other, but most experimenters have combined the two, taking objective records wherever possible, and recording, too, the verbal report or introspections of the subject.

(3)

The question of the extent to which an emotion depends upon its accompanying bodily changes is largely a matter of physiological research, and in consequence the experiments in this field have been performed for the most part by physiologists. One notable experiment is that of Sir Charles Sherrington (1906), the eminent English physiologist. Sherrington transected the spinal cords of a number of dogs in the neck region, thereby severing all connection between the brain and the body organs of the trunk. All sensations from the viscera and the skin were completely destroyed by this operation, only the sensations resulting from face, head, neck, and forelimb stimulation remaining intact. In spite of this drastic reduction of the animal's source of sensory impressions from its own body and skin, emotions persisted with little or no apparent reduction in intensity. One operated dog, for example, showed marked rage and antipathy toward an attendant. She growled, snarled, and bared her teeth, giving the same picture of anger seen in normal animals. At the same time this animal displayed affectionate behavior toward the person who customarily fed and stroked her. An interesting feature of this experiment was the retention by a dog of what might be called "disgust" behavior. Normal dogs, Sherrington found, refuse to eat dog meat, no matter how much it is disguised by being mixed with other foods or covered with milk. Always they exhibit disgust and aversion toward it; probably the odor has much to do with this. Sherrington's "spinal dogs," as these operated animals were called, exhibited the same disgust when given a bowl containing dog meat, refusing to touch it or to eat it no matter how much they were urged.

Much of the recent work on the nervous and physiological bases of the emotions has been carried on by W. B. Cannon, of the Harvard Medical School, and his associates. Cannon has investigated with much thoroughness the rôle of the autonomic nervous system in emotional activity. The autonomic nervous system, as its name implies, is normally active in those functions of the body which involve little or no volition, or knowledge, on the subject's part. It controls the vegetative functions of the body, such as the activity of the heart, lungs, stomach, and internal glands, as well as circulatory and sweat-gland changes. The two main branches of the autonomic nervous system are the thoracic-lumbar or sympathetic (the middle part) and the cranio-sacral (consisting of the upper and lower parts). Cannon has found that the sympathetic branch is active in intense or unpleasant emotions such as fear and rage. Its general function in the body is to intensify certain sorts of activity; for example, it increases the heart-beat, raises the blood-pressure, and increases breathing rate. The cranio-sacral branch, on the other hand, acts as a check and balance to the sympathetic. It inhibits rapid heart-beat, speeds up salivary and gastric secretion (thus aiding digestion), and maintains muscular tonus. During pleasant emotional states—joy, contentment, etc.— the cranio-sacral branch of the autonomic is ascendant over the sympathetic.

For the purpose of discovering whether an intact sympathetic is necessary for emotional experiences, Cannon (1927) removed the entire sympathetic division of the autonomic from a number of cats. This operation removed all sensation from the viscera such as might conceivably be present in fear or rage. Despite the operation, the animals all showed marked signs of anger in the presence of a barking dog; these signs including hissing, growling, retraction of the ears, and baring of the teeth.

The two experiments briefly outlined indicate clearly that the body sensations are not absolutely necessary to emotional states, even if they are normally present. Other experiments which point in the same direction are those in which powerful drugs have been employed to bring about rapid heartbeat, trembling, blushing of the skin, rapid breathing rate—i.e., all of the changes which ordinarily are found in emotional reactions. Logically it would seem that if an individual's emotion is simply his awareness of such stirred-up states in his own body, he should feel rage or fear when so disturbed by drugs. But this result does not occur. Cannon and his associates have shown in a long series of tests that adrenalin (the secretion of the adrenal glands, which lie just above the kidneys) has almost the same effect upon body behavior as violently unpleasant emotions such as intense excitement, fear, and anger. When adrenalin is injected into the blood stream of a normal person, the result is a decidedly stirred-up physiological state; but the subject reports no real emotion, rather he reports that he feels as though he *might* be afraid without any actual fear. In connection with this finding Cannon has pointed out, too, how alike are the bodily or physiological changes in different emotional states as well as in emotional and non-emotional states such as those resulting from strong muscular exercise, exposure to cold, and the like, and how unlike are the conscious states involved. Such observations as these would seem to render the James-Lange theory untenable—at least without some modification. One case of pathological loss of sensation in a human being may be cited before leaving this topic. Dana (1921) reports the case of a woman patient, who owing to a fracture of the neck and the resulting spinal cord injury, had suffered complete paralysis of the muscles of the trunk, arms, and legs, and complete loss of sensitivity. This person lived for a year showing little or no change in personality: grief, joy, and affection seemed unaltered. Such a case can hardly be squared with the James-Lange theory.

Cannon (1927) has recently proposed as a substitute for the James-Lange theory the hypothesis that emotions result from the interactivity of the cerebral cortex and the thalamus. The thalamus, sometimes called the diencephalon, or the between-brain, is a large mass of gray matter lying just below the cerebral cortex. It is a great sensory receptive center for impulses from the body and is a kind of vestibule for the cortex. Cannon (1925) found that when the cortex was entirely removed from a cat, the decorticated animal still showed great emotional excitement ("a sort of sham rage"), which strongly supports the view that rage, and probably other emotions as well, depend upon impulses from the sub-cortical regions. Following this lead Bard (1928) has shown, after some fifty operations on cats in which the cortex and various parts of the brain stem were removed at the same time, that the center for the emotional display of rage is located in the lower thalamus. According to Cannon's theory, then, at the same time that the thalamus discharges into the cortex it also releases motor impulses which produce complex internal changes. In turn these sensory changes in the body are sent back by way of the thalamus and so reinforce or intensify the emotional consciousness. Cannon cites considerable clinical evidence to show that the thalamus is closely connected with emotional or affective experiences. Normally this old and more primitive part of the brain is under inhibition from the cortex; and when it is "released" through disease or injury, there is often an extensive and uncontrolled emotional display (e.g., laughing or crying). The difference between one emotion and another is explained as being due to central (cortical) factors, that is, to the meaning which the emotion-arousing stimulus has for the individual. The chief result of Cannon's theory so far has been to switch the emphasis from body changes to brain changes.

(4)

Two experiments planned with the idea of finding out whether definite emotional patterns exist physiologically and can be accurately measured by instruments will be described in this section. These studies, the one by Blatz (1924) and the other by Landis (1926), are illustrative of the best techniques now available in work of this sort.

Blatz's experiment was concerned with discovering whether there is a definite picture of physiological disturbance corresponding to what we call fear. His subjects, about forty in all, included both men and women. They were told that the purpose of the experiment was the study of heart-rate differences over a fairly long period of time. Each subject was carefully tied in a chair and required to sit alone and blindfolded in a dark room for one half-hour. During this period cardiac, respiratory, and electrical changes (of the skin) were carefully recorded. The force and regularity of the heart-beat were measured by an electro-cardiograph (a delicate galvanometer) and were recorded on a photographic film. Breathing records, taken by means of an electric pneumograph, were photographed on the same film. Changes in the electrical behavior of the skin, a phenomenon known as the psychogalvanic reflex,[1] were obtained from the galvanometric

[1] The psychogalvanic reflex requires a word of explanation. If electrodes are attached to two different points on the skin and are connected with

readings. (See Figure 21.) After three half-hour sittings, Blatz found that his subjects gave consistently normal records, i.e., the slight nervousness and timidity which appeared at first due to the strangeness of the situation had been entirely lost. So much was this so, in fact, that many of the subjects fell asleep before the half-hour was up. These preliminary records constitute what may be called a control series.

The chair used in this experiment was hinged in front so that when suddenly released it would fall over backwards, carrying the subject with it. A powerful door-check stopped the fall gradually after the chair had passed through an arc of 60°. At the fourth sitting, Blatz allowed his subject without warning to fall over backwards. This backward drop was intended to set up a fear response, so that the records taken at the time would give a physiological picture of the emotion which we subjectively call fear. That the fall really caused fear can hardly be doubted. All of the subjects reported a genuine fear at first, followed later on, oftentimes, by anger or amusement. In addition, they struggled, yelled out, called the experimenter by name, and in various ways gave evidence of emotional upset. The effects produced by the fall may be briefly summarized as follows (records were taken before, at the time of, and six minutes after the fall):

a sensitive galvanometer, an electric current (as shown by deflections of the galvanometric needle) will be found to flow between the two points. This current indicates the difference in electrical potential between the two points, and is found to increase markedly during emotional states; hence it is often taken as an index of the intensity of the emotional state. The galvanic deflection is called the psychogalvanic reflex. It is due presumably to changes in sweat-gland secretion. The sweat-glands are controlled largely by the sympathetic branch of the autonomic nervous system, which, as we have seen (page 226), is active in intense emotional reactions. The assumption, then, is that fear or anger, say, cause an increased outpouring of sweat secretion; this sweat, in turn, lowers the skin resistance to the electric current, thus giving an increased galvanic deflection.

1. Breathing was much disturbed. The subjects tended to inhale in short gasps, exhaling somewhat more slowly, so that the respiratory ratio $\frac{inspiration}{expiration}$ decreased.

2. Heart rhythm was markedly irregular. The heart-rate was accelerated at first, sometimes by as much as twenty beats. This initial increase was usually followed by a retardation and then another period of acceleration.

3. In the psychogalvanic reflex there were marked galvanic deflections. These began from one-half second to three seconds after the drop and ranged from one to ten units over the scale.

In addition to these organic disturbances, there were also gross muscular movements, struggles to escape, reflex movements and threshings of the arms and legs, and yelling. In later tests, when the subject expected a fall (having been forewarned), the physiological effects were much less intense than when the fall was unexpected. Adaptation was rapid, the second and third falls producing much less upset than the first.

This experiment gives a very definite picture of general physiological disturbance, but there is no pattern or regularity of response which is constant from person to person or for a given individual. There is too much variability in all of the measures taken to warrant the assumption that we have a clear-cut physiological state which can be labeled "fear" or "terror."

In a somewhat similar experiment, Landis (1926) studied the effects of severe emotional upset upon respiration, blood-pressure, gastro-intestinal activity, and basal metabolism. Respiration, both thoracic (chest) and abdominal, was secured by means of pneumographs. Blood-pressure, which can be best described briefly, perhaps, as the pressure in the arteries resulting from both the force of the heart-beat and the artery tension, was obtained by means of a sphygmo-graph [2] attached to the upper arm. Gastric contractions were obtained by having the subject swallow a small balloon attached to a rubber tube, so that changes in the size of the balloon resulting from stomach contractions were recorded directly. Rectal contractions were secured by using a similar balloon arrangement placed in the rectum. Basal metabolism (roughly, the amount of carbon dioxide given off in breathing) was obtained by having the subject breathe into a specially designed apparatus. All of these measures of physiological change or variability were recorded simultaneously by means of tambours and writing points upon a moving smoked paper. Landis had three subjects in this experiment.

After normal records had been taken over a period of three weeks, the following schedule was begun: Each subject went without food for forty-eight hours and without sleep for thirty-six hours. At the end of this time an electric shock was administered which was "as much as the subject could bear without struggling," and which lasted until the subject signaled that he could endure the pain no longer. Each subject was then given a stimulant, and records were taken hourly for a five-hour period and daily afterward for five days. Landis's results in brief were as follows:

1. Basal Metabolism. Basal rate increased about 30 per cent on the average (with much variability) during the time of anticipation before the shock; it then fell off rapidly until, after six to eight hours, it was practically normal again. Anger, which occurred occasionally, was accompanied sometimes by an increase and sometimes by a decrease in metabolic rate.

2. Blood-Pressure. There was a rapid rise in blood-pres-

[2] This instrument consists essentially of a rubber sleeve attached to the arm. When it is inflated to the point where the flow of blood is cut off, the blood-pressure is measured either graphically or on a scale, by a tube leading off from the inflated sleeve.

sure upon the onset of the shock, together with a rapid and irregular heart-beat. Upon continuation of the stimulus the heart-beat became more regular and the pressure decreased. Landis states that these changes are quite similar to the shock symptoms following a surgical operation.

3. Respiration. Breathing was faster and more shallow, with some tendency toward gasping.

4. Gastric and Rectal Contractions. The electric shock stimulus had a variable effect on gastric contractions. In one subject gastric contractions were marked, while in another they ceased temporarily. The third subject could not retain the apparatus, and hence gave no record. Rectal contractions ceased in all subjects upon the onset of stimulation.

On the day following the experiment, each subject wrote out an account of his experiences, attitudes, and feelings. All stressed fatigue, nausea, occasional fits of anger, irritability, and lack of coördination, with surprisingly little emphasis upon definite feelings of pleasantness or unpleasantness. There was little or no awareness of physiological changes, and no agreement as to the specific emotion felt. As in Blatz's experiment, no evidence appeared to indicate that a given picture or consistent pattern of physiological changes invariably accompanied a reported emotional state. The only physiological pattern which seemed to correspond regularly to a given subjective state was that of *surprise,* or the oncoming of an emotional upset. Surprise is marked by a sudden loss of rhythm in heart-beat, irregular breathing, and gastric contraction. This is the only reported emotional state which fits into the James-Lange definition. Surprise, however, while it marks the onset of an emotion, is hardly an emotion in itself.

The earliest attempt to discover experimentally how accurately one can judge the probable emotional state of a person from a photograph is that of Feleky (1914). To each of 100 judges this investigator submitted eighty-six photographs of herself posed to represent a wide range of emotional states, together with a list of common names for emotions. The judges were instructed to write on a sheet opposite the number of each photograph the emotion which they believed it portrayed. The emotions which were represented ranged from fear, rage, and suspicion to surprise, sympathy, and religious feeling. On the whole, the most striking result was the wide range of emotions attributed to any one photograph. Anger, fear, rage, were in general poorly judged; fear and suspicion were often confused, and rage was frequently called "horror." Expressions depicting sneering and disgust were agreed upon best, though often called "scorn" and "contempt." This experiment is limited, of course, in its practical application, since one never strikes and holds a pose when normally upset. It does indicate, however, that we judge an individual's emotional state very poorly from photographs of facial portrayal of emotions.

If the observer hears the voice, sees the reaction, and knows the stimulating situation confronting the living person, his judgment is improved, but is yet far from perfect. A recent experiment carried out by Sherman (1928) shows this clearly. In this test, a group of thirty-two graduate students in psychology were shown moving pictures portraying the reactions of infants to four kinds of stimuli: hunger, sudden dropping through a distance of two to three feet toward a table, restraint of head and face, pricking with a needle. The stimuli themselves were not seen by the observer, having been deleted from the film. Little agreement appeared as to what was the emotional reaction exhibited by the child. Thirteen observers called the hunger response anger, seven called it hunger, seven fear, three pain, one grief, and one consternation. Fifteen called the response to dropping anger, only five fear. In another test, a group of medical students and nurses were shown the stimuli which produced the emotional responses as well as the responses themselves. Judgment under these conditions was much improved, fear being most often named for the dropping response, anger for restraint, and pain for the needle-prick. When the films were arranged so that the infant's emotional response was shown preceded by some stimulus other than that which actually produced the emotion, accuracy of judgment was much decreased, showing that the observers had based their opinions more on the stimulus situation than on the responses. No doubt this is generally true of other than laboratory situations. We judge a person's probable emotional state from the expected effect of the stimulus upon him more often than from his overt responses. Watson has stated that there are three well-defined emotional patterns in babies, namely, rage, fear, and love. Sherman's work makes the existence of such clearly observable patterns extremely unlikely. Fear or anger responses in babies vary in pattern from situation to situation and from baby to baby.

Landis (1924) has performed an experiment designed to discover whether reported emotions are accompanied by definite and easily recognized facial expressions. A series of photographs were taken of his subjects while they were undergoing various emotion-producing situations. There were seventeen of these situations in all, several of the more striking being as follows: smelling a bottle containing ammonia, falsely marked lemon; looking at pornographic pictures; decapitating a live rat; severe electrical shock. Twelve women, twelve men, and one boy acted as subjects. In order the better to analyze the kind and amount of movement exhibited by the facial muscle groups, these were traced out upon the face of each subject with burnt cork to make them show up better in the photographs.

The subjects characterized the emotional value of the situations in various ways, by profanity, outcries, and verbal descriptions. Situations provoking disgust, anger, surprise, and sex excitement were numerous enough to be studied in connection with the photographs of facial expressions taken during these states. After many comparisons of this sort Landis writes: "With no verbal report of a given emotion did a muscle, group of muscles, or expression occur with sufficient frequency to be considered characteristic of that emotion. There is no expression typically associated with any verbal report." Incidental findings of interest were that men employ more facial expressions than women, and that smiling was the most common response.

(6)

The question has arisen whether the respective intensities of an individual's emotional states are highly correlated, i.e., whether the individual who gives a highly intense fear response to a standardized situation tends to react in the same highly emotional way to situations provoking anger, joy, or grief; and similarly for reactors whose emotional responses have low intensity. Wechsler (1925) has attempted to answer this question, using the galvanic reflex as his indicator of emotional intensity. The psychogalvanic reflex has been described on pages 229-30 as a skin phenomenon which results from a difference in electrical potential between two points on the skin and which in turn is probably dependent upon changes in sweat-gland secretion. A diagram of a simple set-up for securing the galvanic reflex is shown in Figure 20, while in Figure 21 is shown an ordinary D'Arsonval galvanometer. There is considerable reason to doubt the specificity to emotion of the psychogalvanic reflex, although this has been claimed for it by several experimenters. Body resistance, upon which the psychogalvanic reflex depends, is known to change during the course of the day, while fatigue, deep respiration, and muscular exertion all provoke more or less deflection in the absence of any reported emotion. Wechsler has clearly shown, however, that emotional states do produce quite wide psychogalvanic reflexes; and hence in an experi-

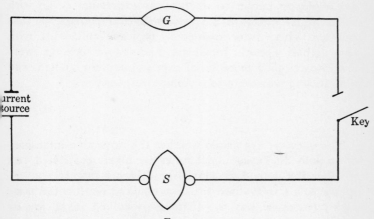

FIG. 20

SIMPLE DIAGRAM TO SHOW HOW THE PSYCHOGALVANIC REFLEX (*p.g.r.*)
MAY BE MEASURED

G is the galvanometer and *S* is the subject, who is in circuit with *G* and a source of current, usually 2-4 volts. When the circuit is closed by the key there will be an initial galvanometric deflection on the scale (see Figure 21) which is recorded by the experimenter. When the subject is stimulated, the deflection measured from this point is a measure of the *p.g.r.* A Wheatstone bridge is often employed to bring the initial deflection back to zero, so that all *p.g.r.*'s may be taken from this reference point.

ment in which the stimuli have been selected so as to give emotional reactions, the extents of the reflex may be fairly taken as indicators of relative emotional intensity.

Eleven different stimuli were employed, such as pricking the subject with a needle, sounding an automobile "klaxon" horn suddenly, and ringing a bell. All of these, with the possible exception of two or three, were calculated to surprise or annoy the subject, provoking anger, pain, or mild fear. The subject's response to each situation was measured by the galvanometric reading. In accordance with the extent of the psychogalvanic reflex response, the thirty subjects were ranked in order of merit for the eleven situations. The correlation or correspondence of these rankings ranged from o

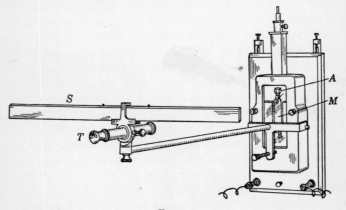

FIG. 21

D'ARSONVAL GALVANOMETER

Changes in the subject's resistance produced by emotional stimuli cause movements of the magnet, *M*, to which is attached a small mirror, *A*. As *A* turns to the right or left, these deflections may be read from the scale, *S*, by the experimenter, through the telescope *T*.

or negative (just no relationship) to .80 or more (close relationship), with an average at .58. In the case of the high correlation of .80, this very close correspondence was undoubtedly due to the similarity of the two situations involved; the first was the response to an automobile horn sounded suddenly, and the second to the same stimulus repeated. This experiment is far from conclusive either way, but on the whole and within the limits of the laboratory situation, there is no evidence to indicate that persons are emotional in general or unemotional in general. A highly emotional response (wide galvanic deflection) to one situation is no guarantee of an equally large upset in another and different situation.

(7)

One of the best-known illustrations of the method of impression is the free association test. Used as a means of diagnosing emotional difficulties or complexes, the association test method was first employed by the psychoanalyst Carl Jung (1910). Jung's method was to present to his subject or patient a set of words (usually 100), to each of which he was instructed to give the first word or first association which occurred to him as quickly as possible. The stimulus words were selected to cover a wide range of situations, and to include many which would presumably have emotional value for the subject. These so-called "critical words" were included with many indifferent or innocuous words. By way of illustration Table XV gives a selection of twenty-five presumably critical words from Jung's list. The theory underlying the association method as used by Jung and other analysts is that the extreme timidity, embarrassment, useless fears, anxieties, and worries which occur in nervous or neurotic persons, and to a lesser degree in normal persons, center around forgotten and little-understood emotional episodes in the person's life. Those words in the list which remind the testee of these occurrences, or "tap" his complexes, should therefore provoke a highly personal or emotional association, accompanied, say, by laughter or blushing. Lengthened reaction time, repetition of the stimulus word, or an entire lack of response are interpreted by Jung as the avoidance of unpleasant associations connected with the stimulus word. Such reactions are called "complex indicators." A complex, as the psychoanalyst generally uses the term, denotes a group or constellation of ideas centered around some particular episode which possesses much emotional significance to the testee. Thus an individual much excited or disturbed over religious matters is said to have a "religious complex"; other individuals are described as having sex complexes, or inferiority complexes, the latter term being generally used to cover feelings of inadequacy of all kinds.

TABLE XV

A SELECTION OF TWENTY-FIVE CRITICAL WORDS FROM JUNG'S
LIST OF 100 ASSOCIATION WORDS *

dead	old
to dance	to beat
sick	to wash
angry	to fear
to swim	brother
pity	false
to die	anxiety
to pray	to kiss
money	bride
despise	pure
unjust	contented
to marry	woman
ridicule	

* From The American Journal of Psychology (1910), 21, 219.

On the principle of strict "psychic" determinism in mental life (Freud), every reaction should be completely explicable in terms of its antecedents, all of which are inevitably linked up with it in some way. So it is argued that any word which is tied up in the subject's experience with an original emotional upset, if followed up, will finally lead back to the source of his difficulty or complex. To illustrate simply, a highly emotional or lengthened response to the word *ridicule* might enable the analyst to discover by further questioning that the source of the patient's trouble began with a peculiarly shaped nose or a speech impediment which had led others to tease and bedevil him to the point where feelings of inadequacy and the misery arising therefrom had seriously interfered with his normal life. In Table XV the words *kiss, bride, pray, ridicule, anxiety,* and the like might conceivably lead to reactions which would be considered complex indicators.

The association method in one form or another has been widely used by psychoanalysts. Perhaps the chief objection of psychologists to association tests as indicators of complexes or of repressed and usually unconventional thoughts and wishes is that they may easily prove too much. Nearly every person has at some time or another worried about religious matters or sex adjustments, or has felt inferior, and if sufficiently guided and prodded by an analyst could probably reveal several complexes. This is particularly true of the sex life, since society is so organized at present as greatly to curb and limit freedom of expression in such matters.

By far the most extensive use of free association has been made by Kent and Rosanoff (1910) in their comparison of the responses given by the normal and the insane. These investigators used a list of 100 words containing stimuli having probable emotional value, i.e., covering the usual worries and anxieties, as well as presumably indifferent words such as *table, chair, stove.* This list was given to 1,000 normal and 247 insane adults, the responses to each word being carefully tabulated. Probably the most striking result obtained from this mass of material was the large percentage of "individual" responses given by the insane as compared with the normal. If a person gives a response not given by any one else in the group, it is considered to be an "individual response." The normal group gave about 7 per cent individual responses, the insane group 27 per cent. A large number of individual responses is considered by the authors to be probably indicative of eccentric thinking or other peculiarity, while a large number of "common" responses (those given by others) indicates conformity to the standards of the group. Each response, together with the frequency of its occurrence, has been tabulated for each of the 100 words in the list. From these tables one can determine how commonplace or how exceptional his associations are.

(8)

From the experimental points of view, the "detective" use of the free association test is a more direct and better controlled use of the word-reaction method. This method, as its name implies, was intended to discover the real culprit from among several persons suspected of a crime. In the psychological laboratory, the "crime" is usually a stunt of some kind through which one person out of several possible candidates is put. It is so arranged that neither the experimenter nor the class knows who is the "guilty" person. The object of the association test is to select this guilty individual from among the several suspects by means of his telltale associations. Usually these responses will be abnormally long or emotionally tinged (accompanied by laughter or embarrassment), or they will bear directly upon the stunt, thus giving the culprit away.

Jung has employed the word-reaction method in the following experiment, which may be used as an illustration. The supervisor of a hospital reported to him the theft of a pocket-book from one of the nurses in her charge. The purse contained a fifty-franc note, one twenty-franc piece, some centimes, a small silver watch-chain, a stencil, and a receipt from Dosenbach's Shoe Shop in Zurich. The purse had been taken from a clothes-closet in which it had been placed by the nurse. Owing to various circumstances which need not be described in detail, suspicion narrowed down to three nurses, all of whom were asked to submit to the association test. The critical words were the name of the robbed nurse, *cupboard, door, open, key, yesterday, bank-note, gold, seventy, fifty, twenty, money, watch, pocket-book, chain, silver, to hide, fur, dark reddish leather* (color of the purse), *centimes, stencil, receipt, Dosenbach.* Other words not bearing directly upon the theft but having emotional value were *theft, to take, to steal, suspicion, blame, court, police, to lie, to fear, to discover, to arrest, innocent.* These critical words were distributed among twice as many indifferent words, the total constituting the final test.

To each of the three nurses the test was then given, the response and the time of reaction (in fifths of a second) being taken for each word. The median reaction times of the three nurses, whom we will designate A, B, and C, to the indifferent and the critical words are given in the following table:

REACTION TIME (FIFTHS OF A SECOND) OF A, B, AND C TO THE INDIFFERENT AND CRITICAL WORDS

	A	*B*	*C*
Indifferent words	10	11	12
Critical words	16	13	15
Difference	6	2	3

Although A's "normal" reaction time—as shown by her responses to the indifferent words—is the shortest of all, she is considerably slower than either B or C in replying to the critical words. This, of course, is evidence, though surely not conclusive, against A. Jung next computed the number of "imperfect reproductions" given by each nurse. An imperfect reproduction or reaction is one which is haltingly or stumblingly given, with repetition or evident emotional upset. Such responses are considered by Jung to grow out of an association of strong feeling tone aroused by the critical word which is carried over to several succeeding responses. The subject, so to speak, becomes "rattled," and gets more flustered as the experiment goes on. The result of this tabulation showed that A gave 65 per cent imperfect reactions, B 56 per cent, and C 30 per cent. The actual responses were distributed as follows:

NUMBER OF IMPERFECT REACTIONS GIVEN TO INDIFFERENT AND CRITICAL WORDS BY A, B, AND C

	A	B	C
Indifferent words	10	12	11
Critical words	19	9	12
Difference	9	3	1

A has an excess of 9 responses to the critical words, B has three, and C has only 1. By this test, then, suspicion again points to A. Still another check was made in terms of the percentage excess of complex indicators given to the critical words, over and above those given to the presumably indifferent stimuli. A's excess is 100 per cent, B's 0, and C's 50 per cent. On the basis of these statistical results and upon careful study of the character of the responses, Jung decided that the greatest suspicion fell on A. Confession by A later on confirmed this judgment.

The method of expression has also been used in attempting to discover guilt or deception. Both Marston (1917) and Larson (1923) have employed changes in blood-pressure as evidences of lying or deception with much apparent success. Marston believes that a rise in systolic blood-pres-

sure of from eight to ten millimeters in conjunction with
a response to a possibly compromising question is sufficient
to indicate that the subject is lying. Larson, who first used
the association test method and later the method of direct
questioning, has employed blood-pressure rises with success in several cases involving actual crimes. Blood-pressure,
however, is affected by so many factors, and the technique
is still experimental to such a high degree, that it is probably too early to regard the findings from such tests as
final evidence of a deceptive consciousness.

(9)

In the first part of the chapter we outlined four somewhat contradictory views of what constitutes an emotion
(pages 222-223). According to the first view, an emotion is a
mental or conscious phenomenon largely independent of
the body changes which are its usual but somewhat incidental accompaniments. In the second view, an emotion
is considered to be the individual's perception of the sensory
changes arising from glandular, muscular, and circulatory
changes in his own body (this is the James-Lange theory).
The third view regards an emotion as a felt impulse or set
toward a certain type of activity plus a mass of sensations
resulting from stirred-up body states. The fourth view is
the behavioristic dictum that an emotion is simply the
reaction pattern itself, the conscious state, if admitted at
all, being of no consequence.

Let us now attempt to evaluate these views as best we
may in the light of the experimental evidence at our dis-
posal. The first view, that an emotion is simply a conscious
or mental state, is clearly too narrow. The part played by
the body changes in preparing the individual to meet
danger or some other emotion-producing situation is too

real to be ignored. Furthermore, we cannot omit from a treatment of emotional reactions the rôle of the skeletal muscles nor the enormous importance of the glands in producing emotional states. The second view—that expressed by the James-Lange theory—is probably untenable in view of the experiments of Sherrington and Cannon; while the fourth view (the behavioristic) is unproven and very probably not true. Certainly experiments carried out with the best technique now available have failed to find for a given emotion either a definite physiological pattern or a very characteristic behavior reaction.

This leaves us, finally, the third viewpoint, which fortunately seems to be fairly satisfactory, since it provides both for the conscious side of the emotion and for the body changes which may accompany it. The "pattern" for an emotion, according to this view, does not lie in the mass of physiological changes, which are largely undifferentiated from one emotion to another, but rather in the impulse or set of the organism. In fear, for example, the set is to get away—to escape the influence of the stimulus—while in joy the impulse is to continue the influence of the stimulus. Typically the impulse precedes the bodily changes, which are often biologically valuable as preparatory reactions. This view seems to be consistent with the most recent theory of the emotions, that of Cannon, described on page 228.

This chapter has tried to show how, as a direct result of recent experimental attacks, there is now a respectable amount of definite information regarding the emotions. Much is now known about the nervous and physical basis of emotional states; many of the complex physiological, circulatory, and electrical changes accompanying emotions have been measured; and techniques have been developed for investigating the causes of certain abnormal emotional states. Much remains to be done, of course. Future research will further define and differentiate emotions both on the physiological and psychological side. And genetic studies will aid in showing how emotions develop, how they become organized, and, possibly, how they may be better controlled for the benefit both of the individual and of society.

Suggested Readings

1. A comprehensive survey of the experimental literature on emotion will be found in Chapter 13, *The Expressions of the Emotions,* by Carney Landis in *Foundations of Experimental Psychology* (1929).
2. For an account of the part played by organic states in emotion, see W. B. Cannon's *Bodily Changes in Pain, Hunger, Fear, and Rage,* 2d edition (1929).
3. Jung's article on the *Association Method* will be found in the American Journal of Psychology (1910), 21, 219-269.
4. An interesting modification of the James-Lange theory and a discussion of the importance of the emotions is given in F. H. Allport's *Social Psychology* (1924), Chapters III and IV.

Chapter 11

KÖHLER'S EXPERIMENTS IN PERCEPTION AND LEARNING AND THEIR IMPORTANCE FOR *GESTALT* PSYCHOLOGY

(1)

THE point of view and method of interpretation represented under the name *Gestalt theorie,* or *Gestalt* psychology, had its rise in Germany as recently as 1912. Max Wertheimer is generally credited with being the founder of the movement in Germany, but Kurt Koffka, of the University of Giessen, and Wolfgang Köhler, of the University of Berlin, through various academic appointments in this country have become the principal champions of the *Gestalt* viewpoint in America.

Perhaps the simplest way of showing just what this new school of psychology stands for is to indicate first what it is not. "The psychologist," says Titchener, "seeks, first of all, to analyze mental experience (consciousness) into its simplest components." [1] "The rule, or measuring rod, which the behaviorist puts in front of him," says Watson, "always is: Can I describe this bit of behavior I see in terms of stimulus and response?" [2] To both of these programs—surely as far apart as the poles—*Gestalt* psychologists stand strongly opposed. It is false analysis, they say, to hold that the complex behavior of a man, or an animal either, for that matter, can be explained genetically as an

[1] *Textbook of Psychology* (1913), p. 37.
[2] *Behaviorism* (1925), p. 6.

Courtesy of Clark University Press

WOLFGANG KÖHLER

(1887–   )

accumulation or outgrowth of fairly specific stimulus-response bonds—the so-called "bundle hypothesis." And it is equally invalid, they hold, to apply strict analysis to complex sensory data. The real data of experience are organized wholes, or *Gestalten,* and never mosaics; we do not encounter specific elements either in consciousness or in behavior. And so instead of the world being to the infant "a buzzing confusion" (William James), from which here and there bits must be laboriously picked out and tied together or integrated, even for the very young child there is a certain degree of orderly arrangement in sensory data to which he may respond without previous learning. Later on adults behave toward the patterns or total organization of objects around them rather than toward specific stimuli. *Gestalten,* or "configurations," therefore, as the word has been translated, are the primary business of psychology. Hence, *Gestalt* psychology concerns itself with these directly experienced wholes; it studies how they come about, what laws govern their changes, and upon what factors they depend.

(2)

The first problems to be attacked from the standpoint of *Gestalt* psychology lay in the field of visual perception. One of the most significant of these was the question whether our sensory experiences or responses are governed by specific stimuli in the visual field or by the *relations* among the stimuli. Köhler (1918) attempted to answer this question in the following interesting experiment. First he trained two hens (generally notorious for their lack of intelligence) to expect food from the brighter only of two papers (a dark and a light) glued side by side on a wooden board. The hen was placed in a wire coop on one side of which apertures were so arranged that the fowl could easily thrust its head out to peck grain from the paper-covered board next to the coop. Grain was scattered in equal amounts upon both papers. Whenever the hen pecked at the grain upon the light or positive paper she was allowed to eat, but whenever she pecked at the grain upon the dark or negative paper, she was at once shooed away. After 400 to 600 trials in which the positive and negative papers were frequently interchanged to prevent any association by the fowl of the positive stimulus with the right or left side, the hen at last learned to select the positive and to avoid the negative stimulus with great regularity. This part of the experiment constitutes what is called the training series. In the critical tests which followed, Köhler kept the positive (light) paper on the board, but substituted for the negative (and darker) paper another paper still lighter than the positive stimulus to which the hen had been trained to go. The question now was whether the hen would continue to peck at the *specific* light paper from which she had been laboriously trained to eat, or whether she would respond to the brightness *relation* and select the still brighter but neutral paper to which she had never gone. Köhler's results are highly interesting and fairly conclusive. Using four hens, two trained to go to the brighter of the two papers and two trained to go to the darker of the two, the neutral paper or new stimulus was selected in about 70 per cent of the trials and the original positive stimulus in 30 per cent. These results show, Köhler thinks, that there are in nature simple organizations of brightness differences which are extremely primitive, to be sure, but yet so fundamental that even so stupid a creature as a hen will respond to the relation "brighter than," rather than to the specific stimulus to which she has been carefully trained to go.

Köhler repeated this experiment with chimpanzees and also with a three-year-old child. The child was allowed to learn by the method of trial and error that the brighter of two colored boxes only contained candy. Forty-five trials were necessary in order to establish this differential response to the point where no errors were made, i.e., the brighter was always chosen. In the critical tests which followed, a new and brighter box was presented along with the old positive stimulus, the negative darker box being removed. Köhler reports that in this series the child "invariably" took the new bright box, instead of the one from which it had formerly got candy. This again is good evidence, he says, that humans react toward situations as related wholes, and not to bits or portions of the environment.

The pioneer experiment designed to test out this matter of relations and the inherent tendency toward organization within the visual field is the now famous *phi*-phenomenon of Wertheimer (1912). This experiment, which is almost as striking as Köhler's, should be briefly mentioned in the present connection. First a beam of light is thrown at regular intervals through a long slit upon a screen in a darkened room, producing a series of flashing white lines against a black background. The appearance and disappearance of these lines will depend, of course, upon the time-interval between the flashes. Now if a second beam of light is projected through a second slit, slightly below the first, and slightly later in time, logically, it would seem, we should see *two* parallel lines, one lying below the other and lagging somewhat after it. The actual result is very different. What the observer does see, if the timing is carefully adjusted, is a *single* line oscillating forward and backward. The addition of the second line has greatly changed the stimulus-value of the first. Instead of a simple addition of stimuli, we have a new construction which cannot be analyzed into two separate lines. This new fact, in Wertheimer's view, is a *Gestalt* or whole which cannot by any effort or intention on our part be split up into its two component parts. Our perceptions, he says, are not built up additively like a tower of building blocks; rather they fall at once into patterns which may not be separated into elemental sensations and images without spurious analysis. In actual experience, such elements simply do not exist as real entities.

(3)

Gestalt psychologists are opposed to the idea that presented stimuli have meaning for the observer only in so far as he is able to bring past experience to bear upon them. On the contrary, they insist that experiences may have form and pattern (and meaning) simply because their elements "come" organized. This phenomenon is illustrated, Köhler thinks, in those cases wherein persons born blind later acquire sight. It is to be noted, he says, that while such individuals do not recognize geometrical forms, e.g., squares and circles, *as such,* they do *understand* the question when asked what a given form is. This must mean, says Köhler, that nebulous organizations and arrangements of the visual field are present even though the stimulus situations, here geometrical forms, are not yet tagged with verbal symbols, i.e., names. The visual field is chaotic, relatively speaking, only when there are serious brain lesions or diseased conditions in the optical centers of the brain, so that only bits can be grasped visually at one time. Köhler cites a study of Gelb and Goldstein upon a patient in this condition. This man had learned to rely largely upon motor and kinesthetic experiences to piece out his visual data. When his name was written in large letters, for instance, and presented to him, he would perceive the first few letters as a group and then guess the remainder from the context and from the amount of movement needed to span the whole name. But if several lines were drawn across his name, the patient could no longer see it as a name, i.e., a whole, since the bits which he *did* see represented two confused patterns, and not two separate independent groups. Nothing was added from other parts of the field to give either pattern complete organization, and in consequence no *Gestalt* appeared.

(4)

To the *Gestalt* psychologists, the distinction between "figure" and "ground" is regarded as one of considerable importance in the psychology of perception. For them every organized whole or pattern exists as a figure against a more general, and usually a vaguer, background. In the auditory field, for example, a melody, which is a *Gestalt,* is heard against a background of silence or against a vague mixture of miscellaneous noises. In like manner, every visual configuration, a sunset or a prize-fight, is projected against a larger and less clearly defined background.

In a notable series of experiments E. Rubin (1915), a Danish psychologist, has studied extensively this figure-ground relationship in the sphere of visual perception. Usually the figure stands out clearly from the ground; and for this reason it is in ambiguous figures in which figure and ground are interchangeable that the distinctions between the two can be most clearly seen. In Figure 22 such an ambiguous figure is shown. Note that the four-pointed "cross," the one with radii, stands out rather easily as a figure against the concentric circles which form the ground. Now interchange figure and ground by fixating intently upon the circles, and note that the arcs in the *new* figure, again a four-pointed "cross," are *true arcs*, i.e., cut-off sections of circumferences, whereas before they were visible parts of unbroken circles. The circles behave differently depending upon whether they are in the figure or in the ground. Rubin and other *Gestalt* psychologists have developed certain characteristic differences which they believe distinguish figure and ground: The figure is more clearly formed or outlined—is a better *Gestalt*—than the ground; it is more vivid; it holds its color better; it is more solid and substantial. Koffka (1922) illustrates some of these

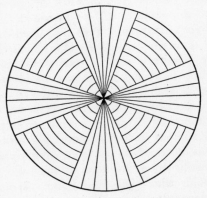

Fig. 22

AN AMBIGUOUS FIGURE TO ILLUSTRATE FIGURE-GROUND RELATIONSHIP
(From Koffka, 1922.)

principles in the following way. Look, he says, through a stereoscope at a slide one side of which is solid blue and the other of which consists of a circle made up of alternate blue and yellow sectors. The yellow figure easily stands out against the blue background, but the blue sectors have a hard time of it as "figure" against a yellow background, being overwhelmed by the solid blue opposite.

(5)

Gestalt psychologists have not confined themselves to the subject of visual perception, but have extended their methods and interpretations into other and diverse fields. Particularly in their studies of animal learning, they have many experiments to their credit which are of much value whether explained according to their system or not. To many psychologists these experiments seem more substantial and less artificial, perhaps, than much of the perception work. As illustrative of this type of work several experiments of Köhler with chimpanzees will be described.

Köhler's ape experiments were conducted during the years 1913-1917, upon the small island of Tenerife, located in the Canary Islands, a short distance off the African coast. Here a colony of chimpanzees was established, and owing to the isolated and tropical nature of the country, experiments could be carried on under conditions closely similar to those in the animal's native habitat. In one experiment a chimpanzee was not fed in the morning as usual, but instead his food was fastened to the roof of his cage and a box thrown casually upon the floor of the cage some distance from the point where the fruit hung suspended. The ape had never used a box as an implement, and hence ignored it completely, although he could easily have reached the fruit by pulling the box over and climbing upon it. The animal spent many hours in unsuccessful effort, trying to reach the fruit by jumping up toward it, climbing up the walls, and the like. Finally the experimenter dragged the box over beneath the suspended fruit, stepped upon it, reached up and touched the banana. He then got down and threw the box some distance away. Almost immediately the chimpanzee pulled the box over under the fruit, climbed upon it, and pulled down the food. A variation of this experiment was tried by Köhler with another ape which he considered particularly stupid. This animal had often seen other chimpanzees use boxes as platforms from which to reach food, but he had never actually done the trick himself.

To see whether he might not have learned from his fellows what to do when put into a situation requiring the employment of a box as a platform, Köhler fastened a banana to the roof of his cage, threw in a box, and left the animal to his own devices. The ape's subsequent behavior is quite enlightening as a demonstration of how hopeless the solution of even a simple task may be unless the relations involved are clearly apprehended. This monkey at once ran to the box, but instead of dragging it under the fruit, he either climbed upon it and jumped up, or else climbed upon the box, hopped down, and quickly ran over to jump up from the ground under the fruit.

This experiment, says Köhler, shows how necessary for learning it is to see the situation involving the task as a whole or entirety. The first ape did not connect box and fruit until the relation was demonstrated to him by the experimenter. Once the relation was perceived, the box ceased to be simply a box and became an implement—something to be used in getting fruit. More technically speaking, at the instant this relation was seen, the *Gestalt* was formed. The stupid ape, it appears, knew that the box and jumping up were both involved in the task of getting the fruit, but that was as far as his analysis went. Had the connections ground-box-fruit been made in their proper sequence, the situation would have been organized at once, and the grouping would have become meaningful. But by the stupid ape this last *Gestalt* was never formed; instead there were for him two separate groupings, box-jumping-up and jumping-up-fruit.

(6)

In another experiment Köhler attempted to see whether Sultan, apparently his most intelligent chimpanzee, could combine two sticks into one useful implement. The sticks

were two hollow bamboo rods, the one being enough smaller
than the other so that it could be fitted easily into the end
of the larger to form a single long stick (see Figure 23).
All of the animals had frequently used single sticks to pull

Fig. 23

A Chimpanzee Fitting a Small Stick into the Bore of a Larger One
(Adapted from Köhler's *The Mentality of Apes.*)

in bananas and other fruit placed outside of the bars of
their cages. But none had been given the task of joining two
sticks into a single one and using the resulting long stick
as an implement with which to pull in fruit.

The set-up of the experiment was as follows. The chimpanzee was put into a cage along with the two sticks, and several pieces of fruit were placed outside of the bars too far away to be reached by either stick alone, but within easy reach of the joined stick. Judged in the light of this rather simple situation, the animal's behavior seems incredibly stupid to human eyes. First he tried to reach the fruit with one stick and then with the other. This failing, he next pushed one stick out as far as possible, and then with the second stick pushed the first one on until it finally touched the fruit. This actual contact, Köhler notes, seemed to give the animal great satisfaction, but it didn't give him the fruit! At last, as the animal seemed no closer to a solution than at the start, the experimenter gave him a hint by sticking one finger into the opening of the larger stick directly before his eyes. But this cue failed to help any, and after an hour or so of futile effort, the ape apparently lost interest and gave up the task as hopeless. He continued to play with the two sticks, however, and after some manipulation, holding the one stick in the left hand and the other in the right, he accidentally got them together as shown in Figure 23. The first connections were loose, so that the sticks frequently fell apart, but the animal persisted, with great eagerness pulling in not only all of the fruit, but all other small moveable objects, such as stones and sticks, within reaching distance. On the following day, after some desultory pushing of the one stick by the other (repetition of the old useless behavior), Sultan quickly joined the two and got the fruit.

This experiment, as interpreted by *Gestalt* principles, shows again the growth of elements at first unconnected into an organized whole. Until the ape perceived the two sticks as capable of forming a single unit in the situation, reaching-the-food, no *Gestalt* appeared. When the two sticks became one implement, however, a new pattern was at once formed. Many illustrations of the growth of such patterns or *Gestalten* are cited by Köhler. A box will often be employed as a platform for reaching fruit if it is in close proximity to the fruit; but not if it is in a far corner of the cage. A stick will be used to pull in fruit from the outside of the bars if it is close enough to where the fruit is lying to "get into the same picture" with it, but not if it is at some distance, or is only potentially present as in the branch of a tree which has been thrown into the cage. The point made by the gestaltists is that, to be used as an implement, the box or the stick must exist as such in an organized visual whole, the relations of whose parts are perceived. When the relations involved are quickly grasped, i.e., when the animal almost at once gets the whole picture of connections and mutual implications, as, for instance, climb-on-box-get-fruit, it is said to have "insight." A situation is experienced without insight when its various parts are simply seen as parts with no dependence or orderly arrangement. Insight into a problem, then, involves seeing the problem with its various implications as all of one piece.

(7)

Beside building up a thoroughgoing experimental basis for their theoretical concepts, the *Gestalt* psychologists have advanced cogent and searching criticisms of other methods and points of view. Köhler's criticism of the methods employed in many animal experiments conducted by behaviorists seems worthy of mention. In learning problems of the "choice reaction" type, the animal is trained to go to one stimulus, a red light, say, and to avoid another stimulus, a green light, by being fed when he chooses the one and shocked when he takes the other. In such experiments,

Köhler points out, instead of giving the animal an electric shock in the feet when he responds to the negative stimulus it would be much more logical from the point of view of the animal's own experience to have the negative stimulus do something to the animal—move forward or frighten him in some way. Not only would this be closer to the natural situation for the animal, but the connection between reward and the one stimulus, and punishment and the other, would be much more obvious and sensible. The latter situation, Köhler thinks, would furnish a good *Gestalt;* the former, which is traditional in animal experimentation, a poor one, since it is well-nigh impossible for the animal to organize into one situation punishment-in-feet-for-taking-the-wrong-light. As noted in Chapter 5, page 113, both Köhler and Koffka have criticized the animal experiments of Thorndike on much the same ground. The animals in these experiments, they say, were forced to learn by trial and error, since there was no possible way—in the light of their experience—in which they could organize such acts as opening a latch or pulling a loop into the situation getting-out-of-a-box-and-getting-food. Much of the so-called stupid learning of animals, Köhler believes, grows out of the setting of almost impossible tasks for the animal, i.e., tasks which cannot readily be organized into a meaningful pattern, if they can be so organized at all.

The work of the *Gestalt* psychologists, most of which has been done in Germany, has inspired several American psychologists to undertake investigations along the same lines. Much of what has been done in the field of perception is highly technical and difficult to describe simply or in brief space. Two studies will serve as illustrations of this type of work. H. R. De Silva (1926) has investigated the factors determining apparent visual movement such as is represented by Wertheimer's *phi*-phenomenon (page 251). Ge-

staltists argue that the apparent movement which occurs in
the *phi* is a clear-cut demonstration that configurations are
non-additive. Actual movements and illusions of movements,
they hold, are fundamentally the same, the latter being
limiting cases of the former. To some extent De Silva sub-
stantiates this viewpoint. The perception of real or actual
movement, however, he finds to be dependent mainly upon
speed or velocity, while the perception of apparent movement is conditioned, instead, upon the separation in space
of the stimuli and upon their degree of intensity. Especially,
he emphasizes the subjective factors present in the perception of apparent movement. W. S. Hulin (1927) has
studied apparent tactual movement by applying two pressure points upon the skin of the forearm. These tactual
stimuli were applied sometimes together and sometimes as
much as .3 second apart; spatially they were separated in
eight steps from from five to 150 millimeters. Hulin's subjects were instructed to report when they experienced apparent movement from one point to the other. Only 30
per cent of the 13,000-odd judgments given by seven observers indicated the experience of apparent movement, i.e.,
configurations in the tactual field. Apparently, therefore,
tactual *Gestalten* are directly dependent upon definite temporal and spatial relations existing among the stimuli, and
are not generally found phenomena.

One of the most interesting investigations, growing out
of Köhler's work with chimpanzees, is a study by A. Alpert
(1928) of the rôle of insight in the learning of very young
children. Forty-four nursery school children varying in age
from nineteen to forty-nine months were subjects. Situations
closely resembling the problems set by Köhler for his apes
were devised. For example, a toy would be placed on a shelf
out of reach and a box or chair left near by; if the child used
the box or chair as an implement—stood upon it—the toy

could be secured. Again a toy would be placed outside of the bars of a play-pen and a stick left handy near-by with which the desired object could be fished in; sometimes this problem was complicated by providing two sticks and a toy, a short stick, which was too short itself to reach the toy, but which could be used in raking in the long stick, and a long stick with which the toy could be fished in. The question at issue in these experiments was whether the child would show the same sudden insight into the task as was exhibited by several of Köhler's apes. Alpert discovered what she called "immediate insight"—a quick, sure solution, more often than Köhler found for his apes. In many cases, however, insight was gradual or partial, preceded by what seemed to be a certain amount of fumbling trial and error. It is impossible to say just how much tentative trial and observation preceded many of the successful solutions where insight was judged to be immediate, but on the whole it was probably more often present than not (see page 114). If comparisons are valid—which is doubtful—we can say definitely that the young children were more intelligent in their solutions than the chimpanzees.

(8)

In spite of the vigor and enthusiasm with which the *Gestalt* psychology has been presented by its advocates, it has not, as yet, won many converts either on the Continent or in America. Objection has been raised both to its theoretical assumptions and to its experimental procedures. It has been urged, for instance, that the term *Gestalt* connotes nothing essentially new. Perception has long been regarded by non-*Gestalt* psychologists as a unifying response or as a "combining activity" (Woodworth); groups and outlines are grasped first and the elements and details afterward.

Binet found long ago (1899) that when line drawings are exposed for brief periods, as in a tachistoscope, the drawing is first glimpsed as a whole and the details gradually added in successive presentations. Nor is the distinction between figure and ground an especially original one. The well-known phenomena exhibited in binocular rivalry [3] and in the ambiguous figures, for example, show how a detail can stand out against a background at one instant and become a part of it later on. It should be said, however, that the gestaltists have carried the study of the figure-ground relation and the laws governing it further than have other workers.

In the field of learning, much criticism has been leveled at the term *insight*. The contention is that this expression, while descriptive, adds nothing in the way of explanation. Insight, according to the *Gestalt* psychologists, appears in quick learning when the man or animal suddenly grasps the principles involved in the task or sees the proper relationships forthwith. But as indicated elsewhere, it is very difficult to know just how much trial-and-error learning has preceded the flash of insight. It may be that such is always the case, provided the learning is closely analyzed. In hard and little-comprehended tasks, we know that both men and animals resort to hit-or-miss learning until by chance the successful move or act is hit upon. In simpler problems, of course, there is usually a marked reduction of random activity and oftentimes the sudden appearance of insight, as there is also in those activities in which the individual is able to bring to bear information or knowledge from previous and somewhat similar situations. It would seem plausible, then, that insight, genetically looked at, may well be the end-result of a much reduced trial-and-error period. The

[3] Binocular rivalry occurs when two dissimilar pictures are placed in a stereoscope. The result is a competition or rivalry between the two, first the one and then the other picture being suppressed.

previous tentative trials exist, to be sure, but are not represented in the particular learning curve under scrutiny, prior to the appearance of insight. It has been pointed out elsewhere (pages 113-114), in another connection, that the insight shown by Köhler's apes was clearly a function, in part at least, of the tasks set the animals.

Criticism has been made also of Köhler's animal work on the score that the experimenter's presence on several occasions during an experiment, constitutes an uncontrolled factor. Animals are quick to pick up cues from an entirely innocent experimenter, as has often been shown in the cases of horses and dogs which calculate or perform other supposedly "intellectual" feats that turn out upon investigation to be anything but "intellectual" (see pages 117-118). Again, the results of many *Gestalt* experiments are not statistically well established. In the experiment quoted on page 250, for instance, the hens responded to the relation of brightness in 70 per cent of the trials. Although this result makes the relational response more probable than the specifically learned one, it is not sufficient to establish it with certainty. Many further trials and larger groups are needed to do this.

In the preceding sections we have sketched in brief outline the point of view and some of the experimental findings of the *Gestalt* psychologists and have given, as well, some of the more obvious criticisms which have been directed against this new school. Whether psychologists agree with the *Gestalt* psychologists' viewpoint or not, most of them are agreed as to the intrinsic value of their experimental work. As a fresh and vigorous movement with emphasis upon experiment, there can be little doubt but that *Gestalt* psychology is destined to play an important rôle in the future development of psychology.

Suggested Readings

1. A good description of some of the representative experimental work on perception done by the *Gestalt* psychologists is given in Kurt Koffka's *Perception: An Introduction to the Gestalt-Theorie,* Psychological Bulletin (1922), 19, 531-585.
2. For an authoritative discussion of the principles of the *Gestalt* psychology and its present status, see Wolfgang Köhler's *Gestalt Psychology* (1929).
3. The articles by Koffka and Köhler in *Psychologies of 1925* will prove helpful to the beginning student.
4. Köhler's experiments with chimpanzees are described in his *The Mentality of Apes* (1925).

Chapter 12

WEBER'S AND FECHNER'S LAWS AND THE RISE OF PSYCHOPHYSICS

(1)

ALL of us, no doubt, are familiar with the fact that our perceptions of differences in the magnitude, extent, and amount of things around us do not vary directly with the changes in the objects themselves. Thus every one would agree that a faint tone does not need to be increased as much as a loud tone for the *change* to be noticed, and that a four-year-old boy does not have to grow as much as his sixteen-year-old brother for the increase in height to be perceived. Most of us, too, would be ready to admit that one pound added on to a ten-pound load is more clearly felt as an increased weight than one pound added on to a fifty-pound load; and that an error of one inch in measuring one foot is far cruder work than an error of one inch in measuring one mile. But few, probably, of those who have noted these facts have given much thought to the question of how our perception of a difference, and the actual difference itself, are related other than to speculate somewhat vaguely, perhaps, that the relation is clearly not one of simple proportion.

As it happens, one of the very earliest attempts to employ experimental methods in psychology was directed toward solving this problem. There were several reasons for this. For one thing the early psychologists were mostly philosophers, and hence were concerned mainly with the problem of how knowledge of the world and ourselves is obtained through the senses. Moreover, there already existed a respectable body of facts concerning the senses, e.g., the ear, the eye, the skin, which furnished a convenient starting-point for investigation. Whatever other reasons there were, the fact remains that the topic of sensation-stimulus dependence bulks large in the history of experimental psychology and has stimulated literally an enormous amount of research. A whole literature, in fact, has grown up around the subject of *psychophysics*, as this branch of psychology is called; and the purpose of this chapter is to outline the development of psychophysics and to evaluate as far as possible, in brief space, its place in modern psychology.

(2)

Psychophysics really began with the work of Ernst Heinrich Weber (1795-1878), although as a separate branch of psychology it did not originate with him. During the years from 1829 to 1834, Weber, who was professor of anatomy in the University of Leipzig, published in Latin a long series of experiments on cutaneous and kinesthetic (or muscular) sensation under the title *De Tactu*. Weber was interested primarily in discovering how accurately small differences between weights can be perceived when the weights are lifted by hand or are allowed to rest freely on the surface of the skin. He was interested also in how small a difference between two lines can be ascertained or perceived by the eye. In a series of experiments with weights held between the fingers and lifted by hand, Weber discovered that a weight of thirty ounces could just barely be distinguished as lighter than a weight of thirty-one ounces, and as heavier than one of twenty-nine ounces. This proportion he found to hold closely for drams [1] as well as

[1] A dram = 1/16 ounce avoirdupois.

for ounces, i.e., thirty drams could just be felt as lighter than thirty-one and heavier than twenty-nine drams. With practised subjects, the same proportion held for lighter weights:—14.5 ounces or 14.5 drams, for instance, could just be distinguished from 15 ounces or 15 drams, respectively. Smaller differences than these, said Weber, are very rarely "sensed," while greater differences are too often perceived to be considered just noticeable. In experiments concerned with judging the length of lines, Weber discovered that a different but consistent principle of proportion held good. A line of 101 millimeters could just be distinguished as longer than one of 100 millimeters, while a line of 51 millimeters was judged to be just observably longer than one of 50.5 millimeters.

On the basis of these results, Weber formulated the famous generalization known subsequently as Weber's Law. In comparing objects, he says, it is clear that we perceive not the *actual difference* between the two objects, but the *ratio* of this difference to the magnitudes of the two objects compared. To put it in other words, the observed difference between two objects is not absolute and completely independent of the objects themselves, but is relative to the *size* of the stimuli and is (roughly) a *constant fraction* of one of them, the so-called "standard stimulus." The constant fraction must be discovered by experiment, and is called the "difference limen," or D L. For weights lifted by hand, the D L was determined by Weber to be $\frac{1}{30}$ to $\frac{1}{40}$, and for lines approximately $\frac{1}{100}$. To illustrate the meaning of the D L more concretely, if thirty ounces can just be distinguished from thirty-one ($\frac{1}{30} \times 30 = 1$), then sixty ounces should be just distinguishable from sixty-two ($\frac{1}{30} \times 60 = 2$), and ninety from ninety-three ($\frac{1}{30} \times 90 = 3$). In each case the just noticeably different stimulus is separated from the standard stimulus by a certain fractional amount of the standard, and this fraction or D L remains substantially constant no matter what the actual size of the objects compared.

Weber's Law may be expressed more concisely and in better mathematical form as follows: let R stand for the standard stimulus,[2] i.e., that object or thing with which other objects or things are to be compared. Then if dR is the increment by which R must be increased in order to produce a just noticeable change in the sensation (S) aroused by R —for example, a judgment of just barely heavier, or just observably longer—Weber's Law may be summed up in the following equation:

$$\frac{dR}{R} = C \text{ (a constant)}$$

As we have already seen, Weber put the constant for lifted weights, i.e., $\frac{dR}{R}$ at $\frac{1}{30}$, and the D L for lines at $\frac{1}{100}$.

Unfortunately Weber's conclusion that the just noticeable increase in a stimulus is a constant fraction of that stimulus is not as clear-cut as it appears at first glance. The trouble lies in the expression "just noticeable." This term is really ambiguous, since it is often necessary to specify just how often a stimulus-increase must be correctly noted in order to be called just noticeable. The usual practice has been to take that difference which is judged correctly 75 per cent of the time as being sufficiently noticeable. But other percentages will serve, the 75 per cent point being chosen simply because it lies midway between 50 per cent correct (which denotes simply a chance difference), and 100 per cent correct (which denotes a difference so large as always to be correctly perceived). To illustrate, if a 102-millimeter line is called longer than a standard line of 100 millimeters

[2] $R = Reiz$, the German word for "stimulus," and is regularly used in psychophysics.

seventy-five times in 100 comparisons, then according to Weber's Law fifty-one millimeters should be called longer than fifty millimeters, 204 millimeters longer than 200, and 510 millimeters longer than 500, in 75 out of 100 trials or judgments. All of these ratios, $\frac{1}{50}$, $\frac{2}{100}$, $\frac{4}{200}$, and $\frac{10}{500}$, are equal, of course, and the D L is $\frac{1}{50}$. We may now state Weber's Law more clearly and less ambiguously as follows: the increase in any given stimulus which is correctly perceived in 75 per cent (or any designated per cent) of the trials is a constant fraction of the size of the stimulus.

The equation $\frac{dR}{R} = C$ was Weber's final statement of his law, and constitutes his chief contribution to the study of the relation between sensory judgments and stimulus intensities. It remained for Gustav Theodor Fechner (1801–1887) to take up where Weber left off and, building upon Weber's Law, to erect the intricate and highly complex structure called psychophysics. Fechner, who besides being Professor of Physics at Leipzig was also a philosopher and something of a mystic, saw in Weber's generalization a means of studying quantitatively the relation between the physical and mental worlds. In his *Elements of Psychophysics,* first published in 1860, Fechner defined psychophysics as "an exact science of the functional relation or relations of dependency between body and mind." The physical world for Fechner was represented by the physical stimuli, and the psychical world by the sensations within the organism aroused by these stimuli.

Fechner made two assumptions which enabled him to amplify and extend Weber's Law. First, he assumed that a large sensation may be thought of as the sum of a number of sensation units; and secondly he assumed that just noticeable differences (*j.n.d.'s*) between sensations are always equal and hence are suitable units for measuring sensation

Courtesy of C. H. Stoelting Co., Chicago

GUSTAV THEODOR FECHNER

(1801–1887)

changes. Accepting Weber's equation $\dfrac{dR}{R} = C$ as fundamentally correct, Fechner on the basis of experiments extending over many years,[3] reformulated Weber's Law to
read as follows: When stimuli increase by equal ratios, the
sensations aroused by them increase by equal increments or
steps. What Fechner meant by this statement, and how it
depends upon his assumptions may be seen most clearly,
perhaps, in Figure 24.

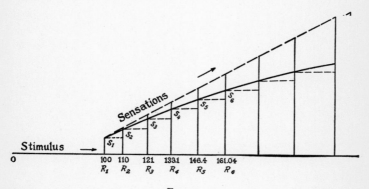

FIG. 24

GRAPHIC REPRESENTATION OF THE RELATION BETWEEN INCREASES IN THE
INTENSITY OF THE STIMULUS AND INCREASES IN THE INTENSITY OF THE
SENSATION

In the diagram we begin with two stimuli, a standard and
a variable comparison-stimulus, each designated by the
value 100 on the horizontal scale. These two stimuli may
be thought of as two lights of brightness value 100, or two
lines each 100 inches long, or two tones each of an absolute intensity designated by 100. To represent these values

[3] During the years 1855-1859 Fechner alone made 67,072 weight comparisons, acting both as experimenter and as subject.

on the stimulus scale (the X-axis, or horizontal line), we lay off an arbitrary distance from zero to the point marked 100. Then on the vertical line above 100 (R_1) we lay off an arbitrary distance to represent the strength of the sensation (S_1) produced by stimulus 100. Suppose now that we increase very slowly the comparison stimulus 100, and that when this stimulus reaches the value 110 or R_2 it is judged by the subject to be *just noticeably greater* than the other or standard stimulus, which remains, of course, at 100 or R_1. The sensation value S_2 (on the vertical line) corresponding to stimulus 110 (R_2) will now equal the sensation S_1 (corresponding to stimulus 100) plus one *j.n.d.* unit, on Fechner's assumption that the *j.n.d.* may be taken as the unit of sensation-change. In Figure 24 the *j.n.d.* is taken as a small and arbitrary increment which when added to S_1 gives S_2. Now let us begin with our two stimuli, the standard and comparison, both at the value 110 on the scale, and increase the comparison stimulus slowly until it is again just noticeably greater than the constant standard, still at 110. This point should be reached theoretically at 121 (110 + $^{11}\!\!/_{10}$), since in the previous trial our D L was found to be $\frac{1}{10}$ (100 + $^{10}\!\!/_{10}$). The sensation S_3 corresponding to stimulus 121 (R_3) is S_2 plus one *j.n.d.*, or S_1 plus two *j.n.d.*'s and accordingly the distance S_1 plus two *j.n.d.* units is laid off above stimulus 121 or R_3. The other stimuli in Figure 24, viz., 133.1 (R_4), 146.4 (R_5), 161.04 (R_6), have all been calculated in the same manner as 121 and 110; in each case one tenth of the preceding stimulus magnitude has been added on to the stimulus scale to give a just noticeable increase on the sensation scale and to accord with Weber's Law. The sensation value (vertical distance) corresponding to the stimulus on the base-line is in every instance equal to the sensation aroused by the preceding stimulus plus one *j.n.d.* unit.

The stimuli, the physical series, in Figure 24 are increasing in *geometrical progression* as we go from 100 to 161.04, while the sensations, the psychical series, are increasing in *arithmetic progression*.[4] Whenever we have two series which correspond point by point, the one increasing geometrically, the other arithmetically, we know from mathematics that the relation between the two variables must be logarithmic. Hence the sensation values (A P) may be here thought of as the logarithms of their corresponding stimulus-values (G P). The logarithmic relationship between a geometric and an arithmetic series may be simply illustrated by the common logarithms of 10 and its multiples. From any table of logarithms we find that

$$\log 1 = 0$$
$$\log 10 = 1$$
$$\log 100 = 2$$
$$\log 1000 = 3$$
$$\log 10,000 = 4$$

On the *left-hand* side the numbers increase by a constant multiple (10), while on the *right-hand* side the logarithms increase by a constant increment (1). The first series is a geometric, the second an arithmetic, progression. If we let our numbers represent stimuli and our logs represent their corresponding sensations, we have the situation pictured in Figure 24. Note carefully that if the sensation values should increase in *direct proportion* to the increase in the

[4] A geometric progression (G P) is a series in which each term (except the first) is derived from the preceding one by multiplying by a constant number or *ratio:* e.g., 4, 12 (4 × 3), 36 (12 × 3), 108 (36 × 3). In the present case we have 100, 110 (100 × 11/10), 121 (110 × 11/10), 133.1 (121 × 11/10), 146.4 (133.1 × 11/10), 161.04 (146.4 × 11/10). An arithmetic progression (A P) is a series in which each term (except the first) is derived from the preceding by the *addition* of a constant number, e.g., 3, 7 (3 + 4), 11 (7 + 4), 15 (11 + 4), 19 (15 + 4). In Figure 25 we have, S_1, S_2 (S_1 + 1 *j.n.d.*), S_3 (S_2 + 1 *j.n.d.*), S_4 (S_3 + 1 *j.n.d.*), S_5 (S_4 + 1 *j.n.d.*), S_6 (S_5 + 1 *j.n.d.*).

stimuli, rather than by equal steps, we should have the rapidly rising oblique line represented by the dots, instead of the more slowly rising logarithmic curve shown in the diagram.

The discovery of the logarithmic relationship obtaining between stimuli and their sensations enabled Fechner to restate Weber's Law in mathematical terms as follows: Sensations are proportional to the logarithms of their exciting stimuli, or, in the form of an equation:

$$S = C \log R$$

wherein S is the sensation, R the stimulus, and C a constant to be determined from the experiment. This equation is generally known as the Weber-Fechner Law or simply as Fechner's Law. The first two quantities, of course, are variables, the third, C, is fixed for a given series of stimuli, e.g., weights, lines, or brightnesses, but varies from one sense modality to another. C's value depends partly upon the sense modality, partly upon the precision of measurement, and partly upon the choice of the zero point for sensation intensities.

Fechner's logarithmic law is, to be sure, an extension and modification of Weber's Law, but it is also much more than this. Weber's equation, $\frac{dR}{R} = C$, says nothing whatever about sensation intensities; it states simply that, for a given proportion of correct judgments (usually 75 per cent), the ratio of the stimuli is constant, no matter what the absolute magnitudes of the objects compared. Fechner's equation, on the other hand, expresses a functional relationship between physical stimuli and their corresponding sensation intensities, a relationship which Fechner, at least, believed to hold true over the whole range of perceptible stimuli.

(3)

As an expression of the general law of the relativity of all judgments, or the dependence of a change for its value upon the magnitude of the thing changed, Weber's Law serves to describe quite well many facts of everyday perception. Familiar examples (see also page 266) readily come to mind: An inch is more perceptible when added to a man's finger than when added to his height; a room lighted by an electric light is scarcely brightened at all by the addition of a candle, but the brightness of the same room, when lighted by a single candle, is markedly increased by the addition of another candle; to hear a pin drop the room must be very quiet; five pounds added to a baby's weight is a much greater increase than five pounds added to a man's weight. Such illustrations as these serve to show the general soundness of Weber's principle, but there are distinct limitations to the law which must be recognized in trying to evaluate it. In the first place, while Weber's Law holds with a fair degree of accuracy in the perception of linear magnitudes (such as lines), in the perception of weights both by passive pressure on the skin and by active lifting, for intensity of lights and sounds, and for judgment of duration and movement, it does not hold for the perception of pitch differences. A person can perceive the same absolute change in pitch equally well whether the vibration rate is changed from a standard set at 200, 400, or 800 vibs. per second. Secondly, Weber's Law holds only in the *middle range* of stimulus intensities; it breaks down with very weak or very strong stimuli. Expressed differently, the ratio $\frac{dR}{R}$ remains fairly constant for the middle range of stimuli, but increases markedly when the stimuli become very strong or very weak. Probably the experiments which show this most clearly are those performed by König and Brodhun in 1888-1889. These investigators, using light intensities varying from very faint to very bright, found the D L or *j.n.d.* to be a constant fraction (.017 to .018) of the stimulus over a wide range of *medium* brightnesses. The difference limens were considerably larger, however, for very *faint* and for very *intense* lights, as may be seen from König and Brodhun's data, part of which are reproduced in Table XVI below.

TABLE XVI

The stimuli are given in an arbitrary unit. The *ratios* give the fraction which the just noticeable difference is of its stimulus (after König and Brodhun). Note that from about 400 to 100,000 the ratio is approximately constant.

Stimulus:	1	2	4	10	40	40	100	200	400	1,000
Ratio:	.256	.175	.120	.070	.048	.037	.030	.025	.022	.020

Stimulus:	2,000	4,000	10,000	20,000	40,000	100,000	200,000	400,000
Ratio:	.018	.017	.016	.017	.018	.021	.029	.038

These variations in *j.n.d.* are attributable in some degree at least to adaptation and various slight disturbances. But such factors are not sufficiently influential, in a careful experiment such as this one, to account for the wide discrepancy in D L throughout the range of intensities, and we are forced to conclude that Weber's Law does not hold generally.

Does Fechner's Law fare any better than Weber's as a universal principle? The answer is not encouraging. In the first place, Fechner's Law, like Weber's, does not hold for pitch; and furthermore, like Weber's, it holds only for the middle range of stimuli. In the second place, Fechner's two assumptions have not stood the test of later experiment, nor of adverse criticism. Psychologists have not been slow to point out that a large sensation is not, psychologically at least, the sum of many elementary sensations, but is a new experience, just as water is not simply the sum of oxygen and hydrogen, but is essentially a new product. Moreover, the *j.n.d.* is by no means a fixed unit. The just noticeable difference between two lights or two tone intensities, for instance, will vary from one observer to another, and for the same observer from time to time. Theoretically, there is no "just noticeable difference," since even very small differences will occasionally be recorded, while large differences will sometimes not be perceived. The third objection to the universality of Fechner's Law is based upon the difficulty of fixing definitely the point of zero sensation. We know from mathematics that the logarithm of 1 is zero. Fechner fitted this into his formula, $S = C \log R$, by assigning the value 1 to that stimulus which arouses a just barely perceptible (zero) sensation. But the eye, the ear, and the skin, unfortunately, rapidly become adapted to faint lights, faint sounds, and faint touches; and this adaptation, plus fatigue, slight distractions, and lapses of attention, shift and distort the zero point of sensation. Thus it would seem that the variability and instability inherent in the sensory receptors themselves must limit the universality of Fechner's Law.

In spite of these theoretical objections to Fechner's Law and the limitations in its range of applicability, it is only fair to say that the principle of logarithmic relationship between stimulus changes and our perceptions of these changes has been found exceedingly useful in many practical problems of physics and engineering. Several instances of such use may be illustrated. The relation of visual acuity to the brightness of the field has been found to be logarithmic. If *absolute acuity* (A) "is the reciprocal of the smallest visual angle for which neighboring contrasted portions of the field can be separated," and if B is the brightness of the field, then $A = c + k \log B$ (Woodworth, 1926). The constants c and k are dependent upon the units employed, the character of the field, and the eye itself. This equation is simply Fechner's Law, $S = C \log R$. It holds for the middle range of intensities. In the field of biophysics, Hecht (1929) has shown that in a certain variety of clam the relation between the reciprocal of the clam's latent time of response (e.g., its reaction time to light) and the intensity of stimulation is logarithmic, for a constant exposure time. If we let $X = 1/\text{latent time}$, and $I = \text{intensity}$, then $X = k \log I$, which again is Fechner's Law.

Experiments in audition have shown that the relation between "loudness" as sensed by the ear and the physical intensity (vibration amplitude) of the sounding body is logarithmic. Thus Fletcher (1929) in his *Speech and Hearing* (page 153) gives the equation $a = \log J$, wherein $a = $ loudness measured in "bels" and J is the physical intensity of the sound in microwatts. A bel equals ten decibels, the latter unit being the smallest change in loudness which the ear can detect. A decibel or "sensation unit" is thus clearly analogous to the Fechnerian *j.n.d.* The decibel is the unit most often used by telephone engineers in this country.

From these illustrations it would appear that Fechner's Law is still considerably alive, although it is surely a limited principle rather than the universal law he considered it to be. As far as psychology is concerned, the present worth of both Weber's Law and Fechner's Law would seem to lie in the fact that they do subsume quantitatively a large group of facts within the middle range of stimulus intensities.

(4)

The interpretation of Fechner's Law has led to much discussion and many theories. Fechner himself regarded his law, $S = C \log R$, as essentially a psychophysical equation expressing the fundamental relationship between the physical world and the mental world. Sensations, or mental states, he said, do not change as rapidly as do their physical stimuli; instead they lag more and more behind to give finally the logarithmic relationship which we have discussed above. According to Fechner's view, the fundamental relationship between "body" and "mind" is logarithmic.

Few psychologists have agreed with Fechner in this somewhat mystical interpretation of his experimental data. A far more common explanation has been in physiological terms. The lag between stimulus and sensation which Fechner noted is frequently interpreted as a physiological lag between the exciting stimulus and the bodily effect aroused by it. Physiologists have found, for instance, in working with isolated muscle groups, that as the stimuli increase in intensity, the muscular responses also increase, but by relatively smaller and smaller amounts. An analogous relation may well exist between changes in the external stimulus and changes in sense-organ (plus nerve and brain) stimulation.

Still other explanations of the lag which appears between stimulus and body response have been given in terms of (1) variability of response, and (2) relativity of judgment. The first explanation, which was first suggested by Woodworth (1914), stresses the increase in variability of a large bodily response over that of a small one. With the physical increase in the stimulus, he says, both the sensory stimulation and the body response involve more and more sensory elements and muscle groups. The more of these elements involved in a given response, the greater the probable overlapping with other responses, and the less distinct each becomes. Hence a large or intense stimulus must needs be increased to a greater degree than a small and weak one in order for the change to be perceived. This is essentially what occurs in Weber's Law and Fechner's Law. The other explanation, that in terms of relativity, was first advanced by Wundt, and is a purely psychological interpretation. All judgments, Wundt says, are governed by the general principle of relativity: changes are estimated always in terms of the thing which has been changed, and derive their importance from our common-sense evaluation of this relation. Several illustrations of the general principle of relativity have been given on page 275. Relativity of judgment serves to describe what actually happens in a sensible way; but it does not explain in any precise fashion the mathematical relationships implied in Weber's and Fechner's Laws.

(5)

In previous sections we have seen that both Weber's Law and Fechner's Law grew out of an effort to generalize and quantify the relationship existing between stimulus changes and their corresponding sensory changes. In the study of this relationship, which Fechner called psychophysics, two chief questions arise: (1) What is the *least* difference that can be perceived between two given stimuli, i.e., what is the D L, or difference threshold? (2) What is the *least* amount of a given stimulus that will just produce a sensation at all (the absolute threshold)? [5] It is clear, of course, that we must first find our thresholds—our *j.n.d.'s*—before we can generalize or establish a principle of relationship between stimuli and sensations. Heretofore we have assumed tacitly that D L's can be found without telling exactly how this is done. We shall now consider the question of technique, or the psychophysical methods, as they are called, which grew out of the attempt to answer these two questions.

The history of the psychophysical methods goes back to Weber's experimental work on lifted weights in 1829, but their origin and development is linked up chiefly with Fech-

[5] This second question grows out of the first and is concerned particularly with the location of the lowest limit of sensitivity in the sense organ.

ner's work. Many later investigators have introduced modifications in the psychophysical methods since Fechner's time, among whom should be mentioned, at least, Müller, Urban, Fullerton and Cattell, and Jastrow. Though developed primarily for the purpose of studying the psychophysical relationship, these methods fortunately have a much wider usefulness as practical techniques for the study of acuity of perception or efficiency of judgment under various conditions.

There are, in general, three psychophysical methods: the *method of minimal change,* the *method of constant stimuli,* and the *method of average error.* These will be considered in order.

1. The Method of Minimal Change. This method was developed from the earlier *method of just noticeable differences,* and is, as its name implies, concerned with determining the smallest change in a given stimulus or between two stimuli which can be just perceived or sensed. It can best be made clear by an illustration. Let L be a standard light intensity (e.g., four, eight, or sixteen candle-power) which illuminates equally the two ground-glass windows P and Q of a photometer.[6] (See Figure 25.) In determining the just noticeable difference in brightness or the threshold of sensibility, there are four stages. (1) We begin with the two windows P and Q of equal brightness, and slowly increase the brightness

[6] The photometer is an instrument for measuring an observer's sensitivity to changes or differences in light intensity. A simple photometer (Woodworth's model) much used in the laboratory consists of a rectangular box containing a light which is reflected equally upon two small white surfaces. These surfaces are viewed by the observer through two ground-glass windows in the side of the box. Movement of the light-source within the box, either to the left or to the right, changes the relative illumination of the two windows; as the one becomes lighter, the other becomes darker, and vice versa. The distance which the light must be moved in order to make the difference in the illumination of the two windows just noticeable can be read from a scale on the outside of the box.

of Q until it is judged to be just perceptibly brighter than P. Call this point A. (2) Next, with Q much brighter than P, we decrease the brightness of Q (the variable) until it is judged to be of *equal* brightness with (or not perceptibly different from) P. Call this second determination B. (3) As

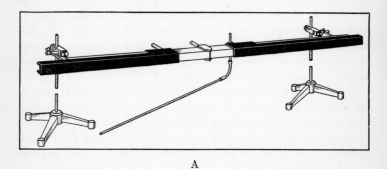

A

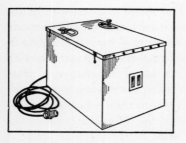

B   C

Fig. 25

Some Apparatus Used in Psychophysical Experiments

A.—Galton bar used in studying the accuracy of estimation of visual extents.
B.—A photometer often used in measuring brightness discrimination.
C.—These weights are used in experiments on weight discrimination, or in studies of the kinesthetic sense.

in (1) above, we begin again with the windows P and Q of the same brightness, but this time we decrease Q's brightness very slowly until the observer judges it to be just less bright (darker) than P. This is point C. (4) Finally, following (2) above, we begin with Q much darker than P and increase its brightness until the two stimuli are judged to be equal. This is point D. From the average of these four points, A, B, C, and D, we can obtain the "general threshold," i.e., the brightness-difference which is just capable of being perceived. Needless to say, observations must be repeated again and again to insure reliable results.

Table XVII illustrates the method of minimal change in an experiment similar to the one outlined above. Note that the ten trials taken under the four different sets of conditions have been averaged separately, and that they show considerable variation the one from the other. If we average the four determinations, A, B, C, and D, the result, 4.2, gives the general threshold, the average just observable difference, or the average D L. This value is a measure of the observer's keenness of discrimination under the given conditions. Other interesting comparisons may be made. By averaging A and C, for instance, and then B and D, we can compare the accuracy of perception when the change is from equality to difference with that when the change is from difference toward equality. When we do this, it is evident that judgment was more accurate when the difference between the standard and the comparison was *decreasing* than when it was *increasing*. The upper threshold, *i.e.*, $\dfrac{A + B}{2}$, is determined from those settings in which the comparison stimulus is *brighter* than the standard; and the lower threshold, i.e., $\dfrac{C + D}{2}$, is determined from those settings in which the comparison is *darker* than the standard. It is clear from Table

XVII that the upper threshold was considerably smaller than the lower threshold, and hence perception of brightness changes was more accurate under the first set of conditions than under the second.

TABLE XVII

DETERMINATION OF THE JUST NOTICEABLE DIFFERENCE IN LIGHT INTENSITY BY THE METHOD OF MINIMAL CHANGE

The standard was a four candle-power lamp, and ten trials were taken at each of four stages. In one half of the trials, at each stage the standard was on the right, and in one half, on the left. (Data adapted with some changes from the original by the writer.)

Average setting

(A) From equality upward, i.e., the comparison stimulus becomes brighter 4.6

(B) Toward equality downward, i.e., the comparison stimulus becomes darker 2.7

(C) From equality downward, i.e., comparison becomes darker 5.6

(D) Toward equality upward, i.e., comparison becomes brighter 3.9

General threshold $\dfrac{(A + B + C + D)}{4}$ 4.2

Average increasing difference $\dfrac{(A + C)}{2}$ 5.1

Average decreasing difference $\dfrac{(B + D)}{2}$ 3.3

Upper threshold $\dfrac{(A + B)}{2}$ 3.7

Lower threshold $\dfrac{(C + D)}{2}$ 4.8

2. *The Method of Constant Stimuli.* Like the method of minimal change, this method was also developed from an

earlier method, the *method of right and wrong cases*. Though it may be employed with other stimuli, as for example, linear extents (lines), this method has most often been used to measure tactual and kinesthetic sensitivity through the lifting of weights, and hence we shall illustrate with lifted weights data. (See Figure 25.) Suppose that we have selected a standard weight of 100 grams, and comparison weights of 88, 92, 96, 104, 108, and 112 grams. The problem is the determination of the amount by which the 100-gram standard must be increased or decreased for the change to be just observable. Instead of changing the standard by small amounts, however, we compare it over and over again, first with the lighter and then with the heavier weights, noting in each case the number of correct judgments. Judgments may be recorded as heavier, as lighter, or as equal. To illustrate, in comparing 100 grams and 108 grams, the judgment "heavier" might be given 80 per cent of the time, "equal" 12 per cent, and "lighter" 8 per cent of the time, and such results as these will be secured with each weight pair, 100-88, 100-104, 100-112, and so on. When there are an equal number of heavier and lighter comparison stimuli, the standard weight is usually lifted first and the comparison weight second, the judgment of heavier, lighter, or equal expressing the subject's opinion of the relation between the variable (the second) weight and the standard (the first) weight. That weight above 100 grams which gives just 50 per cent "heavier" judgments determines the upper threshold, or the just perceptibly heavier difference; while that weight below 100 grams which gives just 50 per cent "lighter" judgments determines the lower threshold, or the just perceptibly lighter difference. The average of these two values is the general threshold, or the average difference limen. It is seldom that a weight difference will be found experimentally which gives exactly 50 per cent "heavier" or 50 per cent "lighter" judgments, so that interpolation is nearly always necessary. The two 50 per cent points may be determined fairly accurately from graphs, and somewhat more precisely from formulas for interpolation between percentages actually found.

The procedure for the method of constant stimuli above outlined is the older, or classical, form in which the method was developed by Fechner, Müller, and Urban. It is an accurate and precise method when used with highly trained subjects, but with those less well trained it is open to considerable objection, because of the allowance of equal judgments. We have no way of controlling the number of judgments which a subject will call "equal," and hence, if he is extremely cautious, a large part of his data will be so classified, and hence not directly usable.

In 1896 Fullerton and Cattell showed in a series of experiments that if a subject will guess when inclined to say equal, he is more often right than wrong, as there is usually present some slight basis for a judgment, although it may be too small to be very convincing. These investigators simplified the method of constant stimuli, permitting only *two* judgments—"heavier" or "lighter." They made it up, in a sense, to the subject for thus forcing his judgment by allowing him to qualify each judgment by a degree of confidence, "sure," "fairly sure," "a guess." In this simpler form of the method of constant stimuli, that weight difference which gives 75 per cent "heavier" judgments determines the upper threshold, while that giving 75 per cent "lighter" judgments fixes the lower threshold. Of course, the 75 per cent threshold is arbitrary, but it is, perhaps, the most reasonable value, since it lies midway between 50 per cent (chance) and 100 per cent (certainty) (see page 269). The average of the upper and lower thresholds gives the general threshold, or average D L. This D L, it will be noted, cannot properly be called a *j.n.d.* unless we assume that the difference which is perceived correctly in 75 per cent of the trials is in fact just noticeable. As this is a very questionable assumption at best, it is more accurate to call such a D L the "75 per cent threshold."

Certain data selected from an experiment on weight-lifting (Garrett, 1922) are given in Table XVIII to illustrate the method of constant stimuli in its simpler form. Since 300 comparisons were made of each weight-pair, e.g., 100-96, 100-112, and so on, the percentages of correct judgments are quite reliably determined. From the table it is seen at once that the lower threshold is eight grams, since the comparison 100-92 gave exactly 75 per cent correct judgments. Unfortunately the upper threshold cannot be obtained so readily. It is clear, however, that it must lie between four and eight grams, since the weight-pair 100-104 gave 66 per cent correct judgments and the pair 100-108, 85.3 per cent correct judgments. The value most likely to give 75 per cent correct would seem by simple proportion to lie approximately at 106 grams, half-way between 104 and 108. This 75 per cent point can be more accurately determined from tables prepared for the purpose or by graphical methods. If we put the lower threshold at eight grams and the upper threshold at six grams, the general threshold is the arithmetic mean of these two values, or seven grams. This indicates that, on the average and in many trials, the difference between 100 grams and 107 or 100 grams and 93 should be correctly perceived 75 per cent of the time. In order to verify Weber's Law for these data, it would be necessary to show that for a standard of 200 grams, the 75 per cent threshold is fourteen grams; for a standard of 500 grams, it is thirty-five grams; and so on. That is, the D L in each case must be a constant fraction of the standard stimulus.

TABLE XVIII

DISCRIMINATION OF LIFTED WEIGHTS: METHOD OF CONSTANT
STIMULI

The combined records for six observers, each of whom made fifty comparisons of each weight-pair, giving 300 comparisons for each pair and 1,800 for all six weight-pairs.

Weights compared	Percentage of right judgments
100-88	84.3
100-92	75.0
100-96	56.3
100-104	66.0
100-108	85.3
100-112	90.7
Lower threshold (75%)	8 gms.
Upper threshold (75%)	6 gms. (approx.)
General threshold	7 gms.

3. The Method of Average Error. This method is based on the assumption that measurements of just noticeable differences are essentially measurements of observational errors, i.e., of the limitations or obtuseness of the subject's sensory and nervous mechanism. Ordinarily a subject is given a fixed standard stimulus and an adjustable or variable one which he is instructed to make equal to the standard. The amount by which the observer misses this standard is a measure of his "error of observation."

We may illustrate this method with the Galton bar, which is often used in the measurement of just non-perceptible differences between linear magnitudes. The Galton bar consists of a strip of flat enameled wood about 2.5 centimeters in height and 100 centimeters in length. It is divided in the center by a small wedge, and on the reverse side contains a graduated scale, by which the length of each half can be measured. Two sliding sleeves of metal permit varying distances to be set off from the center or o-point. The whole apparatus is mounted against a black background. (See Figure 25.) Now suppose a standard length of twenty centimeters to be set off on the right-hand half of the bar and the subject to be instructed to adjust the slide on the left-hand half from a much smaller setting than twenty centimeters up to apparent equality with this standard. Twenty trials at least should be made, and the average amount of error (overestimation or underestimation) calculated. A second series of trials is then taken from a too-large setting (greater than twenty centimeters) down to equality with the standard, and the average error again found. The whole procedure must be repeated with the standard set off on the left and the variable on the right half of the bar. The amount of variation or fluctuation in the subject's settings, the amount by which he misses the standard, gives a measure of his *average error*. The tendency of the subject repeatedly to overestimate or underestimate the standard is called his *constant error*.

Table XIX illustrates the method of average error with data for eighty trials on the Galton bar, the standard length being twenty centimeters. Note that one half of the trials were taken with the standard on the right and one half with the standard on the left to avoid any "place error." Each set of forty trials is equally divided between settings from too small and too large; viz., one half of the time the variable was set shorter and one half of the time longer than the twenty-centimeter standard. The average of all eighty trials is 19.05 centimeters, which indicates a *constant error* of .95 centimeter (20 — 19.05). This is the amount by which, on the average, the observer fell short of the standard, or the amount by which he *overestimated* his settings. The extent to which the observer, on the average, missed the standard is given by his *average error* of 1.04 centimeters. To calculate the A E (average error), we sum up all of the deviations made in the eighty trials from the twenty-centimeter standard and divide by the number of trials. The calculation of the A E is not shown in the table, but can easily be made from the original data. To verify Weber's Law, the A E found for a ten-centimeter standard should be one half as large as the A E for our twenty-centimeter standard.

When the observer made his settings from the too-small position (average 18.6), he fell short of the standard to a greater degree than when he made his adjustments from a too-large position (average 19.5). Obviously in both cases he overestimated his settings, however, since both averages are less than the twenty-centimeter standard.

TABLE XIX

DATA FOR EIGHTY TRIALS ON THE GALTON BAR, FORTY WITH STANDARD ON THE LEFT AND FORTY WITH STANDARD ON THE RIGHT

(Adapted by writer with several small changes.)

Standard left—forty trials cms.		*Standard right—forty trials* cms.	
From too small.....	18.5	From too small.....	18.7
From too large.....	19.2	From too large.....	19.8
General average	19.05		
Average (from too-small settings)....	18.6		
Average (from too-large settings)....	19.5	Constant error...	.95
		Average error ...	1.04

(6)

The evaluation of Fechner's work is not an easy task. Many and various opinions have been expressed regarding it, from the enthusiastic commendation of Titchener, who regarded Fechner as the father of mental measurement, to the caustic remarks of William James,[7] who wrote: "Fechner's book was the starting point of a new department of literature, which it would be perhaps impossible to match for qualities of thoroughness and subtlety, but of which, in the humble opinion of the present writer, the proper psychological outcome is just *nothing*." As is usually the case, the truth is somewhere between these two rather extreme views, but the judgment of time inclines toward Titchener's rather than James's view.

It must be remembered—to take the negative side first—that much of Fechner's psychophysics has not stood the test of later research. His concept of a large sensation as the sum of many smaller sensations, as well as his idea that *j.n.d.*'s are equal all over the scale of intensities, have both been pretty definitely rejected by present-day psychologists. Also his psychophysical law, as we saw, has been found to have a decidedly limited instead of, as he thought, a universal application. It is becoming increasingly evident that modern psychology is interested more in the larger aspects of behavior than in the study of sensation and small sensory changes. The development of mental tests with their emphasis upon individual differences has, no doubt, had much to do with this shift in orientation, while behaviorism, with its emphasis upon the wholeness of the organism's activities, has played a not unimportant rôle. The present-day psychologist is interested in the psychophysical methods as tools to be used in the study of problems involving the determination of sensory acuity, sensory efficiency, and the accuracy and precision of movement. Or he may be interested in the possibility of adapting these techniques more directly to problems of mental measurement. Rarely is he interested in

[7] *Principles of Psychology* (1890), vol. I, p. 534.

Weber's or Fechner's principles as such, or in the measurement of the stimulus-sensation relation. To illustrate concretely, in 1910 E. L. Thorndike devised his Handwriting Scale, the first scale for the measurement of an educational product, proceeding on the supposition that equally often noticed differences between specimens of handwriting are equal. According to this principle, if the difference between handwriting specimens A and B is noted by competent judges as often as the difference between specimens X and Y, then the difference between A and B is, in effect, equal to the difference between X and Y. Thorndike's assumption, as well as his technique, are direct outgrowths from the psychophysical methods. More recently, Thurstone (1927) has adapted and extended the psychophysical concepts on the theoretical side and has applied them to the problem of scale-making and to the study of attitudes and preferences.

Despite the modern trends away from Fechner's psychophysics, therefore, and the limitations of his law, as one reads through the experimental work in psychology since Fechner's time, and since James's, too, he cannot help but be impressed with the very large influence exerted by psychophysics and the psychophysical methods. Fechner's work was important because it showed conclusively that problems in psychology can be subjected to quantitative methods and are amenable to exact mathematical treatment. The far-reaching result of this point of view is seen to-day in the rapid development of mental tests, of educational and achievement tests and scales, and in the widespread use of statistical methods in the study of human problems. In short, it is probably not too much to say that, beginning with Fechner, psychology ceased to be a branch of philosophy and began to be an experimental science.

Suggested Readings

1. An interesting account of Fechner and his work is given in G. Murphy's *Historical Introduction to Modern Psychology* (1929), Chapter 5; see also E. G. Boring's *A History of Experimental Psychology* (1929), Chapter 13.

2. For a clear discussion of the various psychophysical methods, see C. S. Myers's *Experimental Psychology* (1925), Revised Edition, Part I, Chapter XV.

3. An interesting interpretation of the Weber-Fechner Law in terms of variability can be found in the article on psychophysics by R. S. Woodworth in *Psychological Researches of James McKeen Cattell*, Archives of Psychology (1914), 30.

Chapter 13

EXPERIMENTAL STUDIES IN THE VISUAL PERCEPTION OF DISTANCE AND DEPTH

(1)

IN the history of experimental psychology, no topic has excited more research and led to more discussion than that of how we perceive or come to know the positions and relations of objects in space. The reasons for this interest are fairly obvious. Not only do our sense impressions obtained from the environment lie at the basis of all mental activity, but in addition there is the enormous practical importance of such data for everyday existence. The two senses best fitted for the perception of objects in space are touch and vision, since both the skin and the retina are spread out spatially in two dimensions. Of these two, vision is easily the more important. Seeing and hearing, in fact, are usually called the "higher" senses in contrast to tasting and smelling, the "lower" senses. This differentiation is due not so much to the greater complexity of eye and ear, but to the immense value of the sense data derived from them. A man who loses his sense of taste or smell is handicapped, to be sure, but such a loss is not comparable to loss of sight.

The immediate stimuli to visual perception are light-rays reflected from objects upon the two retinas (the inner surfaces of the eyes) by way of the aperture called the pupil. Figure 26 gives a simple schematic representation of how this occurs. The retina is a slightly concave surface in two dimensions, length and width, and yet, as we all know, our perceptions of distance, depth, and motion are given in three dimensions. How, we may ask, is this possible? And why aren't the objects of our experience—houses, trees, and people—spread out before us as though pinned upon a large flat board parallel to our retinas? This has been a much debated question in psychology, and much of the experimental data on the subject goes back to the researches of the great German physicist, Hermann von Helmholtz (1821-1894). Beside elaborate studies in the physiology of the eye and on the physical facts of optics, Helmholtz accumu-

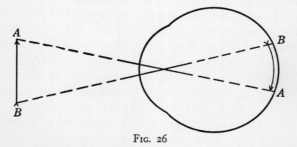

Fig. 26

How the Image of an Object *AB* is Focused on the Retina

lated many data of direct psychological interest upon the question of space perception. It is largely upon such data that the empirical theory of space perception is based. This theory holds that our knowledge of distance and depth is secured largely, if not entirely, through the mutual co-operation and check-up of vision, touch, and locomotion. The nativistic theory, on the other hand, explains facts in three dimensions as natively given and unlearned. Many data can be marshaled to support each of these theories. Probably most psychologists to-day are inclined to accept the empirical view with the reservation that there must be a substantial framework to visual perception which is natively given.

(2)

The invention of the reflecting stereoscope by Wheatstone in 1833 permitted a direct experimental attack upon the problem of how we see objects in three dimensions. Wheatstone's stereoscope was a scientifically accurate instrument, but somewhat clumsy and impracticable for ordinary work. For this reason it has been generally displaced by the re-

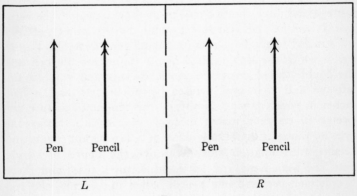

L   R

FIG. 27

STEREOSCOPIC SLIDE DRAWN TO GIVE PERCEPTION OF DISTANCE

fracting stereoscope invented by David Brewster somewhat later (*circa* 1843). Essentially the stereoscope is an optical instrument by means of which two plane pictures may be presented, the one to the right eye and the other to the left, to give a single fused picture in three dimensions. This somewhat striking result follows from the facts that man is a two-eyed animal and that his eyes are separated spatially, so that when they are focused upon a common object, each views it from a slightly different position. In other words, two pictures are secured in binocular vision, and it is largely the fusion of these two which gives us our visual perception of three dimensions. Simple stereoscopic effects, i.e., without instruments, may be obtained in the following way. Hold a pen and a pencil straight out in front of the face, about one foot away, and a little to the left of an imaginary line passing through the nose. Now move the pencil slightly to the right of the pen and about two inches away from the face. Close the right eye and draw on a sheet of paper the two objects as they appear to the left (open) eye. Now close the left eye and draw the two objects as they appear to the right eye. It will be sufficient to represent the two objects simply by straight lines. Your picture should now look like Figure 27, in which the single-tufted arrow represents the pen and the double-tufted arrow the pencil. Be sure and separate the left-eye and right-eye pictures by about two and a half inches in your drawing. Now hold the completed picture out twelve to eighteen inches in front of the face. Focus the eyes as though you were looking at a far-distant point, and keeping this fixation steadily, move the figure in slowly until the right-hand and left-hand pictures fuse, and there is only one pen and one pencil. When this occurs, the pen will seem nearer than the pencil. A simple explanation of this interesting phenomenon lies in the fact that the distance between the left and right pencils is greater than the distance between the left and right pens (this can easily be verified from your picture). Hence, the eyes must converge more from the parallel position to make the pens combine than the pencils. The greater the convergence, the nearer the object, and so we see the pen as nearer to us than the pencil. It is a common experience that near objects require greater convergence to be brought to a focus than far objects; and so convergence is a direct cue to relative distances.

In Figure 28, the principle upon which the refracting stereoscope works is represented schematically. The picture

seen by the left eye is placed at *A*, and the picture seen by
the right eye at *B*. Owing to the refraction of the light-rays
by the prisms *P* and *P'*, the two pictures are combined by
the two eyes *E* and *E'* and seen as a single fused image at
X. The impression of distance and depth got from pictures
combined stereoscopically is astonishingly real. In taking pictures for ordinary stereoscopic work, the camera first takes

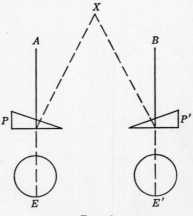

Fɪɢ. 28

Tʜᴇ Pʀɪɴᴄɪᴘʟᴇ ᴏғ ᴛʜᴇ Rᴇғʀᴀᴄᴛɪɴɢ Sᴛᴇʀᴇᴏsᴄᴏᴘᴇ (Bʀᴇᴡsᴛᴇʀ's Mᴏᴅᴇʟ)
    The picture for the left eye is placed at *A;* that for the right eye at *B*.
Refraction of the light-rays by the prisms at *P* and *P'* give a single fused
image at *X*.

the right-eye picture; then it is moved about three inches to
the left to take the left-eye picture. Two and one-half to
three inches is approximately the interocular distance. Because of this separation, each eye, as we have said, sees
around different sides of the objects, the right eye around
the right, the left eye around the left, and in this way cues
to distance and depth are secured. If two pictures are taken,

separated by more than three inches—by one foot, for example—striking and often ludicrous results will be obtained when they are combined stereoscopically. On such a slide we see objects as we would see them if our eyes were a foot apart. Seeing around corners, therefore, becomes highly exaggerated, and objects and people are stretched out in amusing proportions.[1]

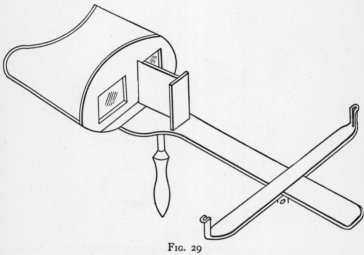

Fig. 29
BREWSTER'S HAND STEREOSCOPE

An illustration of the ordinary Brewster stereoscope is shown in Figure 29. The hood serves to exclude from the eye nearly all of the light which does not come directly through the prisms. The partition between the two prisms restricts each picture to the eye for which it is intended; while the extension slide permits adjustment for eyes of different focal lengths.

[1] Titchener's Stereoscopic Slides (Stoelting), forty-three in number, include several in which the interocular distance is much increased.

The part played by the right-eye and left-eye images in determining our perceptions of objects in three dimensions is even more strikingly shown by the pseudoscope than by the stereoscope. In the pseudoscope, the pictures belonging to the right and left eyes are transposed, so that the right eye sees the left eye's picture, and vice versa. The net result of this is a complete reversal of perspective in the fused picture; near things seem far, and far things seem near. Go back for a moment to Figure 27. If this slide is cut vertically into two equal parts and the parts transposed, the pencil pictures will now be closer together than the pen pictures. Hence, when the right and left pictures are combined, more convergence is required to combine the pencils than the pens, and accordingly the pencil is judged to be nearer. In simple line drawings and geometrical figures, pseudoscopic effects (reversal of perspective) can usually be secured readily enough, either by transposing the right-eye and left-eye pictures, or by inverting the whole slide. With actual scenes, however, landscapes, objects, and people, for example, it is extremely difficult to get pseudoscopic effects when the result would be meaningless, or contrary to experience. Few people, for instance, have ever seen a human face pseudoscopically, i.e., concave, as the "central" or associative facts of experience are too strong. The required reversal of lifetime habits is not readily achieved.

(3)

There are a number of factors upon which our perceptions of three dimensions depend besides this matter of the fusion of left-eye and right-eye pictures. These criteria may be divided conveniently into physiological and psychological. Under physiological factors should be included convergence, accommodation, muscular strain on the eye muscles, and double images.

1. Convergence. It is a familiar fact that objects near at hand require greater convergence of the two eyes in order to focus upon them than objects some distance away. These sensations of strain furnish cues to distance. Convergence, however, is not of much value except in the perception of objects fairly close at hand. When the eyes are focused on objects thirty feet or more away, the lines of sight are practically parallel, and convergence is no longer a real factor.

2. Accommodation to distance is effected by the eye through changes in the crystalline lens. The lens is a translucent prism-like structure which lies behind the pupil and between it and the retina. Light-rays coming through the pupil are refracted by the lens, and focused upon the retina. When a photographer wants to adjust his camera for distance, he lengthens or shortens the distance between the lens and the screen. The eye, on the other hand, adjusts to distances by increasing or decreasing the thickness (refractive power) of the lens. This pull, or release, of the muscles controlling the lens for different degrees of accommodation supplies us with other cues to distance and depth. But since far objects require little accommodation, this factor, like convergence, is limited mainly to objects close by.

3. Muscular strain on the eye muscles. Each eye is moved by six little muscles arranged in pairs. When we compare the length of two lines, or gauge the width of a ditch or creek or the height of a building, the degree of strain on the eye muscles is a valuable factor in determining our judgment of distance.

4. Double Images. The doubling-of-images factor is of especial psychological interest because it is so seldom noticed in everyday life. In fact, Helmholtz has remarked that the existence of double images "remains unknown to many people even in adult life." Their existence may readily be shown, however, in the following simple way. Focus on a point on the opposite wall some ten to fifteen feet away, and then (holding this fixation) bring a pencil up directly before the eyes and about twelve inches away. The pencil will appear double—unless your focus slips—and Figure 30 shows why this is true. When you focus upon F the pencil images since they fall upon non-corresponding retinal

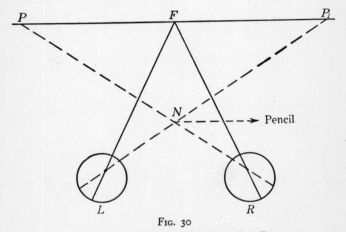

FIG. 30

THE DOUBLING OF "NEAR" OBJECTS IN FAR FIXATION

When the eyes are focused at F, the pencil at N is seen as two pencils at P and P_1, in the plane of F.

points (points which do not give single vision) appear as two pencils at P and P' in the plane of fixation. If you close the left eye, the pencil image (seen now by the right eye) is on the left side; and if you close the right eye, the pencil image (seen by the left eye) is on the right side. That is, the images are crossed, and hence crossed images always mean an object *nearer* than the fixation point. If the focus is upon the near object, it is the far object that doubles, as you can readily demonstrate by focusing upon your pencil (twelve inches away) and doubling a picture on the wall in the same line of vision. In this case the doubled images are not crossed, as Figure 31 shows, and hence uncrossed images always mean an object farther away than the fixation point.

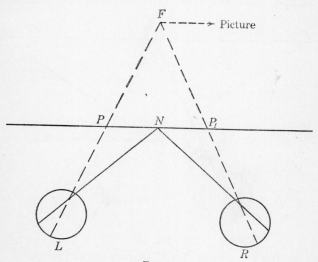

FIG. 31

THE DOUBLING OF "FAR" OBJECTS IN NEAR FIXATION

When the eyes are focused at *N*, the picture (or other object) at *F* is seen double at *P* and P_1, in the plane of *N*.

(4)

More important, perhaps, than the physiological factors in space perception are the so-called psychological factors. These depend upon learning and are the result of everyday contacts with near and far objects. Among such influences we may mention superposition, clearness of outline (aërial perspective), shade and shadows, relative movement, and size of image on the retina.

1. Superposition. This factor is of value in relative distance judgments. When a tree, for instance, partially obstructs our view of a house, the immediate inference is that the tree stands between us and the house, and hence must be nearer.

2. Clearness of outline generally means nearness; dimness and blurring, distance. On a very clear day we are often astonished by the apparent nearness of distant objects, while individuals accustomed to fog and an obscured sky are often completely misled by distances in a high altitude where rain is almost unknown.

3. Differences in lighting, shadows and shade, are especially valuable cues in the perception of depth. Brightly lighted objects in the visual field are generally higher than those dimly lighted, since light usually comes from above; again, on a plane surface depressions or concavities are darker, while protrusions or convexities are brighter. Artists depend to a considerable degree upon light and shade to represent distances and depth. Again, near objects seem "down" in the foreground, and far objects "up" closer to the horizon, and these facts are regularly employed in pictures to give the proper perspective.

4. Relative movement is clearly an important factor in space perception. Objects move toward us and away from us, before and behind other objects, and in this way give us cues as to relative position and relative distance. We are all familiar with the fact that when we are moving, on a train for instance, far objects move along with us and near objects in the direction opposite to our movement. Figure 32 shows in a simple way how this happens. As the observer moves from position 1 to 2 and then to 3, N (the near object) moves from 3 to 2 to 1 in the reverse direction, while F (the far object) apparently moves along with the observer.

5. *Size of Retinal Image.* From Figure 26 it is obvious that at the same distance from the eye a large object will subtend a greater visual angle than a small object, and that the retinal images will vary proportionally. Also it is clear that the farther away an object is from the eyes, the smaller its retinal images will be. Retinal images, then, furnish valuable data as to distance and size, provided, of

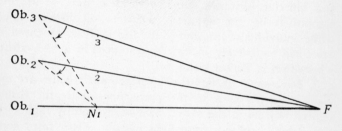

Fɪɢ. 32

DɪAGRAM TO DEMONSTRATE THE APPARENT MOTION OF NEAR AND FAR OBJECTS WHEN THE OBSERVER IS IN MOTION

As observer moves from 1→2→3, any near object (N) rapidly falls farther and farther behind a far object (F), the far object being on the same line with the near at position 1. In consequence of the relatively much greater backward movement of N, F is interpreted as moving along with the observer.

course, the actual dimensions of some of the physical objects are known through other means. The man a block away takes up no more retinal space in your eyes than the ink-bottle on your desk, but the two objects are interpreted as being at different distances from the eyes and not as being of the same size. Since the retinal images vary both for size and distance, this factor is a rather dubious cue unless supplemented by other sense data.

(5)

If reference is made again to Figure 26, it will be noted that, with reference to the physical object, the retinal image is inverted. This inversion is due, of course, to the refractive mechanism of the lens. How is it that we see objects right side up when their retinal images are upside down? This question, which has often been proposed as a philosophical enigma, is puzzling only if we fail to appreciate properly the enormous rôle of experience and learning in perception. What we see, of course, is not the inverted retinal image, but the object in the field from which light-rays are reflected. The image on the retina is simply part of the total physiological process involved in getting the perception; we are no more conscious of it than of the sensory impulse traversing the optic nerve. It must be remembered, too, that the retinal image is spatially correct with reference to its various parts, even though inverted, so that objects are perceived in their right relations. Up-ness and down-ness, right and left, what we see and how we see it, depend upon all of the factors which we have mentioned plus hundreds of associated tactual and muscular experiences and contacts. We see things, feel them, fall over and walk to them, in this way coming to know them.

An exceedingly interesting experiment carried out by Stratton (1897) has a direct bearing upon this question of the relation of retinal images to our perceptions of space. Stratton fastened before his right eye a tube containing two convex lenses. This instrument, of course, gave a retinal image which was right side up, and hence an inversion of objects appeared in the visual field. The left eye was covered over by a hood which excluded light, but allowed free ocular movements. Over a period of eight days (a total of eighty-seven hours), Stratton wore this instrument, observing carefully meanwhile any changes and new arrangements in the visual field. To prevent as far as possible conflicts between the new and the old (normal) perceptions, at night when the instrument was removed, the eyes were carefully bandaged. On the first day, as might have been predicted, everything was topsy-turvy; things on the right were reached for on the left and things lying on the floor reached for toward the ceiling. However, this confusion gradually abated, until by the end of the third day little was left of the nervous strain so clearly apparent at first. By the eighth day the confusion in the visual field had almost entirely disappeared; things could be reached for in their correct positions, and objects appeared normal (right side up) again. Stratton notes, however, that even then there were often sudden slips or inversions, which, however, could usually be corrected by reaching for the object or moving toward it. This experiment is valuable in showing that the retinal image, although absolutely necessary, of course, to vision, is but one cue in the total process whereby we perceive objects in space. It demonstrates, furthermore, how flexible are the connections between hand and eye and how readily modifiable and adaptable our various sensory experiences are. Ordinary everyday experiences demonstrate the same thing. So we learn to shave in a mirror, although right and left are reversed, and to operate a microscope, although the field is inverted. To repeat, it is clear that the retina simply gives us the image in its proper relations; how we place these relations in space depends upon myriad associated tactual and muscular impressions.

(6)

In describing briefly on pages 301 and 304-5 the various factors which contribute to our knowledge of position in space, we did not deal directly with the rôle of eye movements in visual perception. It is readily recognized, however, that this must be a valuable factor, for our knowledge of objects and their structures is not attained by a steady fixation upon them, but by a series of short "views" as the eyes flit over the object and its surroundings. Careful studies by psychologists have shown that eye movements fall into two main classes, "jump" movements and "pursuit" movements. Jump movements occur when our eyes are moved voluntarily over an object; pursuit movements, when the eyes are controlled, so to speak, by the moving objects upon which they are fixated and move along with them.

Dodge (1901) has made probably the most careful studies of angular eye movements of the jump type, using the method of photography. Earlier investigators, for example Huey (1900), had attempted to register eye movements by mechanical means. A small disc was glued to the cornea of the subject's eye, and a fine thread led from this to a delicate writing point. When the eye moved, its excursion was recorded by the writing point on a smoked drum. Besides many obvious objections to this procedure as far as the subject was concerned, there was also undoubtedly some inaccuracy and lag in the transfer by this system. The records, too, tended to blur at the beginning and end of the movement, which made measurements unreliable. Photography of the eyes in motion eliminates most of these difficulties. With his subject seated in a dark room, and position of the head kept constant by means of a head rest, Dodge reflected a beam of light from the cornea upon a moving sensitive plate. As the plate moved downward vertically between two grooves, the subject was instructed to move his eyes from a given point to another in the same horizontal line. Focus, or rest points, showed up as bright spots on the film, intermediate movements as white lines, or streaks.

The time required to shift the focus from point A to point

B was measured by photographing an oscillating spring pendulum along the edge of the moving plate. The vibrations of this time marker showed up as a series of teethlike indentations which could easily be counted. Since the pendulum rate of vibration was known, it was possible to measure the time intervening between the fixation at *A* and that at *B*. As might be expected, the time of an angular movement of

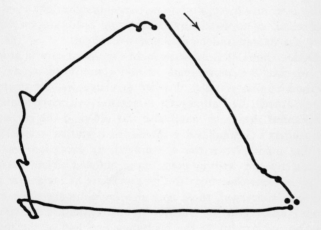

Fig. 33

<small>Photographic Record of the Eye's Movement in Tracing the Outline of a Circle</small>
(After Stratton.)

the eyes depends largely upon the extent of the excursion. Dodge found that the time required for the eyes to move through an angle of five degrees is about .03 second, the time for twenty degrees is about .06 second, and the time for forty degrees is .1 second. These results are based upon the records of three subjects. The reaction time of the eye to a beam of light cast upon the retina—i.e., the time intervening between the stimulus and the eye's movement—was determined by Dodge to be around .165 second.

The jerky character of eye movements in ordinary seeing has been clearly shown by Stratton (1906), who also employed the photographic method. Contrary to everyday opinion, the eye does not move in a smooth sweep, unless the movement is of the pursuit variety. In such movements, as previously noted, the eye simply follows the moving object, and is not controlled by the observer. In looking at an object or a picture, however, Stratton found that the eye moves in a series of jerks or jumps, even though the subject thinks he is moving his eyes smoothly. Like Dodge, Stratton also placed his subject in a dark room and photographed the eye movements by reflecting light from the cornea upon a sensitive plate. The way in which the eye moves in looking around a circle is shown in Figure 33. The dots represent pauses.

(7)

One of the most careful studies of eye movements in reading was made by Dearborn (1905), who also used the method of photographic registration employed by Dodge and Stratton. Dearborn found that the number of fixations per line for ordinary printed matter varied from four to seven for eight subjects. The number of "stops" in a line is fairly variable, depending upon the difficulty of the material read as well as upon the education and mental ability of the reader. Dearborn also found, as Erdman and Dodge had earlier reported (1898), that the fixation pauses of the eye in reading consume about 95 per cent of the total reading time. This fact, plus the high speed of eye movement, makes clear perception during eye movement practically impossible. In spite of this our visual world, as we all know, is a continuous affair, and not a patchwork of clear visual spots here and there, bridged over in between by blurs. There are many reasons why this is true. In the first place, our visual field, when the eyes are at rest, is continuous and unbroken. There is clear vision, too, of moving objects in pursuit movements, although in following rapidly moving objects the background is blurred. But more important than these is the continuous "filling-in" by data got from the other senses. This background of information and learned material in terms of which our immediate perceptions are "sized up" and made meaningful is sometimes called our "apperceptive mass." A familiar example is the speed with which educated adults read easy or familiar prose. The eye sweeps along over the page, hitting important or "key" words here and there, the gaps being filled in by the context of associated information.

Early in the chapter we referred briefly to the two theories of visual space perception, the nativistic and the empiristic. No doubt, most of the facts here presented have seemed to favor the empirical theory, although the physiological factors of accommodation, convergence, and muscular strain weigh heavily. No one, of course, can say definitely just where the influence of native factors leaves off and the influence of learned factors begins. Here again we are faced with the same dilemma encountered in the familiar controversies of instinct versus learning, heredity versus environment. Certainly learning can do nothing without the native equipment of a spatially correct retinal image and the physiological factors which furnish cues to movement. Nor could the eye alone build up visual space as we know it unless aided by associated observations from the other senses. Both sets of factors are important and necessary, and we could dispense with neither.

Suggested Readings

1. The interested student should consult C. S. Myers's *Experimental Psychology* (1925), Part I, Chapter XXII, and E. B. Titchener's *Experimental Psychology, Students' Manual, Qualitative* (1916), Chapter IX, for a full discussion of experimental method and for many illustrations of illusions.

2. Chapter IX in E. S. and F. R. Robinson's *Readings in General Psychology* (1923) contains much interesting material on perception.

Chapter 14

FRANZ'S AND LASHLEY'S EXPERIMENTAL STUDIES OF THE RÔLE OF THE BRAIN IN LEARNING

(1)

THE experimental work of Shepherd I. Franz and Karl S. Lashley offers one of the best examples of the physiological approach to problems of learning and habit-formation. Both of these scientists are physiologists as well as psychologists. Franz received the doctor's degree in psychology from Columbia University in 1899, and in 1902 began a series of studies on the rôle of the brain in learning, using cats and monkeys as experimental subjects. For many years he was psychologist at the Government Hospital for the Insane in Washington, where he did much striking work in the reëducation of individuals who had sustained brain injury. Lashley took the Ph.D. degree from the Johns Hopkins University in 1914. He is probably the most eminent American worker in the field of physiological psychology.

The main task which both Franz and Lashley set for themselves in their investigations was to determine what regions of the brain cortex function in specific learned acts, and how much of the brain tissue so functions. Their method, in brief, was to compare the learning ability of animals before and after destruction of certain brain areas by operation, or to compare the learning of "operated" animals with that of normal animals. For example, a group of rats are trained to thread a maze, the number of trials and the time being recorded; parts of the brain tissue are then removed and after recovery from the operation the animals are retested to see to what extent the loss of brain structure affects their behavior. Or again, animals whose brains have already been partially destroyed are trained to get out of a box, and their records are compared with those of normal animals.

Operations involving different brain areas have been performed upon rats, cats, and monkeys, and their effects upon the acquisition of both sensory and motor habits of different degrees of complexity have been recorded. These experiments have much significance for human learning. Since the human brain cannot be experimented with, it is only in the event of disease or wounds that brain injury can be correlated with loss of mental function. In pathological conditions like these, however, complications arising from bodily disease or injury must be seriously considered, and these influences may be so extensive that a definite conclusion as to the specific effect of the brain injury itself is often hard to reach. This situation does not arise in operative work with animals; parts of the brain cortex can be experimentally destroyed and the resulting effects upon learning behavior directly noted. In many cases the experimental findings from the higher animals, e.g., the apes, can be carried over almost unaltered to human learning, and even in the lower species the problems of learning are fundamentally the same as in man. In a careful review of the literature on cerebral function, Lashley (1929) finds that while there is undoubtedly greater specialization as we go up the evolutionary scale, the problem of the relation of brain areas to learning does not differ greatly in man from that in other mammals. A marked advantage of experimentation with animals should also be noted; namely, that it permits us to observe the rôle of the brain in behavior much less complex and more easily controlled than in man.

(2)

In his pioneer studies Franz (1907) investigated the function of the frontal lobes in the retention of associations formed in learning. His experiments were carried out with cats and with monkeys. The cats were trained to escape from boxes quite similar to those used by Thorndike in his studies of animal learning (see page 107). These boxes were about twelve inches high, fifteen inches wide, and twenty inches long. The bottom, back, and sides were solid, the front and top being covered with three-quarter inch slats. The door was six inches wide by eight inches high, and was hinged at the bottom so that it would fall forward when the latch or other mechanism holding it was released. Three boxes were used. Two could be opened by pushing or knocking against a cord attached in different ways to the door; the third by pressing a button up or down. This third box is shown in Figure 34.

The stimulus to activity was food—meat, fish, or milk—placed just outside of the box. Given a training period of about a week, a normal and hungry cat can learn to escape from a box like these described in from two to six seconds. After the animal had learned the habit to this high point of efficiency, Franz gave it an anesthetic and operated upon the brain, cutting away both frontal lobes from the rest of the cortex without, however, removing the severed parts from the skull.[1] After the animal had recovered from the anesthetic and the shock following operation, which usually required two to three days, it was retested in the box from which it had previously learned to escape. In all

[1] In man the frontal lobes, which lie just behind the forehead, have long been thought to be active in complex and highly learned activities, such as thinking, reasoning, and planning. Presumably they function also in animals when learning tricks or other fairly complex acts.

three cats used in this experiment the habit of escape, though repeatedly tested for, failed to reappear. But the cats still made impulsive efforts to escape; also they retained old and much-used habits, such as purring when petted, rubbing against the experimenter's legs, and responding to call. When they were held before a cage of mice, normal emotional re-

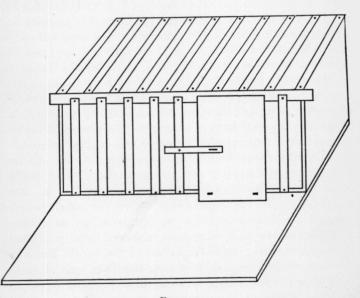

Fig. 34

Puzzle Box Used by Franz in Learning Experiments with Cats

sponses were exhibited, such as increased heart-beat, following the mice rapidly with the eyes, and attempts to jump. Only the *recently acquired habit* of opening the box seemed to be lost. Franz was careful not to use any animal in which post-operative infection had set in, and in every case the cat was later killed and its brain examined to make sure that the frontals had actually been cut away from the rest of the brain.

The loss of learned responses following extirpation of the frontal lobes holds for monkeys as well as for cats. In his experiments with monkeys, Franz used small animals of the rhesus (short-tail) and the ring-tail variety. Two tasks were arranged, the one called the food box, and the other the hurdle. The problem set by the food box was opening the door of a small food compartment which was attached to the cage in which the animal lived. The door of the food box was held by a button much like the door of the box in Figure 34. In the hurdle problem the animal had to perform several acts in order, going from one bar to another, crawling through a hole, and so forth, before reaching the food. All of the animals were hungry when placed in the test situations so that active and vigorous behavior was readily secured.

Six monkeys were used in this experiment. As soon as they had thoroughly learned the habits, parts of their frontal lobes were removed, with the same precautions as those employed in the cat experiments. When the monkeys were retested after recovery from the operation, all were found to have lost the trick of opening the food box or of going through the more complex activities of the hurdle. But as in the case of the cats, habits of long standing, such as eating out of the experimenter's hand and jumping upon his shoulder, remained. The monkeys were described as normally active and apparently normal emotionally, screaming and chattering as before the operation.

(3)

Objection might be raised to the conclusion reached in the above experiment, namely, that newly formed associations and habits are dependent upon the frontal lobes. In the first place, the shock of the operation (surgical shock) might alone be sufficient to break up the new association; second, the mere excision of brain tissue in any part of the brain (not the frontal lobe particularly) might explain the loss of the habit. To settle these issues, Franz performed two control operations. In the one, a cat was trained as before to escape from a box. After the trick was learned, she was anesthetized and her skull opened, but no excision of brain tissue was made. The wound was simply closed and bandaged as in the other operations. Twenty-four hours after the operation, this cat was retested in the box and found to retain the habit perfectly. Other repetitions of this experiment checked the result. In the second control test, a cat which had been trained to escape from two boxes was operated, but this time a portion of the parietal lobe [2] instead of the frontal was cut away from the underlying parts of brain tissue. Three days after the operation this animal got out of the box in a little over seven seconds, which was about twice the time required before the operation. Shortly afterward it reduced its escape time to the former level, showing, apparently, that the associations involved in the habits had not been actually disturbed. Seven weeks later, the right frontal lobe *only* in this same cat was excised. Four days after this operation, though extremely slow, the animal was able to do the trick. In another cat which had learned perfectly how to get out of the box, both parietal lobes were destroyed. Three days after the operation, this animal performed the trick as well as before. These control experiments indicate quite clearly (1) that only when *both frontals* are injured are the recently acquired associations lost; and (2) that the loss of the habit cannot be explained as due either to surgical shock resulting from the operation or to mere cutting of the brain tissue.

[2] The parietal lobes lie in back of the frontals, and in man are concerned chiefly with sensory and associative functions.

(4)

In all of Franz's experiments described so far, the habits and associations lost as the result of frontal injury were of quite recent origin; old and well-established habits persisted. To see whether this would hold true for highly trained escape habits, Franz in a second series of experiments trained four monkeys over a much longer period of time until the escape habit was firmly established—almost second nature, so to speak. The frontal lobes of these highly trained animals were then destroyed, and after recovery it was found that the escape habit functioned almost, if not quite, as perfectly as before the operation. In another series of experiments with several cats, the frontals were severed from the rest of the brain *before* the animals had learned to get out of any of the boxes. When these animals were trained later, it was found that they could learn the habits as well as normal cats.

These experiments are highly interesting and suggestive since they indicate that one part of the brain must take over the function of another part vicariously, or by substitution. It seems quite evident from Franz's results that, in cats and monkeys at least, recently formed associations are normally carried on by the frontal lobes, since the habits are lost when the frontals are removed. But if the habits are well formed, i.e., fairly well mechanized, they persist even when parts of the frontals are lost, being carried on apparently through the agency of other parts of the brain. That these other centers may acquire the habit in the first place is indicated by those experiments in which cats whose frontal lobes had been excised *before* training still learned the habit. These findings are directly opposed to the old idea of specific centers in the brain which control definite functions. Such areas, if they actually exist, must be considerably more diffuse, and they must also be more loosely organized, than was originally believed.

Several cases of restitution of function taken from Franz's work with humans will be instructive in this connection. These cases are concerned with the reëducation of patients whose brains had been injured by disease or wounds. An aphasic, fifty-seven years old, had recently suffered a paralytic stroke.[3] His right side was paralyzed, and his language was jumbled and often unintelligible. Many irrelevant words were employed and objects were often named incorrectly. The attempt was made to retrain this patient by having him relearn (1) the names of ten familiar colors; (2) a short stanza of poetry; and (3) the Lord's Prayer. Beginning with an accuracy score of 44 per cent right in naming colors, after three months, in which the trials varied in number from day to day and were sometimes omitted, this man increased his accuracy score to 96 per cent right. Almost the same results were obtained in relearning numbers. An interesting finding here was that the number 5 (probably because of its common use) was most often used spontaneously. In trying to learn poetry—the first stanza of "The Village Blacksmith" was the selection used—the patient read aloud the first one or two lines five times and then tried to recite. Repetition was continued until reproduction was perfect, whereupon the next few lines were attempted, and so on. After five days of work the patient was able to repeat six lines of the selection sufficiently well to indicate that he was gradually learning it. The Lord's Prayer, formerly well known to this patient, was correctly given after twenty-five readings spaced over three days. A post-mortem examination of this man's brain (he

[3] Aphasia is the loss of ability to understand spoken or written language (sensory type); or the loss of the ability to say the correct word to express one's thought (motor type). Aphasia is, in general, the result of injury to the associative areas of the cortex, most often, probably, in the frontal and temporal lobes.

died of pneumonia shortly after the experiments described) showed considerable destruction in the lower part of the cortex, i.e., in the temporal lobes. Franz points out that the slow but steady reëducation of this man suggests the possibility of the reëstablishment of old brain connections or the opening-up of new ones. This seems reasonable in the light of the experimental work on animals which has been described.

A second case illustrates the powerful stimulating effect of positive suggestion. In this instance the patient was an ex-soldier, a young man who had been struck by a high-explosive shell. The result of his injuries was paralysis of face, arm, and leg on one side, and this condition had persisted for nine months. This man entered the examination room hobbling on a cane. At once he was ordered sharply by the examiner to put down his cane and take a seat in a chair some twelve feet away. Although he insisted at first that he couldn't walk without a cane, upon being told that the examiner was quite sure that he could, he laid the cane aside and awkwardly, but unassisted, walked to the chair. Here the authority and the prestige of the examiner proved to be a sufficiently positive stimulus to reinstate a partly lost function. Either the old nerve connections conducted under "pressure" or other and new connections substituted for them.

The effect of a powerful incentive or an emotional stimulus in making a patient "forget" his disabilities is well illustrated in the case of another partially paralyzed man who had walked with a cane for nineteen years. During a baseball game this individual hit the ball, and in great excitement, without pausing to get his cane, he ran quickly to first base, beating out the throw. It is significant that in spite of this achievement he then demanded his cane, saying that he couldn't walk without it. In many cases of this sort it seems, as already noted, that old pathways in the brain and nervous system are still partially intact, or that others are able to substitute for them. The patient's attitude is often the controlling factor in stirring these connections into life. If the suggestion is strong enough, or if the patient can be sufficiently aroused to activity, say by anger or by fear, recovery of function may follow.

(5)

The work of Lashley to be reported here, like that of Franz, was directed toward discovering the effect of brain-destruction upon specific learned acts. His experimental animals were white rats. In one series of experiments (1920 and later), a group of rats were trained in a very simple sensory habit of brightness discrimination. The problem box used (Yerkes Discrimination Box) contains two alleyways, either of which can be illuminated by a transparent screen placed at the far end of the box. When the rat takes the lighted side, it is admitted to the food compartment through a small door; when it takes the dark side it receives no food, but receives instead a shock through an electric grill placed on the floor of the alley. The light can be shifted from the left to the right alley irregularly so that the animals cannot form a place association or habit. About 100 trials are required for the rats to fix the habit illuminated alley → food. Training was continued at the rate of ten trials per day until twenty consecutive errorless trials were obtained. After one group of animals had learned the habit perfectly, various amounts of the posterior parts of both cerebral hemispheres [4] were destroyed by operation, and after recovery the rats were tested for retention. Another group of animals untrained in the brightness discrimination habit were *first* subjected to

[4] The posterior parts of the hemispheres are called the occipital lobes and are active in the learning of visual habits.

brain operations which involved different thirds of the occipital cortex. These rats were then tested to see how long it would take them to acquire the habit. The results of these tests are quite convincing. On the one hand, those animals which had learned the habits with uninjured brains were found *after* the operation to have lost the habit entirely. But with practice they were all able to reacquire it, the number of trials needed being roughly proportional to the *extent*, but entirely independent of the *place* of brain destruction. The correlation between the percentage of cortex destruction and efficiency of learning is about .45 (Lashley, 1929). On the other hand, those rats whose brains had been injured *before* being tested in the discrimination box learned the habits just as quickly as did the uninjured animals. This experiment seems to establish clearly (1) that the occipital lobes are ordinarily active in brightness discrimination, but (2) that these regions are not necessary for it, since other parts apparently do take over the function. (3) It shows, too, that the brightness discrimination habit must depend upon the activity of the whole posterior region of the cerebrum rather than upon a specific region, since the habit is weakened by the extent of the injury, but is independent of the point where it occurs.

In another group of trained rats, the parietal brain areas were destroyed by operation. Upon being retested, these animals, while considerably slower than before, in no case showed complete loss of the brightness discrimination habit. This clearly suggests that the occipital areas were the regions originally concerned in learning this activity. We have already seen, however, that when parts of the occipital lobe were destroyed *before* training, the rats were still able to learn the brightness discrimination habit as well as normal rats. This led Lashley to propose the following query: Is there any particular area of the brain which takes over the functions of the injured occipital parts? To answer this question, he first destroyed various parts of the occipital lobes in twelve rats and then trained them until they had learned the brightness discrimination habit up to his standard. A second operation was then performed on the same rats, various regions of the remaining parts of the cortex being destroyed. Each operation injured about one third of the still intact cortex, the injuries sampling the remaining area in such a way as to cover (when all twelve rats are considered) the entire two hemispheres. In no animal was *all* of the cortex destroyed, however, as complete decortication has not as yet been successfully performed in the rat. These twice-operated animals were then retested for retention of the brightness discrimination habit, with the result that none were found to have lost it! From this last experiment we are forced to the highly important conclusion that after occipital injury *no specific area* of the cortex carries on the brightness discrimination habit vicariously; or stating the same thing in a different way, that apparently *any* part of the cortex is able to take over the brightness discrimination habit in the absence of those occipital areas whose function it normally is. Since the entire cortex was not removed in any animal used in these tests, it is uncertain whether or not some cortical tissue is necessary for the retention of the brightness discrimination habit. It may be, of course, that subcortical centers can substitute in the absence of the whole cortex.

These results which have been quoted from Lashley's work are quite securely established. More than 150 rats in all were used in these experiments, and there were adequate controls, so that the results cannot be attributed to surgical shock or to actual blindness in the animals. Postmortem examinations to verify the extent of the lesions were also made.

(6)

In another series of experiments, Lashley (1920 and later) studied the effects of brain injury upon the learning and retention of a motor habit. Animals were first trained to secure

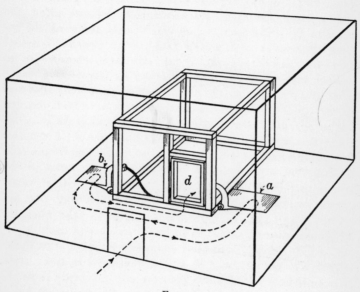

Fig. 35

DOUBLE-PLATFORM BOX USED IN EXPERIMENTS IN LEARNING WITH WHITE RATS

The door *d* is opened when the platforms *a* and *b* are successively pressed down. (From Lashley, 1920.)

food in the problem box shown in Figure 35. In this box, called the double platform box, it is necessary for the animal to depress platforms *a* and *b* in the fixed order *a* → *b* in order to open the door, *d*, which leads to the food compartment. These platforms are about four by two inches and are raised one inch from the floor; a fairly slight pressure is sufficient to depress either of them. This task requires a more complex motor response than that needed in the inclined plane box used in earlier experiments by Franz and Lashley (1917). In the inclined plane box, the animal had to climb upon the food compartment (a small box placed within the cage) and depress one small platform in order to open the door of the food box. In the double platform box, as noted, two platforms instead of one had to be depressed.

Nineteen rats were trained in the double platform box after about one third, on the average (14 to 50 per cent), of the cerebral cortex had been destroyed by operation. These operated animals learned the habit as readily as the normal (control) rats, actually requiring only about three-fifths as much practice, as shown in Table XX. This rather

TABLE XX

THE AVERAGE NUMBER OF TRIALS AND THEIR RANGE FOR NORMAL AND OPERATED RATS IN LEARNING THE DOUBLE PLATFORM BOX
(After Lashley.)

Group	Injury	Average No. trials	Range	No. of animals	Average per cent of brain-destruction
1	Normal	142.6	63-204	10	0
2	One hemisphere destroyed ..	87.2	49-141	6	37
3	Occipital injury	68.8	45-107	4	28
4	Parietal injury	80.0	41-101	5	22
5	Frontal injury .	90.0	90	2	16
6	Fronto-parietal injury	39.0	27-51	2	28
	All operated rats.....	79.0	27-141	19	28

remarkable outcome may be partly explained as a result of the somewhat lesser distractibility of the operated rats with a consequent lessening of their random activity. That is, brain-destruction may actually favor quick learning. Lashley has found, for instance, that operated rats slightly paralyzed and with motor disturbances required about 30 per cent less trials than other operated rats which showed no motor defects. Animals with brain injuries jump over the platforms less often than normal rats, more often bumping into and eventually depressing them. The task of opening the door of the food compartment seems then actually to have been easier for the injured rats, though it is hard to see how this advantage can entirely explain the wide differences found between normal and operated animals in favor of the latter. Lashley writes in regard to this point: ". . . various lines of evidence point to the conclusion that irrelevant factors at least did not change a real inferiority of the operated animals into an apparent superiority; that the normal and operated groups are most probably equal in learning ability."

In later experiments (1921), rats first trained in the double platform habit were later subjected to operations which destroyed various parts of their frontal and occipital brain areas. The habit, though much disturbed, was not totally lost as a result of such destruction. This suggests that normally the frontal lobes are active in the formation and retention of motor habits, but that substitution of function by other areas is immediate and quite effective.

(7)

Lashley (1929) has recently checked and extended many of his results on learning and retention in animals. Tests of the learning ability and retention of both motor and sensory habits were made with four mazes of different patterns and the brightness discrimination box previously described on page 322. The experimental group was made up of fifty animals, all of which were subjected to brain operations involving from 1½ to 81 per cent of the total surface area of the cerebrum. A few of the significant findings in these careful and extensive experiments may be summarized briefly. In substantiation of his earlier work Lashley found (1) that the capacity to form motor habits (e.g., to learn mazes) is reduced by brain-destruction, the reduction being independent of the place of the injury but roughly proportional to the amount of destruction. (2) The more complex the problem set, the greater the effect upon learning produced by any given injury. (3) Simple sensory habits, such as that of brightness discrimination, are not greatly affected by cerebral lesions even when the whole sensory area is involved, owing probably to the comparative simplicity of the habit itself. (4) Retention of simple motor habits (learning mazes) after forty days is significantly impaired by cerebral lesion, the degree of impairment depending chiefly upon the extent of the injury and the initial learning ability of the injured rats.

Perhaps the most far-reaching result for human psychology of such experimental studies as these of Franz and Lashley is the very definite finding that learning and retention of sensory and motor habits cannot be explained in terms of fixed nervous pathways, definite brain structures, or specific synaptic connections. Complex learned activities must depend upon much more extensive brain patterns than was formerly thought probable. This may explain why a single operation does not greatly disturb a given pattern, but the more extensive the injury the greater is the likelihood of some disturbance. It may appear as though we are returning to an older and less analytic view to say that the brain functions as a whole in learning, but certainly this view is not as improbable now as it once appeared to be. Localization of cerebral areas as the sensory, the motor, the visual, and so on is, of course, well established. But such areas must be modified to allow for wide flexibility and extended to permit of much functional substitution of one part for another. The clinical evidence, as well as the experimental evidence, indicates that this widespread substitution of brain function in the case of rats, cats, and monkeys holds also to a high degree for man.

Suggested Readings

1. For a critical review of the experimental work of Franz and Lashley, see C. J. Herrick's *Brains of Rats and Men* (1926). This reference, also, gives a comprehensive summary of present knowledge concerning the rôle of the brain in behavior.
2. Many students will find Lashley's own account of his recent experimental work in *Brain Mechanisms and Intelligence* (1929) extremely interesting.

INDEX

6⁰

1 6 5 9   5 8 2